Flowers from a Persian Garden and Other Papers

W. A. Clouston

Flowers from a Persian Garden and Other Papers

Copyright © 2010 by Indo-European Publishing

For information and contact visit our website at:
IndoEuropeanPublishing.com

The present edition is a revised version of an earlier publication of this work, produced in the current edition with completely new, easy to read format, and is set and proofread by Alfred Aghajanian for Indo-European Publishing.

Cover Design by Indo-European Design Team

ISBN: 978-1-60444-275-5

IndoEuropean
Publishing.com
Los Angeles, CA, USA

TO

E. SIDNEY HARTLAND, Esq.,

FELLOW OF THE SOCIETY OF ANTIQUARIES; MEMBER OF THE COUNCIL OF THE FOLK-LORE SOCIETY, ETC.

My dear Hartland,

Though you are burdened with the duties of a profession far outside of which lie those studies that have largely occupied my attention for many years past, yet your own able contributions to the same, or cognate, subjects of investigation evince the truth of the seemingly paradoxical saying, that "the busiest man finds the greatest amount of leisure." And in dedicating this little book to you—would that it were more worthy!—as a token of gratitude for the valuable help you have often rendered me in the course of my studies, I am glad of the opportunity it affords me for placing on record (so to say) the fact that I enjoy the friendship of a man possessed of so many excellent qualities of heart as well as of intellect.

The following collection of essays, or papers, is designed to suit the tastes of a more numerous class of readers than were some of my former books, which are not likely to be of special interest to many besides students of comparative folk-lore—amongst whom your own degree is high. The book, in fact, is intended mainly for those who are rather vaguely termed "general readers"; albeit I venture to think that even the folk-lore student may find in it somewhat to "make a note of," as the great Captain Cuttle was wont to say—in season and out of season.

Leaving the contents to speak for themselves, I shall only say farther that my object has been to bring together, in a handy volume, a series of essays which might prove acceptable to many readers, whether of grave or lively temperament. What are called "instructive" books—meaning thereby "morally" instructive—are generally as dull reading as is proverbially a book containing nothing but jests—good, bad, and indifferent. We can't (and we shouldn't) be always in the "serious" mood, nor can we be for ever on the grin; and it seems to me that a mental dietary, by turns, of what is wise and of what is witty should be most wholesome. But, of the two, I confess I prefer to take the former, even as one ought to take solid food, in great moderation; and, after all, it is surely better to laugh than to mope or weep, in spite of what has been said of "the loud laugh that speaks the vacant mind." Most of us, in this work-a-day world, find no small benefit from allowing our minds to lie fallow at certain times, as farmers do with their fields. In the following pages, however, I believe wisdom and wit, the didactic and the diverting, will be found in tolerably fair proportions.

But I had forgot—I am not writing a Preface, and this is already too long for a Dedication; so believe me, with all good wishes,

Yours ever faithfully,

W. A. CLOUSTON
Glasgow, *February*, 1890

CONTENTS

FLOWERS FROM A PERSIAN GARDEN

I: Sketch of the Life of the Persian Poet Saádí—Character of his Writings—the *Gulistán*, or Rose-Garden—Prefaces to Books— Preface to the *Gulistán*—Eastern Poets in praise of Springtide 1

II: Boy's Archery Feat—Advantages of Abstinence—Núshirván on Oppression—Boy in terror at Sea—Pride of Ancestry—Misfortunes of Friends—Fortitude and Liberality—Prodigality—Stupid Youth— Advantages of Education—The Fair Cup-bearer—'January and May'—Why an Old Man did not Marry—The Dervish who became King—Muezzin and Preacher who had bad voices—Witty Slave— Witty Kází—Astrologer and his Faithless Wife—Objectionable Neighbour 10

III: On Taciturnity: Parallels from Caxton's *Dictes* and preface to *Kalíla wa Dimna*—Difference between Devotee and Learned Man— To get rid of Troublesome Visitors—Fable of the Nightingale and the Ant—Aphorisms of Saádí—Conclusion 19

ORIENTAL WIT AND HUMOUR

I: Man a Laughing Animal—Antiquity of Popular Jests—'Night and Day'—The Plain-featured Bride—The House of Condolence—The Blind Man's Wife—Two Witty Persian Ladies—Woman's Counsel— The Turkish Jester: in the Pulpit; the Cauldron; the Beggar; the Drunken Governor; the Robber; the Hot Broth—Muslim Preachers and Misers 29

II: The Two Deaf Men and the Traveller—The Deaf Persian and the Horseman—Lazy Servants—Chinese Humour: The Rich Man and the Smiths; How to keep Plants alive; Criticising a Portrait—The Persian Courtier and his old Friend—The Scribe—The Schoolmaster and the Wit—The Persian and his Cat—A List of Blockheads—The Arab and his Camel—A Witty Baghdádí—The Unlucky Slippers 36

III: The Young Merchant of Baghdád; or, the Wiles of Woman 43

IV: Ashaab the Covetous—The Stingy Merchant and the Hungry Bedouin—The Sect of Samradians—The Story-teller and the King— Royal Gifts to Poets—The Persian Poet and the Impostor—'Stealing Poetry'—The Rich Man and the Poor Poet 47

V: Unlucky Omens—The Old Man's Prayer—The Old Woman in the Mosque—The Weeping Turkmans—The Ten Foolish Peasants—The Wakeful Servant—The Three Dervishes—The Oilman's Parrot—The Moghul and his Parrot—The Persian Shopkeeper and the Prime Minister—Hebrew Facetiæ 54

TALES OF A PARROT

I: General Plan of Eastern Story-books—The *Túti Náma*, or Parrot-Book—The Frame-story—The Stolen Images—The Woman carved out of Wood—The Man whose Mare was kicked by a Merchant's Horse 60

II: The Emperor's Dream—The Golden Apparition—The Four Treasure-seekers 65

III: The Singing Ass: the Foolish Thieves: the Faggot-maker and the Magic Bowl 73

IV: The Goldsmith who lost his Life through Covetousness—The King who died of Love for a Merchant's Daughter—The Discovery of Music—The Seven Requisites of a Perfect Woman 80

V: The Princess of Rome and her Son—The Seven Vazírs 84

VI: The Tree of Life—Legend of Rájá Rasálú—Conclusion 89

RABBINICAL LEGENDS, TALES, FABLES, AND APHORISMS

I: Introductory: Authors, Traducers, and Moral Teachings of Talmud 94

II: Legends of some Biblical Characters: Adam and Eve—Cain and Abel—The Planting of the Vine—Luminous Jewels—Abraham's Arrival in Egypt—The Infamous Citizens of Sodom—Abraham and Ishmael's Wives—Joseph and Potiphar's Wife—Joseph and his Brethren—Jacob's Sorrow—Moses and Pharaoh 98

III: Legends of David and Solomon, etc. 107

IV: Moral and Entertaining Tales: Rabbi Jochonan and the Poor Woman—A Safe Investment—The Jewels—The Capon-carver 113

V: Moral Tales, Tables, and Parables: The Dutiful Son—An Ingenious Will—Origin of Beast-Fables—The Fox and the Bear—The Fox in the Garden—The Desolate Island—The Man and his Three Friends—The Garments—Solomon's Choice—Bride and Bridegroom—Abraham and the Idols—The Vanity of Ambition—The Seven Stages of Human Life 118

VI: Wise Sayings of the Rabbis 129

AN ARABIAN TALE OF LOVE 145

APOCRYPHAL LIFE OF ESOP 152

IGNORANCE OF THE CLERGY IN THE MIDDLE AGES 159

THE BEARDS OF OUR FATHERS 168

FOOTNOTES 182

FLOWERS FROM A PERSIAN GARDEN

I

SKETCH OF THE LIFE OF THE PERSIAN POET SAADI—CHARACTER OF HIS WRITINGS—THE "GULISTÁN"—PREFACES TO BOOKS—PREFACE TO THE "GULISTÁN"—EASTERN POETS IN PRAISE OF SPRINGTIDE

It is remarkable how very little the average general reader knows regarding the great Persian poet Saádí and his writings. His name is perhaps more or less familiar to casual readers from its being appended to one or two of his aphorisms which are sometimes reproduced in odd corners of popular periodicals; but who he was, when he lived, and what he wrote, are questions which would probably puzzle not a few, even of those who consider themselves as "well read," to answer without first recurring to some encyclopædia. Yet Saádí was assuredly one of the most gifted men of genius the world has ever known: a man of large and comprehensive intellect; an original and profound thinker; an acute observer of men and manners; and his works remain the imperishable monument of his genius, learning, and industry.

Maslahu 'd-Dín Shaykh Saádí was born, towards the close of the twelfth century, at Shíráz, the famous capital of Fars, concerning which city the Persians have the saying that "if Muhammed had tasted the pleasures of Shíráz, he would have begged Allah to make him immortal there." In accordance with the usual practice in Persia, he assumed as his *takhallus*, or poetical name, [1] Saádí, from his patron Atabag Saád bin Zingí, sovereign of Fars, who encouraged men of learning in his principality. Saádí is said to have lived upwards of a hundred years, thirty of which were passed in the acquisition of knowledge, thirty more in travelling through different countries, and the rest of his life he spent in retirement and acts of devotion. He died, in his native city, about the year 1291.

1

At one period of his life Saádí took part in the wars of the Saracens against the Crusaders in Palestine, and also in the wars for the faith in India. In the course of his wanderings he had the misfortune to be taken prisoner by the Franks, in Syria, and was ransomed by a friend, but only to fall into worse thraldom by marrying a shrewish wife. He has thus related the circumstances:

"Weary of the society of my friends at Damascus, I fled to the barren wastes of Jerusalem, and associated with brutes, until I was made captive by the Franks, and forced to dig clay along with Jews in the fortress of Tripoli. One of the nobles of Aleppo, mine ancient friend, happened to pass that way and recollected me. He said: 'What a state is this to be in! How farest thou?' I answered: 'Seeing that I could place confidence in God alone, I retired to the mountains and wilds, to avoid the society of man; but judge what must be my situation, to be confined in a stall, in company with wretches who deserve not the name of men. "To be confined by the feet with friends is better than to walk in a garden with strangers."' He took compassion on my forlorn condition, ransomed me from the Franks for ten dínars, [2] and took me with him to Aleppo.

"My friend had a daughter, to whom he married me, and he presented me with a hundred dínars as her dower. After some time my wife unveiled her disposition, which was ill-tempered, quarrelsome, obstinate, and abusive; so that the happiness of my life vanished. It has been well said: 'A bad woman in the house of a virtuous man is hell even in this world.' Take care how you connect yourself with a bad woman. Save us, O Lord, from the fiery trial! Once she reproached me, saying: 'Art thou not the creature whom my father ransomed from captivity amongst the Franks for ten dínars?' 'Yes,' I answered; 'he redeemed me for ten dínars, and enslaved me to thee for a hundred.'

"I heard that a man once rescued a sheep from the mouth of a wolf, but at night drew his knife across its throat. The expiring sheep thus complained: 'You delivered me from the jaws of a wolf, but in the end I perceive you have yourself become a wolf to me.'"

Sir Gore Ouseley, in his *Biographical Notices of Persian Poets*, states that Saádí in the latter part of his life retired to a cell near Shíráz, where he remained buried in contemplation of the Deity, except when visited, as was often the case, by princes, nobles, and learned men. It was the custom of his illustrious visitors to take with them all kinds of meats, of which, when Saádí and his company had partaken, the shaykh always put what remained in a basket suspended from his window, that the poor wood-cutters of Shíráz, who daily passed by his cell, might occasionally satisfy their hunger.

The writings of Saádí, in prose as well as verse, are numerous; his best known works being the *Gulistán*, or Rose-Garden, and the *Bustán*, or Garden of Odours. Among his other compositions are: an essay on Reason and Love; Advice to Kings; Arabian and Persian idylls, and a book of elegies, besides a large collection of odes and sonnets. Saádí was an accomplished linguist, and composed several poems in the languages of many of the countries through which he travelled. "I have wandered to various regions of the world," he tells us, "and everywhere have I mixed freely with the inhabitants. I have gathered something in each corner; I have gleaned an ear from every harvest." A deep insight into the secret springs of human actions; an extensive knowledge of mankind; fervent piety, without a taint of bigotry; a poet's keen appreciation of the beauties of nature; together with a ready wit and a lively sense of humour, are among the characteristics of Saádí's masterly compositions. No writer, ancient or modern, European or Asiatic, has excelled, and few have equalled, Saádí in that rare faculty for condensing profound moral truths into short, pithy sentences. For example:

"The remedy against want is to moderate your desires."

"There is a difference between him who claspeth his mistress in his arms, and him whose eyes are fixed on the door expecting her."

"Whoever recounts to you the faults of your neighbour will doubtless expose your defects to others."

His humorous comparisons flash upon the reader's mind with curious effect, occurring, as they often do, in the midst of a grave discourse. Thus he says of a poor minstrel: "You would say that the sound of his bow would burst the arteries, and that his voice was more discordant than the lamentations of a man for the death of his father;" and of another bad singer: "No one with a mattock can so effectually scrape clay from the face of a hard stone as his discordant voice harrows up the soul."

Talking of music reminds me of a remark of the learned Gentius, in one of his notes on the *Gulistán* of Saádí, that music was formerly in such consideration in Persia that it was a maxim of their sages that when a king was about to die, if he left for his successor a very young son, his aptitude for reigning should be proved by some agreeable songs; and if the child was pleasurably affected, then it was a sign of his capacity and genius, but if the contrary, he should be declared unfit.—It would appear that the old Persian musicians, like Timotheus, knew the secret art of swaying the passions. The celebrated philosopher Al-Farabí (who died about the middle of the tenth century), among his accomplishments, excelled in music, in proof of which a curious anecdote is told. Returning from the pilgrimage to Mecca, he introduced himself, though a stranger, at the court of Sayfú 'd-Dawla, sultan of Syria, when a party of musicians chanced to be performing, and he joined them. The prince admired his skill, and, desiring to hear something of his own, Al-Farabí unfolded a composition, and distributed the parts amongst the band. The first movement threw the prince and his courtiers into violent laughter, the next melted all into tears, and the last lulled even the performers to sleep. At the retaking of Baghdád by the Turks in 1638, when the springing of a mine, whereby eight hundred jannisaries perished, was the signal for a general massacre, and thirty thousand Persians were put to the sword, a Persian musician named Sháh-Kúlí, who was brought before the sultan Murád, played and sang so sweetly, first a song of triumph, and then a dirge, that the sultan, moved to pity by the music, gave order to stop the slaughter.

To resume, after this anecdotical digression. Saádí gives this whimsical piece of advice to a pugnacious fellow: "Be sure, either that thou art stronger than thine enemy, or that thou hast a swifter pair of heels." And he relates a droll story in illustration of the use and abuse of the phrase, "For the sake of God," which is so frequently in the mouths of Muslims: A harsh-voiced man was reading the Kurán in a loud tone. A pious man passed by him and said: "What is thy monthly salary?" The other replied: "Nothing." "Why, then, dost thou give thyself this trouble?" "I read for the sake of God," he rejoined. "Then," said the pious man, *"for God's sake don't read."*

The most esteemed of Saádí's numerous and diversified works is the *Gulistán*, or Rose-Garden. The first English translation of this work was made by Francis Gladwin, and published in 1808, and it is a very scarce book. Other translations have since been issued, but they are rather costly and the editions limited. It is strange that in these days of cheap reprints of rare and excellent works of genius no enterprising publisher should have thought it worth reproduction in a popular form. It is not one of those ponderous tomes of useless learning which not even an Act of Parliament could cause to be generally read, and which no publisher would be so blind to his own interests as to reprint. As regards its size, the *Gulistán* is but a small book, but intrinsically it is indeed a very great book, such as could only be produced by a great mind, and it comprises more wisdom and wit than a score of old English folios could together yield to the most devoted reader. Some querulous persons there are who affect to consider the present as a shallow age, because, forsooth, huge volumes of learning—each the labour of a lifetime—are not now produced. But the flood-gates of knowledge are now wide open, and, no longer confined within the old, narrow, if deep, channels, learning has spread abroad, like the Nile during the season of its over-flow. Shallow, it may be, but more widely beneficial, since its life-giving waters are within the reach of all.

Unlike most of our learned old English authors, Saádí did not cast upon the world all that came from the rich mine of his genius, dross as well as fine gold, clay as well as gems. It is because they have done so that many ponderous tomes of learning and industry stand neglected on the shelves of great libraries. Time is too precious now-a-days, whatever may have been the case of our forefathers, for it to be dissipated by diving into the muddy waters of voluminous authors in hopes of finding an occasional pearl of wisdom. And unless some intelligent and painstaking compiler set himself to the task of separating the gold from the rubbish in which it is imbedded in those graves of learning, and present the results of his labour in an attractive form, such works are virtually lost to the world. For in these high-pressure days, most of us, "like the dogs in Egypt for fear of the crocodiles, must drink of the waters of knowledge as we run, in dread of the old enemy Time."

Saádí, however, in his *Gulistán* sets forth only his well-pondered thoughts in the most felicitous and expressive language. There is no need to form an abstract or epitome of a work in which nothing is superfluous, nothing valueless. But, as in a cabinet of gems some are more beautiful than others, or as in a garden some flowers are more attractive from their brilliant hues and fragrant odours, so a selection may be made of the more striking tales and aphorisms of the illustrious Persian philosopher.

The preface to the *Gulistán* is one of the most pleasing portions of the whole book. Now prefaces are among those parts of books which are too frequently "skipped" by readers—they are "taken as read." Why this should be so, I confess I cannot understand. For my part, I make a point of reading a preface at least twice: first, because I would know what reasons my author had for writing his book, and again, having read his book, because the preface, if well written, may serve also as a sort of appendix. Authors are said to bestow particular pains on their prefaces. Cervantes, for instance, tells us that the preface to the first part of *Don Quixote* cost him more thought than the writing of the entire work. "It argues a deficiency of taste," says Isaac D'Israeli, "to turn over an elaborate preface unread; for it is the essence of the author's roses—every drop distilled at an immense cost." And, no doubt, it is a great slight to an author to skip his preface, though it cannot be denied that some prefaces are very tedious, because the writer "spins out the thread of his verbosity finer than the staple of his argument," and none but the most *hardy* readers can persevere to the distant end. The Italians call a preface *salsa del libro*, the *salt* of the book. A preface may also be likened to the porch of a mansion, where it is not courteous to keep a visitor waiting long before you open the door and make him free of your house. But the reader who passes over the preface to the *Gulistán* unread loses not a little of the spice of that fascinating and instructive book. He who reads it, however, is rewarded by the charming account which the author gives of how he came to form his literary Rose-Garden:

5

"It was the season of spring; the air was temperate and the rose in full bloom. The vestments of the trees resembled the festive garments of the fortunate. It was mid-spring, when the nightingales were chanting from their pulpits in the branches. The rose, decked with pearly dew, like blushes on the cheek of a chiding mistress. It happened once that I was benighted in a garden, in company with a friend. The spot was delightful: the trees intertwined; you would have said that the earth was bedecked with glass spangles, and that the knot of the Pleiades was suspended from the branch of the vine. A garden with a running stream, and trees whence birds were warbling melodious strains: that filled with tulips of various hues; these loaded with fruits of several kinds. Under the shade of its trees the zephyr had spread the variegated carpet.

"In the morning, when the desire to return home overcame our inclination to remain, I saw in my friend's lap a collection of roses, odoriferous herbs, and hyacinths, which he intended to carry to town. I said: 'You are not ignorant that the flower of the garden soon fadeth, and that the enjoyment of the rose-bush is of short continuance; and the sages have declared that the heart ought not to be set upon anything that is transitory.' He asked: 'What course is then to be pursued?' I replied: 'I am able to form a book of roses, which will delight the beholders and gratify those who are present; whose leaves the tyrannic arm of autumnal blasts can never affect, or injure the blossoms of its spring. What benefit will you derive from a basket of flowers? Carry a leaf from my garden: a rose may continue in bloom five or six days, but this Rose-Garden will flourish for ever.' As soon as I had uttered these words, he flung the flowers from his lap, and, laying hold of the skirt of my garment, exclaimed: 'When the beneficent promise, they faithfully discharge their engagements.' In the course of a few days two chapters were written in my note-book, in a style that may be useful to orators and improve the skill of letter-writers. In short, while the rose was still in bloom, the book called the Rose-Garden was finished."

Dr. Johnson has remarked that "there is scarcely any poet of eminence who has not left some testimony of his fondness for the flowers, the zephyrs, and the warblers of the spring." This is pre-eminently the case of Oriental poets, from Solomon downwards: "Rise up, my love, my fair one, and come away," exclaims the Hebrew poet in his Book of Canticles: "for lo! the winter is past, the rain is over and gone: the flowers appear on the earth; the time of the singing of birds has come, and the voice of the turtle is heard in our land. The fig-tree putteth forth her green fruits, and the vines with the tender grapes give forth a good smell. Arise, my love, my fair one, and come away."

In a Persian poem written in the 14th century the delights of the vernal season are thus described: "On every bush roses were blowing; on every

6

branch the nightingale was plaintively warbling. The tall cypress was dancing in the garden; and the poplar never ceased clapping its hands with joy. With a loud voice from the top of every bough the turtle-dove was proclaiming the glad advent of spring. The diadem of the narcissus shone with such splendour that you would have said it was the crown of the Emperor of China. On this side the north wind, on that, the west wind, were, in token of affection, scattering dirhams at the feet of the rose. [3] The earth was musk-scented, the air musk-laden."

But it would be difficult to adduce from the writings of any poet, European or Asiatic, anything to excel the charming ode on spring, by the Turkish poet Mesíhí, who flourished in the 15th century, which has been rendered into graceful English verse, and in the measure of the original, by my friend Mr. E. J. W. Gibb, in his dainty volume of *Ottoman Poems*, published in London a few years ago. These are some of the verses from that fine ode:

Hark! the bulbul's [4] lay so joyous: "Now have come the days of spring!"
Merry shows and crowds on every mead they spread, a maze of spring;
There the almond-tree its silvery blossoms scatters, sprays of spring:
Gaily live! for soon will vanish, biding not, the days of spring! [5]

Once again, with flow'rets decked themselves have mead and plain;
Tents for pleasure have the blossoms raised in every rosy lane;
Who can tell, when spring hath ended, who and what may whole remain?
Gaily live! for soon will vanish, biding not, the days of spring!

Sparkling dew-drops stud the lily's leaf like sabre broad and keen;
Bent on merry gipsy party, crowd they all the flow'ry green!
List to me, if thou desirest, these beholding, joy to glean:
Gaily live! for soon will vanish, biding not, the days of spring!

Rose and tulip, like to maidens' cheeks, all beauteous show,
Whilst the dew-drops, like the jewels in their ears, resplendent glow;
Do not think, thyself beguiling, things will aye continue so:
Gaily live! for soon will vanish, biding not, the days of spring!

Whilst each dawn the clouds are shedding jewels o'er the rosy land,
And the breath of morning zephyr, fraught with Tátár musk, is bland;
Whilst the world's fair time is present, do not thou unheeding stand:
Gaily live! for soon will vanish, biding not, the days of spring!

With the fragrance of the garden, so imbued the musky air,
Every dew-drop, ere it reaches earth, is turned to attar rare;
O'er the parterre spread the incense-clouds a canopy right fair:
Gaily live! for soon will vanish, Biding not, the days of spring!

7

This Turkish poet's maxim, it will be observed, was "enjoy the present day"—the *carpe diem* of Horace, the genial old pagan. On the same suggestive theme of Springtide a celebrated Turkish poetess, Fitnet Khánim (for the Ottoman Turks have poetesses of considerable genius as well as poets), has composed a pleasing ode, addressed to her lord, of which the following stanzas are also from Mr. Gibb's collection:

The fresh spring-clouds across all earth their glistening pearls profuse now
....sow;
The flowers, too, all appearing, forth the radiance of their beauty show;
Of mirth and joy 'tis now the time, the hour, to wander to and fro;
The palm-tree o'er the fair ones' pic-nic gay its grateful shade doth throw.

O Liege, come forth! From end to end with verdure doth the whole earth
....*glow;*
'Tis springtide once again, once more the tulips and the roses blow!

Behold the roses, how they shine, e'en like the cheeks of maids most fair;
The fresh-sprung hyacinth shows like to beauties' dark, sweet, musky hair;
The loved one's form behold, like cypress which the streamlet's bank doth
....bear;
In sooth, each side for soul and heart doth some delightful joy prepare.

O Liege, come forth! From end to end with verdure doth the whole earth
....*glow;*
'Tis springtide once again, once more the tulips and the roses blow!

The parterre's flowers have all bloomed forth, the roses, sweetly smiling,
....shine;
On every side lorn nightingales, in plaintive notes discerning, pine.
How fair carnation and wallflower the borders of the garden line!
The long-haired hyacinth and jasmine both around the cypress twine.

O Liege, come forth! From end to end with verdure doth the whole earth
....*glow;*
'Tis springtide once again, once more the tulips and the roses blow!

I cannot resist the temptation to cite, in concluding this introductory paper, another fine eulogy of the delights of spring, by Amír Khusrú, of Delhi (14th century), from his *Mihra-i-Iskandar*, which has been thus rendered into rhythmical prose:

"A day in spring, when all the world a pleasing picture seemed; the sun at early dawn with happy auspices arose. The earth was bathed in balmy dew; the beauties of the garden their charms displayed, the face of each with brilliancy adorned. The flowers in freshness bloomed; the lamp of the rose acquired lustre from the breeze; the tulip brought a cup from paradise; the rose-bower shed the sweets of Eden; beneath its folds the musky buds remained, like a musky amulet on the neck of Beauty. The violet bent its head; the fold of the bud was closer pressed; the opened rose in splendour glowed, and attracted every eye; the lovely flowers oppressed with dew in tremulous motion waved. The air o'er all the garden a silvery radiance threw, and o'er the flowers the breezes played; on every branch the birds attuned their notes, and every bower with warblings sweet was filled, so sweet, they stole the senses. The early nightingale poured forth its song, that gives a zest to those who quaff the morning goblet. From the turtle's soft cooings love seized each bird that skimmed the air."

II

STORIES FROM THE "GULISTÁN"

The *Gulistán* consists of short tales and anecdotes, to which are appended comments in prose and verse, and is divided into eight chapters, or sections: (1) the Morals of Kings; (2) the Morals of Dervishes; (3) the Excellence of Contentment; (4) the Advantages of Taciturnity; (5) Love and Youth; (6) Imbecility and Old Age; (7) the Effects of Education; (8) Rules for the Conduct of Life. In culling some of the choicest flowers of this perennial Garden, the particular order observed by Saádí need not be regarded here; it is preferable to pick here a flower and there a flower, as fancy may direct.

It may happen, says our author, that the prudent counsel of an enlightened sage does not succeed; and it may chance that an unskilful boy inadvertently hits the mark with his arrow: A Persian king, while on a pleasure excursion with a number of his courtiers at Nassála Shíráz, appointed an archery competition for the amusement of himself and his friends. He caused a gold ring, set with a valuable gem, to be fixed on the dome of Asád, and it was announced that whosoever should send an arrow through the ring should obtain it as a reward of his skill. The four hundred skilled archers forming the royal body-guard each shot at the ring without success. It chanced that a boy on a neighbouring house-top was at the same time diverting himself with a little bow, when one of his arrows, shot at random, went through the ring. The boy, having obtained the prize, immediately burned his bow, shrewdly observing that he did so in order that the reputation of this feat should never be impaired.

The advantage of abstinence, or rather, great moderation in eating and drinking, is thus curiously illustrated: Two dervishes travelled together; one was a robust man, who regularly ate three meals every day, the other was infirm of body, and accustomed to fast frequently for two days in succession. On their reaching the gate of a certain town, they were arrested on suspicion of being spies, and both lodged, without food, in the same prison, the door of which was then securely locked. Several days after, the unlucky dervishes were found to be quite innocent of the crime imputed to them, and on opening the door of the prison the strong man was discovered to be dead, and the infirm man still alive. At this circumstance the officers of justice marvelled; but a philosopher observed, that had the contrary happened it would have been more wonderful, since the one who died had been a great eater, and consequently was unable to endure the want of food, while the other, being accustomed to abstinence, had survived.

Of Núshírván the Just (whom the Greeks called Chosroe), of the Sassanian dynasty of Persian kings—sixth century—Saádí relates that on one occasion, while at his hunting-seat, he was having some game dressed, and ordered a servant to procure some salt from a neighbouring village, at the same time charging him strictly to pay the full price for it, otherwise the exaction might become a custom. His courtiers were surprised at this order, and asked the king what possible harm could ensue from such a trifle. The good king replied: "Oppression was brought into the world from small beginnings, which every new comer increased, until it has reached the present degree of enormity." Upon this Saádí remarks: "If the monarch were to eat a single apple from the garden of a peasant, the servant would pull up the tree by the roots; and if the king order five eggs to be taken by force, his soldiers will spit a thousand fowls. The iniquitous tyrant remaineth not, but the curses of mankind rest on him for ever."

Only those who have experienced danger can rightly appreciate the advantages of safety, and according as a man has become acquainted with adversity does he recognise the value of prosperity—a sentiment which Saádí illustrates by the story of a boy who was in a vessel at sea for the first time, in which were also the king and his officers of state. The lad was in great fear of being drowned, and made a loud outcry, in spite of every effort of those around him to soothe him into tranquility. As his lamentations annoyed the king, a sage who was of the company offered to quiet the terrified youth, with his majesty's permission, which being granted, he caused the boy to be plunged several times in the sea and then drawn up into the ship, after which the youth retired to a corner and remained perfectly quiet. The king inquired why the lad had been subjected to such roughness, to which the sage replied: "At first he had never experienced the danger of being drowned, neither had he known the safety of a ship."

One of our English moralists has remarked that the man who chiefly prides himself on his ancestry is like a potato-plant, whose best qualities are under ground. Saádí tells us of an old Arab who said to his son: "O my child, in the day of resurrection they will ask you what you have done in the world, and not from whom you are descended."—In the *Akhlák-i-Jalaly*, a work comprising the practical philosophy of the Muhammedans, written, in the 15th century, in the Persian language, by Fakír Jání Muhammed Asaád, and translated into English by W. F. Thompson, Alí, the Prophet's cousin, is reported to have said:

My soul is my father, my title my worth;
A Persian or Arab, there's little between:

11

Give me him for a comrade, whatever his birth,
Who shows what *he is*—not what *others have been.*

An Arabian poet says:

Be the son of whom thou wilt, try to acquire literature,
The acquisition of which may make pedigree unnecessary to thee;
Since a man of worth is he who can say, "I am so and so,"
Not he who can only say, "My father was so and so."

And again:

Ask not a man who his father was, but make trial
Of his qualities, and then conciliate or reject him accordingly
For it is no disgrace to new wine, if it only be sweet,
As to its taste, that it was the juice [or daughter] of sour grapes.

The often-quoted maxim of La Rochefoucauld, that there is something in the misfortunes of our friends which affords us a degree of secret pleasure, is well known to the Persians. Saádí tells us of a merchant who, having lost a thousand dínars, cautioned his son not to mention the matter to anyone, "in order," said he, "that we may not suffer two misfortunes—the loss of our money and the secret satisfaction of our neighbours."

A generous disposition is thus eloquently recommended: They asked a wise man, which was preferable, fortitude or liberality, to which he replied: "He who possesses liberality has no need of fortitude. It is inscribed on the tomb of Bahram-i-Gúr that a liberal hand is preferable to a strong arm." "Hátim Taï," remarks Saádí, "no longer exists, but his exalted name will remain famous for virtue to eternity.[6] Distribute the tithe of your wealth in alms, for when the husbandman lops off the exuberant branches from the vine, it produces an increase of grapes."

Prodigality, however, is as much to be condemned as judicious liberality is to be lauded. Saádí gives the following account of a Persian prodigal son, who was not so fortunate in the end as his biblical prototype: The son of a religious man, who succeeded to an immense fortune by the will of his uncle, became a dissipated and debauched profligate, in so much that he left no heinous crime unpractised, nor was there any intoxicating drug which he had not tasted. Once I admonished him, saying: "O my son, wealth is a running stream, and pleasure revolves like a millstone; or, in other words, profuse expense suits him only who has a certain income. When you have no certain income, be frugal in your expenses, because the sailors have a song, that if the rain does not fall in the mountains, the Tigris will become a dry bed of sand in the course of a year. Practise wisdom and virtue, and relinquish sensuality, for when your money is spent you will suffer distress and expose yourself to shame."z The young man, seduced by music and wine, would not take my advice, but, in opposition to my arguments, said: "It is contrary to the wisdom of the sages to disturb our present enjoyments by the dread of futurity. Why should they who possess fortune suffer distress by anticipating sorrow? Go and be merry, O my enchanting friend! We ought not to be uneasy to-day for what may happen to-morrow. How would it become me, who am placed in the uppermost seat of liberality, so that the fame of my bounty is wide spread? When a man has acquired reputation by liberality and munificence, it does not become him to tie up his money-bags. When your good name has been spread through the street, you cannot shut your door against it." I perceived (continues Saádí) that he did not approve of my admonition, and that my warm breath did not affect his cold iron. I ceased advising, and, quitting his society, returned into the corner of safety, in conformity with the saying of the philosophers: "Admonish and exhort as your charity requires; if they mind not, it does not concern you. Although thou knowest that they will not listen, nevertheless speak whatever you know is advisable. It will soon come to pass that you will see the silly fellow with his feet in the stocks, smiting his hands and exclaiming, 'Alas, that I did not listen to the wise man's advice!'" After some time, that which I had predicted from his dissolute conduct I saw verified. He was clothed in rags, and begging a morsel of food. I was distressed at his wretched condition, and did not think it consistent with humanity to scratch his wound with reproach. But I said in my heart: Profligate men, when intoxicated with pleasure, reflect not on the day of poverty. The tree which in the summer has a profusion of fruit is consequently without leaves in winter.

The incapacity of some youths to receive instruction is always a source of vexation to the pedagogue. Saádí tells us of a vazír who sent his stupid son to a learned man, requesting him to impart some of his knowledge to the lad, hoping that his mind would be improved. After attempting to instruct him for some time without effect, he sent this message to his father: "Your son has no capacity, and has almost distracted me. When nature has given capacity instruction will make impressions; but if iron is not of the proper temper, no polishing will make it good. Wash not a dog in the seven seas, for when he is wetted he will only be the dirtier. If the ass that carried Jesus Christ were to be taken to Mecca, at his return he would still be an ass."

One of the greatest sages of antiquity is reported to have said that all the knowledge he had acquired merely taught him how little he did know; and indeed it is only smatterers who are vain of their supposed knowledge. A sensible young man, says Saádí, who had made considerable progress in learning and virtue, was at the same time so discreet that he would sit in the company of learned men without uttering a word. Once his father said to him: "My son, why do you not also say something you know?" He replied: "I fear lest they should question me about something of which I am ignorant, whereby I should suffer shame."

The advantages of education are thus set forth by a philosopher who was exhorting his children: "Acquire knowledge, for in worldly riches and possessions no reliance can be placed.[8] Rank will be of no use out of your own country; and on a journey money is in danger of being lost, for either the thief may carry it off all at once, or the possessor may consume it by degrees. But knowledge is a perennial spring of wealth, and if a man of education cease to be opulent, yet he need not be sorrowful, for knowledge of itself is riches.[9] A man of learning, wheresoever he goes, is treated with respect, and sits in the uppermost seat, whilst the ignorant man gets only scanty fare and encounters distress." There once happened (adds Saádí) an insurrection in Damascus, where every one deserted his habitation. The wise sons of a peasant became the king's ministers, and the stupid sons of the vazír were reduced to ask charity in the villages. If you want a paternal inheritance, acquire from your father knowledge, for wealth may be spent in ten days.

In the following charming little tale Saádí recounts an interesting incident in his own life: I remember that in my youth, as I was passing through a street, I cast my eyes on a beautiful girl. It was in the autumn, when the heat dried up all moisture from the mouth, and the sultry wind made the marrow boil in the bones, so that, being unable to support the sun's powerful rays, I was obliged to take shelter under the shade of a wall, in hopes that some one would relieve me from the distressing heat, and quench my thirst with a draught of water. Suddenly from the portico of a house I beheld a female form whose beauty it is impossible for the tongue of eloquence to describe, insomuch that it seemed as if the dawn was rising in the obscurity of night, or as if the Water of Immortality was issuing from the Land of Darkness. She held in her hand a cup of snow-water, into which she had sprinkled sugar and mixed with it the juice of the grape. I know not whether what I perceived was the fragrance of rose-water, or that she had infused into it a few drops from the blossom of her cheek. In short, I received the cup from her beauteous hand, and, drinking the contents, found myself restored to new life. The thirst of my soul is not such that it can be allayed with a drop of pure water—the streams of whole rivers would not satisfy it. How happy is that fortunate one whose eyes every morning may behold such a countenance! He who is intoxicated with wine will be sober again in the course of the night; but he who is intoxicated by the cup-bearer will never recover his senses till the day of judgment.

Alas, poor Saádí! The lovely cup-bearer, who made such a lasting impression on the heart of the young poet, was not destined for his bride. His was indeed a sad matrimonial fate; and who can doubt but that the beauteous form of the stranger maiden would often rise before his mental view after he was married to the Xantippe who rendered some portion of his life unhappy!

Among the tales under the heading of "Imbecility and Old Age" we have one of "oldé January that wedded was to freshé May," which points its moral now as it did six hundred years ago: When I married a young virgin, said an old man, I bedecked a chamber with flowers, sat with her alone, and had fixed my eyes and heart solely upon her. Many long nights I passed without sleep, repeating jests and pleasantries, to remove shyness, and make her familiar. On one of these nights I said: "Fortune has been propitious to you, in that you have fallen into the society of an old man, of mature judgment, who has seen the world, and experienced various situations of good and bad fortune, who knows the rights of society, and has performed the duties of friendship;—one who is affectionate, affable, cheerful, and conversable. I will exert my utmost endeavours to gain your affection, and if you should treat me unkindly I will not be offended; or if, like the parrot, your food should be sugar, I will devote my sweet life to your support. You have not met with a youth of a rude disposition, with a weak understanding, headstrong, a gadder, who would be constantly changing his situations and inclinations, sleeping every night in a new place, and every day forming some new intimacy. Young men may be lively and handsome, but they are inconstant in their attachments. Look not thou for fidelity from those who, with the eyes of the nightingale, are every instant singing upon a different rose-bush. But old men pass their time in wisdom and good manners, not in the ignorance and frivolity of youth. Seek one better than yourself, and having found him, consider yourself fortunate. With one like yourself you would pass your life without improvement." I spoke a great deal after this manner (continued the old man), and thought that I had made a conquest of her heart, when suddenly she heaved a cold sigh from the bottom of her heart, and replied: "All the fine speeches that you have been uttering have not so much weight in the scale of my reason as one single sentence I have heard from my nurse, that if you plant an arrow in the side of a young woman it is not so painful as the society of an old man." In short (continued he), it was impossible to agree, and our differences ended in a separation. After the time prescribed by law, she married a young man of an impetuous temper, ill-natured, and in indigent circumstances, so that she suffered the injuries of violence, with the evils of penury. Nevertheless she returned thanks for her lot, and said: "God be praised that I escaped from infernal torment, and have obtained this permanent blessing. Amidst all your violence and impetuosity of temper, I will put up with your airs, because you are handsome. It is better to burn with you in hell than to be in paradise with the other. The scent of onions from a beautiful mouth is more fragrant than the odour of the rose from the hand of one who is ugly."

It must be allowed that this old man put his own case to his young wife with very considerable address: yet, such is woman-nature, she chose to be "a young man's slave rather than an old man's darling." And, *apropos*, Saádí has another story which may be added to the foregoing: An old man was asked why he did not marry. He answered: "I should not like an old woman." "Then marry a young one, since you have property." Quoth he: "Since I, who am an old man, should not be pleased with an old woman, how can I expect that a young one would be attached to me?"

"Uneasy lies the head that wears a crown," says our great dramatist, in proof of which take this story: A certain king, when arrived at the end of his days, having no heir, directed in his will that the morning after his death the first person who entered the gate of the city they should place on his head the crown of royalty, and commit to his charge the government of the kingdom. It happened that the first to enter the city was a dervish, who all his life had collected victuals from the charitable and sewed patch on patch. The ministers of state and the nobles of the court carried out the king's will, bestowing on him the kingdom and the treasure. For some time the dervish governed the kingdom, until part of the nobility swerved their necks from obedience to him, and all the neighbouring monarchs, engaging in hostile confederacies, attacked him with their armies. In short, the troops and peasantry were thrown into confusion, and he lost the possession of some territories. The dervish was distressed at these events, when an old friend, who had been his companion in the days of poverty, returned from a journey, and, finding him in such an exalted state, said: "Praised be the God of excellence and glory, that your high fortune has aided you and prosperity been your guide, so that a rose has issued from the brier, and the thorn has been extracted from your foot, and you have arrived at this dignity. Of a truth, joy succeeds sorrow; the bud does sometimes blossom and sometimes wither; the tree is sometimes naked and sometimes clothed." He replied: "O brother, condole with me, for this is not a time for congratulation. When you saw me last, I was only anxious how to obtain bread; but now I have all the cares of the world to encounter. If the times are adverse, I am in pain; and if they are prosperous, I am captivated with worldly enjoyments. There is no calamity greater than worldly affairs, because they distress the heart in prosperity as well as in adversity. If you want riches, seek only for contentment, which is inestimable wealth. If the rich man would throw money into your lap, consider not yourself obliged to him, for I have often heard that the patience of the poor is preferable to the liberality of the rich."

Muezzins, who call the faithful to prayer at the prescribed hours from the minarets of the mosques, are generally blind men, as a man with his eyesight might spy into the domestic privacy of the citizens, who sleep on the flat roofs of their houses in the hot season, and are selected for their sweetness of voice. Saádí, however, tells us of a man who performed gratuitously the office of muezzin, and had such a voice as disgusted all

16

who heard it. The intendant of the mosque, a good, humane man, being unwilling to offend him, said one day: "My friend, this mosque has muezzins of long standing, each of whom has a monthly stipend of ten dínars. Now I will give you ten dínars to go to another place." The man agreed to this and went away. Some time after he came to the intendant and said: "O, my lord, you injured me in sending me away from this station for ten dínars; for where I went they will give me twenty dínars to remove to another place, to which I have not consented." The intendant laughed, and said: "Take care—don't accept of the offer, for they may be willing to give you fifty."

To those who have "music in their souls," and are "moved by concord of sweet sounds," the tones of a harsh voice are excruciating; and if among our statesmen and other public speakers "silver tongues" are rare, they are much more so among our preachers. The Church of Rome does not admit into the priesthood men who have any bodily shortcoming or defect; it would also be well if all candidates for holy orders in the English and Scottish Churches whose voices are not at least tolerable were rejected, as unfit to preach! Saádí seems to have had a great horror of braying orators, and relates a number of anecdotes about them, such as this: A preacher who had a detestable voice, but thought he had a very sweet one, bawled out to no purpose. You would say the croaking of the crow in the desert was the burden of his song, and that this verse of the Kurán was intended for him, "Verily the most detestable of sounds is the braying of an ass." When this ass of a preacher brayed, it made Persepolis tremble. The people of the town, on account of the respectability of his office, submitted to the calamity, and did not think it advisable to molest him, until one of the neighbouring preachers, who was secretly ill-disposed towards him, came once to see him, and said: "I have had a dream—may it prove good!" "What did you dream?" "I thought you had a sweet voice, and that the people were enjoying tranquility from your discourse." The preacher, after reflecting a little, replied: "What a happy dream is this that you have had, which has discovered to me my defect, in that I have an unpleasant voice, and that the people are distressed at my preaching. I am resolved that in future I will read only in a low tone. The company of friends was disadvantageous to me, because they look on my bad manners as excellent: my defects appear to them skill and perfection, and my thorn as the rose and the jasmin."

Our author, as we have seen, enlivens his moral discourses occasionally with humorous stories, and one or two more of these may fittingly close the present section: One of the slaves of Amrúlais having run away, a person was sent in pursuit of him and brought him back. The vazír, being inimical to him, commanded him to be put to death in order to deter other slaves from committing the like offence. The slave prostrated himself before Amrúlais and said: "Whatever may happen to me with your

17

approbation is lawful—what plea can the slave offer against the sentence of his lord? But, seeing that I have been brought up under the bounties of your house, I do not wish that at the resurrection you shall be charged with my blood. If you are resolved to kill your slave, do so comformably to the interpretation of the law, in order that at the resurrection you may not suffer reproach." The king asked: "After what manner shall I expound it?" The slave replied: "Give me leave to kill the vazír, and then, in retaliation for him, order me to be put to death, that you may kill me justly." The king laughed, and asked the vazír what was his advice in this matter. Quoth the vazír: "O my lord, as an offering to the tomb of your father, liberate this rogue, in order that I may not also fall into this calamity. The crime is on my side, for not having observed the words of the sages, who say, 'When you combat with one who flings clods of earth, you break your own head by your folly: when you shoot at the face of your enemy, be careful that you sit out of his aim.'"—And not a little wit, too, did the kází exhibit when detected by the king in an intrigue with a farrier's daughter, and his Majesty gave order that he should be flung from the top of the castle, "as an example for others"; to which the kází replied: "O monarch of the universe, I have been fostered in your family, and am not singular in the commission of such crimes; therefore, I ask you to precipitate some one else, in order that I may benefit by the example." The king laughed at his wit, and spared his life.—Nor is this tale without a spice of humour: An astrologer entered his house and finding a stranger in company with his wife abused him, and called him such opprobrious names that a quarrel and strife ensued. A shrewd man, being informed of this, said to the astrologer: "What do you know of the heavenly bodies, when you cannot tell what goes on in your own house?"[10]—Last, and perhaps best of all, is this one: I was hesitating about concluding a bargain for a house, when a Jew said: "I am an old householder in that quarter; inquire of me the description of the house, and buy it, for it has no fault." I replied: "Excepting that you are one of the neighbours!"

III

ANECDOTES AND APHORISMS FROM THE "GULISTÁN," WITH ANALOGUES— CONCLUSION

Besides the maxims comprised in the concluding chapter of the *Gulistán*, under the heading of "Rules for the Conduct of Life," many others, of great pith and moment, are interspersed with the tales and anecdotes which Saádí recounts in the preceding chapters, a selection of which can hardly fail to prove both instructive and interesting.

It is related that at the court of Núshírván, king of Persia, a number of wise men were discussing a difficult question; and Buzurjmihr (his famous prime minister), being silent, was asked why he did not take part in the debate. He answered: "Ministers are like physicians, and the physician gives medicine to the sick only. Therefore, when I see your opinions are judicious, it would not be consistent with wisdom for me to obtrude my sentiments. When a matter can be managed without my interference it is not proper for me to speak on the subject. But if I see a blind man in the way of a well, should I keep silence it were a crime." On another occasion, when some Indian sages were discoursing on his virtue, they could discover in him only this fault, that he hesitated in his speech, so that his hearers were kept a long time in suspense before he delivered his sentiments. Buzurjmihr overheard their conversation and observed: "It is better to deliberate before I speak than to repent of what I have said."[11]

A parallel to this last saying of the Persian vazír is found in a "notable sentence" of a wise Greek, in this passage from the *Dictes, or Sayings of Philosophers*, printed by Caxton (I have modernised the spelling):

"There came before a certain king three wise men, a Greek, a Jew, and a Saracen, of whom the said king desired that each of them would utter some good and notable sentence. Then the Greek said: 'I may well correct and amend my thoughts, but not my words.' The Jew said: 'I marvel of them that say things prejudicial, when silence were more profitable.' The Saracen said: 'I am master of my words ere they are pronounced; but when they are spoken I am servant thereto.' And it was asked one of them: 'Who might be called a king?' And he answered: 'He that is not subject to his own will.'"

The *Dictes, or Sayings of Philosophers*, of which, I believe, but one perfect copy is extant, was translated from the French by Earl Rivers, and printed by Caxton, at Westminister, in the year 1477, as we learn from the colophon. I am not aware that any one has taken the trouble to trace to their sources all the sayings comprised in this collection, but I think the original of the above is to be found in the following, from the preface to the Arabian version (from the Pahlaví, the ancient language of Persia) of the celebrated Fables of Bidpaï, entitled *Kalíla wa Dimna*, made in the year 754:

"The four kings of China, India, Persia, and Greece, being together, agreed each of them to deliver a saying which might be recorded to their honour in after ages. The king of China said: 'I have more power over that which I have not spoken than I have to recall what has once passed my lips.' The king of India: 'I have been often struck with the risk of speaking; for if a man be heard in his own praise it is unprofitable boasting, and what he says to his own discredit is injurious in its consequences.' The king of Persia: 'I am the slave of what I have spoken, but the master of what I conceal.' The king of Greece: 'I have never regretted the silence which I had imposed upon myself; though I have often repented of the words I have uttered;[12] for silence is attended with advantage, whereas loquacity is often followed by incurable evils.'"

The Persian poet Jámí—the last of the brilliant galaxy of genius who enriched the literature of their country, and who flourished two centuries after Saádí had passed to his rest—reproduces these sayings of the four kings in his work entitled *Baháristán*, or Abode of Spring, which is similar in design to the *Gulistán*.

Among the sayings of other wise men (whose names, however, Saádí does not mention) are the following: A devotee, who had quitted his monastery and become a member of a college, being asked what difference there is between a learned man and a religious man to induce him thus to change his associates, answered: "The devotee saves his own blanket out of the waves, and the learned man endeavours to save others from drowning."—A young man complained to his spiritual guide of his studies being frequently interrupted by idle and impudent visitors, and desired to know by what means he might rid himself of the annoyance. The sage replied: "To such as are poor lend money, and of such as are rich ask money, and, depend upon it, you will never see one of them again."

Saádí's own aphorisms are not less striking and instructive. They are indeed calculated to stimulate the faltering to manly exertion, and to counsel the inexperienced. It is to youthful minds, however, that the "words of the wise" are more especially addressed; for it is during the spring-time of life that the seeds of good and evil take root; and so we find the sage Hebrew king frequently addressing his maxims to the young: "My son," is his formula, "my son, attend to my words, and bow thine ear to my understanding; that thou mayest regard discretion, and that thy lips may keep knowledge." And the "good and notable sentences" of Saádí are well worthy of being treasured by the young man on the threshold of life. For example:

"Life is snow, and the summer advanceth; only a small portion remaineth: art thou still slothful?"

This warning has been reiterated by moralists in all ages and countries;— the Great Teacher says: "Work while it is day, for the night cometh when no man can work." And Saádí, in one of his sermons (which is found in another of his books), recounts this beautiful fable, in illustration of the fortunes of the slothful and the industrious:

It is related that in a certain garden a Nightingale had built his nest on the bough of a rose-bush. It so happened that a poor little Ant had fixed her dwelling at the root of this same bush, and managed as best she could to store her wretched hut of care with winter provision. Day and night was the Nightingale fluttering round the rose-bower, and tuning the barbut[13] of his soul-deluding melody; indeed, whilst the Ant was night and day industriously occupied, the thousand-songed bird seemed fascinated with his own sweet voice, echoing amidst the trees. The Nightingale was whispering his secret to the Rose,[14] and that, full-blown by the zephyr of the dawn, would ogle him in return. The poor Ant could not help admiring the coquettish airs of the Rose, and the gay blandishments of the Nightingale, and incontinently remarking: "Time alone can disclose what may be the end of this frivolity and talk!" After the flowery season of summer was gone, and the black time of winter was come, thorns took the station of the Rose, and the raven the perch of the Nightingale. The storms of autumn raged in fury, and the foliage of the grove was shed upon the ground. The cheek of the leaf was turned yellow, and the breath of the wind was chill and blasting. The gathering cloud poured down hailstones, like pearls, and flakes of snow floated like camphor on the bosom of the air. Suddenly the Nightingale returned into the garden, but he met neither the bloom of the Rose nor fragrance of the spikenard; notwithstanding his thousand-songed tongue, he stood stupified and mute, for he could discover no flower whose form he might admire, nor any verdure whose freshness he might enjoy. The Thorn turned round to him and said: "How long, silly bird, wouldst thou be courting the society of the Rose? Now is the season that in the absence of thy charmer thou must put up with the heart-rending bramble of separation." The Nightingale cast his eye upon the scene around him, but saw nothing fit to eat. Destitute of food, his strength and fortitude failed him, and in his abject helplessness he was unable to earn himself a little livelihood. He called to his mind and said: "Surely the Ant had in former days his dwelling underneath this tree, and was busy in hoarding a store of provision: now I will lay my wants before her, and, in the name of good neighbourship, and with an appeal to her generosity, beg some small relief. Peradventure she may pity my distress and bestow her charity upon me." Like a poor suppliant, the half-famished Nightingale presented himself at the Ant's door, and said: "Generosity is the harbinger of prosperity, and the capital stock of good luck. I was wasting my precious life in idleness whilst thou wast toiling hard and laying up a hoard. How considerate and good it were of thee wouldst thou spare me a portion of it." The Ant replied:

"Thou wast day and night occupied in idle talk, and I in attending to the needful: one moment thou wast taken up with the fresh blandishment of the Rose, and the next busy in admiring the blossoming spring. Wast thou not aware that every summer has its fall and every road an end?"[15]

These are a few more of Saádí's aphorisms:

Riches are for the comfort of life, and not life for the accumulation of riches.[16]

The eye of the avaricious man cannot be satisfied with wealth, any more than a well can be filled with dew.

A wicked rich man is a clod of earth gilded.

The liberal man who eats and bestows is better than the religious man who fasts and hoards.

Publish not men's secret faults, for by disgracing them you make yourself of no repute.

He who gives advice to a self-conceited man stands himself in need of counsel from another.

The vicious cannot endure the sight of the virtuous, in the same manner as the curs of the market howl at a hunting-dog, but dare not approach him.

When a mean wretch cannot vie with any man in virtue, out of his wickedness he begins to slander him. The abject, envious wretch will slander the virtuous man when absent, but when brought face to face his loquacious tongue becomes dumb.

O thou, who hast satisfied thy hunger, to thee a barley loaf is beneath notice;—that seems loveliness to me which in thy sight appears deformity.

The ringlets of fair maids are chains for the feet of reason, and snares for the bird of wisdom.

When you have anything to communicate that will distress the heart of the person whom it concerns, be silent, in order that he may hear it from some one else. O nightingale, bring thou the glad tidings of the spring, and leave bad news to the owl!

It often happens that the imprudent is honoured and the wise despised. The alchemist died of poverty and distress, while the blockhead found a treasure under a ruin.

Covetousness sews up the eyes of cunning, and brings both bird and fish into the net.

Although, in the estimation of the wise, silence is commendable, yet at a proper season speech is preferable.[17]

Two things indicate an obscure understanding: to be silent when we should converse, and to speak when we should be silent.

Put not yourself so much in the power of your friend that, if he should become your enemy, he may be able to injure you.

Our English poet Young has this observation in his *Night Thoughts*:

> Thought, in the mine, may come forth gold or dross;
> When coined in word, we know its real worth.

He had been thus anticipated by Saádí: "To what shall be likened the tongue in a man's mouth? It is the key of the treasury of wisdom. When the door is shut, who can discover whether he deals in jewels or small-wares?"

The poet Thomson, in his *Seasons*, has these lines, which have long been hackneyed:

Loveliness
Needs not the aid of foreign ornament,
But is when unadorned adorned the most.

Saádí had anticipated him also: "The face of the beloved," he says, "requireth not the art of the tire-woman. The finger of a beautiful woman and the tip of her ear are handsome without an ear-jewel or a turquoise ring." But Saádí, in his turn, was forestalled by the Arabian poet-hero Antar, in his famous *Mu'allaka*, or prize-poem, which is at least thirteen hundred years old, where he says: "Many a consort of a fair one, whose beauty required no ornaments, have I laid prostrate on the field."

Yet one Persian poet, at least, namely, Nakhshabí, held a different opinion: "Beauty," he says, "adorned with ornaments, portends disastrous events to our hearts. An amiable form, ornamented with diamonds and gold, is like a melodious voice accompanied by the rabáb." Again, he says: "Ornaments are the universal ravishers of hearts, and an upper garment for the shoulder is like a cluster of gems. If dress, however," he concedes, "may have been at any time the assistant of beauty, beauty is always the animator of dress." It is remarkable that homely-featured women dress more gaudily than their handsome sisters generally, thus unconsciously bringing their lack of beauty (not to put too fine a point on it) into greater prominence.

In common with other moralists, Saádí reiterates the maxim that learning and virtue, precept and practice, should ever go hand in hand. "Two persons," says he, "took trouble in vain: he who acquired wealth without using it, and he who taught wisdom without practising it." Again: "He who has acquired knowledge and does not practise it, is like unto him that ploughed but did not sow." And again: "How much soever you may study science, when you do not act wisely, you are ignorant. The beast that they load with books is not profoundly wise and learned: what knoweth his empty skull whether he carrieth fire-wood or books?" And yet again: "A learned man without temperance is like a blind man carrying a lamp: he showeth the way to others, but does not guide himself."

Ingratitude is denounced by all moralists as the lowest of vices. Thus Saádí says: "Man is beyond dispute the most excellent of created beings, and the vilest animal is the dog; but the sages agree that a grateful dog is better than an ungrateful man. A dog never forgets a morsel, though you pelt him a hundred times with stones. But if you cherish a mean wretch for an age, he will fight with you for a mere trifle." In language still more forcible does a Hindú poet denounce this basest of vices: "To cut off the teats of a cow;[18] to occasion a pregnant woman to miscarry; to injure a Bráhman—are sins of the most aggravated nature; but more atrocious than these is ingratitude."

The sentiment so tersely expressed in the Chinese proverb, "He who never reveals a secret keeps it best," is thus finely amplified by Saádí: "The matter which you wish to preserve as a secret impart not to every one, although he may be worthy of confidence; for no one will be so true to your secret as yourself. It is safer to be silent than to reveal a secret to any one, and tell him not to mention it. O wise man! stop the water at the spring-head, for when it is in full stream you cannot arrest it."[19]

The imperative duty of active benevolence is thus inculcated: "Bestow thy gold and thy wealth while they are thine; for when thou art gone they will be no longer in thy power. Distribute thy treasure readily to-day, for to-morrow the key may be no longer in thy hand. Exert thyself to cast a covering over the poor, that God's own veil may be a covering to thee."

In the following passage the man of learning and virtue is contrasted with the stupid and ignorant blockhead:

"If a wise man, falling into company with mean people, does not get credit for his discourse, be not surprised, for the sound of the harp cannot overpower the noise of the drum, and the fragrance of ambergris is overcome by fetid garlic. The ignorant fellow was proud of his loud voice, because he had impudently confounded the man of understanding. If a jewel falls in the mud it is still the same precious stone,[20] and if dust flies up to the sky it retains its original baseness. A capacity without education is deplorable, and education without capacity is thrown away. Sugar obtains not its value from the cane, but from its innate quality. Musk has fragrance of itself, and not from being called a perfume by the druggist. The wise man is like the druggist's chest, silent, but full of virtues; while the blockhead resembles the warrior's drum, noisy, but an empty prattler. A wise man in the company of those who are ignorant has been compared by the sages to a beautiful girl in the company of blind men, and to the Kurán in the house of an infidel."—The old proverb that "an evil bird has an evil egg" finds expression by Saádí thus: "No one whose origin is bad ever catches the reflection of the good." Again, he says: "How can we make a good sword out of bad iron? A worthless person cannot by education become a person of any worth." And yet again: "Evil habits which have taken root in one's nature will only be got rid of at the hour of death."

Firdausí, the Homer of Persia (eleventh century), has the following remarks in his scathing satire on the sultan Mahmúd, of Ghazní (Atkinson's rendering):

> Alas! from vice can goodness ever spring?
> Is mercy hoped for in a tyrant king?
> Can water wash the Ethiopian white?
> Can we remove the darkness from the night?

The tree to which a bitter fruit is given
Would still be bitter in the bowers of heaven;
And a bad heart keeps on its vicious course,
Or, if it changes, changes for the worse;
Whilst streams of milk where Eden's flow'rets blow
Acquire more honied sweetness as they flow.

The striking words of the Great Teacher, "How hardly shall they that have riches enter into the kingdom of God!" find an interesting analogue in this passage by Saádí: "There is a saying of the Prophet, 'To the poor death is a state of rest.' The ass that carries the lightest burden travels easiest. In like manner, the good man who bears the burden of poverty will enter the gate of death lightly loaded, while he who lives in affluence, with ease and comfort, will, doubtless, on that very account find death very terrible. And in any view, the captive who is released from confinement is happier than the noble who is taken prisoner."

A singular anecdote is told of another celebrated Persian poet, which may serve as a kind of commentary on this last-cited passage: Faridú 'd-Dín 'Attár, who died in the year 1229, when over a hundred years old, was considered the most perfect Súfí[21] philosopher of the time in which he lived. His father was an eminent druggist in Nishapúr, and for a time Faridú 'd-Dín followed the same profession, and his shop was the delight of all who passed by it, from the neatness of its arrangements and the fragrant odours of drugs and essences. 'Attár, which means druggist, or perfumer, Faridú 'd-Dín adopted for his poetical title. One day, while sitting at his door with a friend, an aged dervish drew near, and, after looking anxiously and closely into the well-furnished shop, he sighed heavily and shed tears, as he reflected on the transitory nature of all earthly things. 'Attár, mistaking the sentiment uppermost in the mind of the venerable devotee, ordered him to be gone, to which he meekly rejoined: "Yes, I have nothing to prevent me from leaving thy door, or, indeed, from quitting this world at once, as my sole possession is this threadbare garment. But O 'Attár, I grieve for thee: for how canst thou ever bring thyself to think of death—to leave all these goods behind thee?" 'Attár replied that he hoped and believed that he should die as contentedly as any dervish; upon which the aged devotee, saying, "We shall see," placed his wooden bowl upon the ground, laid his head upon it, and, calling on the name of God, immediately resigned his soul. Deeply impressed with this incident, 'Attár at once gave up his shop, and devoted himself to the study of Súfí philosophy.[22]

The death of Cardinal Mazarin furnishes another remarkable illustration of Saádí's sentiment. A day or two before he died, the cardinal caused his servant to carry him into his magnificent art gallery, where, gazing upon his collection of pictures and sculpture, he cried in anguish, "And must I leave all these?" Dr. Johnson may have had Mazarin's words in mind when he said to Garrick, while being shown over the famous actor's splendid mansion: "Ah, Davie, Davie, these are the things that make a death-bed terrible!"

Few passages of Shakspeare are more admired than these lines:

> And this our life, exempt from public haunts,
> Finds *tongues in trees*, books in the running brooks,
> Sermons in stones, and good in everything.[23]

Saádí had thus expressed the same sentiment before him: "The foliage of a newly-clothed tree, to the eye of a discerning man, displays a whole volume of the wondrous works of the Creator." Another Persian poet, Jámí, in his beautiful mystical poem of *Yúsuf wa Zulaykhá*, says: "Every leaf is a tongue uttering praises, like one who keepeth crying, 'In the name of God.'"[24] And the Afghan poet Abdu 'r-Rahman says: "Every tree, every shrub, stands ready to bend before him; every herb and blade of grass is a tongue to mutter his praises." And Horace Smith, that most pleasing but unpretentious writer, both of verse and prose, has thus finely amplified the idea of "tongues in trees":

> Your voiceless lips, O Flowers, are living preachers,
> Each cup a pulpit, every leaf a book,
> Supplying to my fancy numerous teachers,
> > From loneliest nook.

> 'Neath cloistered boughs, each floral bell that swingeth,
> And tolls its perfume on the passing air,
> Makes Sabbath in the fields, and ever ringeth
> > A call to prayer;—

> Not to the domes where crumbling arch and column
> Attest the feebleness of mortal hand,
> But to that fane, most catholic and solemn,
> > Which God hath planned:

> To that cathedral, boundless as our wonder,
> Whose quenchless lamps the sun and moon supply;
> Its choir, the winds and waves, its organ, thunder,
> > Its dome, the sky.

> There, amid solitude and shade, I wander
> Through the green aisles, and, stretched upon the sod,
> Awed by the silence, reverently ponder
> > The ways of God.

When Saádí composed his *Gulistán*, in 1278, he was between eighty and ninety years of age, with his great mind still vigorous as ever; and he lived many years after, beloved and revered by the poor, whose necessities he relieved, and honoured and esteemed by the noble and the learned, who frequently visited the venerable solitary, to gather and treasure up the pearls of wisdom which dropped from his eloquent tongue. Like other poets of lofty genius, he possessed a firm assurance of the immortality of his fame. "A rose," says he, "may continue to bloom for five or six days, but this Rose-Garden will flourish for ever"; and again: "These verses and recitals of mine will endure after every particle of my dust has been dispersed." Six centuries have passed away since the gifted sage penned his *Gulistán*, and his fame has not only continued in his own land and throughout the East generally, but has spread into all European countries, and across the Atlantic, where long after the days of Saádí "still stood the forests primeval."

ORIENTAL WIT AND HUMOUR

Sport that wrinkled Care derides,
And Laughter shaking both his sides.—
L' Allegro

I

MAN A LAUGHING ANIMAL—ANTIQUITY OF
POPULAR JESTS—"NIGHT AND DAY"—THE PLAIN-
FEATURED BRIDE—THE HOUSE OF CONDOLENCE—
THE BLIND MAN'S WIFE—TWO WITTY PERSIAN
LADIES—WOMAN'S COUNSEL—THE TURKISH
JESTER: IN THE PULPIT; THE CAULDRON; THE
BEGGAR; THE DRUNKEN GOVERNOR; THE
ROBBER; THE HOT BROTH—MUSLIM PREACHERS
AND MUSLIM MISERS

Certain philosophers have described man as a cooking animal, others as a tool-making animal, others, again, as a laughing animal. No creature save man, say the advocates of the last definition, seems to have any "sense of humour." However this may be, there can be little doubt that man in all ages of which we have any knowledge has possessed that faculty which perceives ridiculous incongruities in the relative positions of certain objects, and in the actions and sayings of individuals, which we term the "sense of the ludicrous." It is not to be supposed that a dog or a cat—albeit intelligent creatures, in their own ways—would see anything funny or laughable in a man whose sole attire consisted in a general's hat and sash and a pair of spurs! Yet *that* should be enough to "make even a cat laugh"! Certainly laughter is peculiar to our species; and gravity is as certainly not always a token of profound wisdom; for

The gravest beast's an ass;
    The gravest bird's an owl;
The gravest fish's an oyster;
    And the gravest man's a *fool*.

Many of the great sages of antiquity were also great humorists, and laughed long and heartily at a good jest. And, indeed, as the Sage of Chelsea affirms, "no man who has once heartily and wholly laughed can be altogether, irreclaimably bad. How much lies in laughter!—the cipher key wherewith we decipher the whole man!... The man who cannot laugh is not only fit for treasons, stratagems, and spoils, but his whole life is already a treason and a stratagem." Let us, then, laugh at what is laughable while we are yet clothed in "this muddy vesture of decay," for, as delightful Elia asks, "Can a ghost laugh? Can he shake his gaunt sides if we be merry with him?"

It is a remarkable fact that a considerable proportion of the familiar jests of almost any country, which are by its natives fondly believed to be "racy of the soil," are in reality common to other peoples widely differing in language and customs. Not a few of these jests had their origin ages upon ages since—in Greece, in Persia, in India. Yet they must have set out upon their travels westward at a comparatively early period, for they have been long domiciled in almost every country of Europe. Nevertheless, as we ourselves possess a goodly number of droll witticisms, repartees, and jests, which are most undoubtedly and beyond cavil our own—such as many of those which are ascribed to Sam Foote, Harry Erskine, Douglas Jerrold, and Sydney Smith; though they have been credited with some that are as old as the jests of Hierokles—so there exist in what may be termed the lower strata of Oriental fiction, humorous and witty stories, characteristic of the different peoples amongst whom they originated, which, for the most part, have not yet been appropriated by the European compilers of books of facetiæ, and a selection of such jests—choice specimens of Oriental Wit and Humour—gleaned from a great variety of sources, will, I trust, amuse readers in general, and lovers of funny anecdotes in particular.

To begin, then—*place aux dames*! In most Asiatic countries the ladies are at a sad discount in the estimation of their lords and masters, however much the latter may expatiate on their personal charms, and in Eastern jests this is abundantly shown. For instance, a Persian poet, through the importunity of his friends, had married an old and very ugly woman, who turned out also of a very bad temper, and they had constant quarrels. Once, in a dispute, the poet made some comparisons between his aged wife and himself and between Night and Day. "Cease your nonsense," said she; "night and day were created long before us." "Hold a little," said the husband. "I know they were created long before me, but whether before

30

you, admits of great doubt!" Again, a Persian married, and, as is customary with Muslims, on the marriage night saw his bride's face for the first time, when she proved to be very ugly—perhaps "plain-looking" were the more respectful expression. A few days after the nuptials, she said to him: "My life! as you have many relatives, I wish you would inform me before which of them I may unveil." (Women of rank in Muslim countries appear unveiled only before very near relations.) "My soul!" responded the husband, "if thou wilt but conceal thy face from *me*, I care not to whom thou showest it." And there is a grim sort of humour in the story of the poor Arab whose wife was going on a visit of condolence, when he said to her: "My dear, if you go, who is to take care of the children, and what have you left for them to eat?" She replied: "As I have neither flour, nor milk, nor butter, nor oil, nor anything else, what can I leave?" "You had better stay at home, then," said the poor man; "for assuredly *this* is the true house of condolence." And also in the following: A citizen of Tawris, in comfortable circumstances, had a daughter so very ugly that nothing could induce any one to marry her. At length he resolved to bestow her on a blind man, hoping that, not seeing her personal defects, he would be kind to her. His plan succeeded, and the blind man lived very happily with his wife. By-and-by, there arrived in the city a doctor who was celebrated for restoring sight to many people, and the girl's father was urged by his friends to engage this skilled man to operate upon his son-in-law, but he replied: "I will take care to do nothing of the kind; for if this doctor should restore my son-in-law's eyesight, *he* would very soon restore my daughter to me!"

But occasionally ladies are represented as giving witty retorts, as in the story of the Persian lady who, walking in the street, observed a man following her, and turning round enquired of him: "Why do you follow me, sir?" He answered: "Because I am in love with you." "Why are you in love with me?" said the lady. "My sister is much handsomer than I; she is coming after me—go and make love to her." The fellow went back and saw a woman with an exceedingly ugly face, upon which he at once went after the lady, and said to her: "Why did you tell me what was not true?" "Neither did you speak the truth," answered she; "for if you were really in love with me, you would not have turned to see another woman." And the Persian poet Jámí, in his *Baháristán*, relates that a man with a very long nose asked a woman in marriage, saying: "I am no way given to sloth, or long sleeping, and I am very patient in bearing vexations." To which she replied: "Yes, truly: hadst thou not been patient in bearing vexations thou hadst not carried that nose of thine these forty years."

[The low estimation in which women are so unjustly held among Muhammedans is perhaps to be ascribed partly to the teachings of the Kurán in one or two passages, and to the traditional sayings of the Apostle Muhammad, who has been credited (or rather *discredited*) with many things which he probably never said. But this is not peculiar to the followers of the Prophet of Mecca: a very considerable proportion of the Indian fictions represent women in an unfavourable light—fictions, too, which were composed long before the Hindús came in contact with the Muhammedans. Even in Europe, during mediæval times, *maugre* the "lady fair" of chivalric romance, it was quite as much the custom to decry women, and to relate stories of their profligacy, levity, and perversity, as ever it has been in the East. But we have changed all that in modern times: it is only to be hoped that we have not gone to the other extreme!— According to an Arabian writer, cited by Lane, "it is desirable, before a man enters upon any important undertaking, to consult ten intelligent persons among his particular friends; or if he have not more than five such friends let him consult each twice; or if he have not more than one friend he should consult him ten times, at ten different visits [he would be 'a friend indeed,' to submit to so many consultations on the same subject]; if he have not one to consult let him return to his wife and consult her, and whatever she advises him to do let him do the contrary, so shall he proceed rightly in his affair and attain his object."[25] We may suppose this Turkish story, from the *History of the Forty Vezírs*, to be illustrative of the wisdom of such teaching: A man went on the roof of his house to repair it, and when he was about to come down he called to his wife, "How should I come down?" The woman answered, "The roof is free; what would happen? You are a young man—jump down." The man jumped down, and his ankle was dislocated, and for a whole year he was bedridden, and his ankle came not back to its place. Next year the man again went on the roof of his house and repaired it. Then he called to his wife, "Ho! wife, how shall I come down?" The woman said, "Jump not; thine ankle has not yet come to its place—come down gently." The man replied, "The other time, for that I followed thy words, and not those of the Apostle [*i.e.*, Muhammed], was my ankle dislocated, and it is not yet come to its place; now shall I follow the words of the Apostle, and do the contrary of what thou sayest [Kurán, iii, 29.]" And he jumped down, and straightway his ankle came to its place.

In the Turkish collection of jests ascribed to Khoja Nasrú 'd-Dín Efendi[26] is the following, which has been reproduced amongst ourselves within comparatively recent years, and credited to an Irish priest:

One day the Khoja went into the pulpit of a mosque to preach to the people. "O men!" said he, "do you know what I should say unto you?" They answered: "We know not, Efendi." "When you do know," said the Khoja, "I shall take the trouble of addressing you." The next day he again ascended into the pulpit, and said, as before: "O men! do you know what I should say unto you?" "We do know," exclaimed they all with one voice. "Then," said he, "what is the use of my addressing you, since you already know?" The third day he once more went into the pulpit, and asked the same question. The people, having consulted together as to the answer they should make, said: "O Khoja, some of us know, and some of us do not know." "If that be the case, let those who know tell those who do not know," said the Khoja, coming down. A poor Arab preacher was once, however, not quite so successful. Having "given out," as we say, for his text, these words, from the Kurán, "I have called Noah," and being unable to collect his thoughts, he repeated, over and over again, "I have called Noah," and finally came to a dead stop; when one of those present shouted, "If Noah will not come, call some one else." Akin to this is our English jest of the deacon of a dissenting chapel in Yorkshire, who undertook, in the vanity of his heart, to preach on the Sunday, in place of the pastor, who was ill, or from home. He conducted the devotional exercises fairly well, but when he came to deliver his sermon, on the text, "I am the Light of the world," he had forgot what he intended to say, and continued to repeat these words, until an old man called out, "If thou be the light o' the world, I think thou needs snuffin' badly."

To return to the Turkish jest-book. One day the Khoja borrowed a cauldron from a brazier, and returned it with a little saucepan inside. The owner, seeing the saucepan, asked: "What is this?" Quoth the Khoja: "Why, the cauldron has had a young one"; whereupon the brazier, well pleased, took possession of the saucepan. Some time after this the Khoja again borrowed the cauldron and took it home. At the end of a week the brazier called at the Khoja's house and asked for his cauldron. "O set your mind at rest," said the Khoja; "the cauldron is dead." "O Khoja," quoth the brazier, "can a cauldron die?" Responded the Khoja: "Since you believed it could have a young one, why should you not also believe that it could die?"

The Khoja had a pleasant way of treating beggars. One day a man knocked at his door. "What do you want?" cried the Khoja from above. "Come down," said the man. The Khoja accordingly came down, and again said: "What do you want?" "I want charity," said the man. "Come up stairs," said the Khoja. When the beggar had come up, the Khoja said: "God help you"— the customary reply to a beggar when one will not or cannot give him anything. "O master," cried the man, "why did you not say so below?" Quoth the Khoja: "When I was above stairs, why did you bring me down?"

Drunkenness is punished (or punishable) by the infliction of eighty strokes of the bastinado in Muslim countries, but it is only flagrant cases that are thus treated, and there is said to be not a little private drinking of spirits as well as of wine among the higher classes, especially Turks and Persians. It happened that the governor of Súricastle lay in a state of profound intoxication in a garden one day, and was thus discovered by the Khoja, who was taking a walk in the same garden with his friend Ahmed. The Khoja instantly stripped him of his *ferage*, or upper garment, and, putting it on his own back, walked away. When the governor awoke and saw that his ferage had been stolen, he told his officers to bring before him whomsoever they found wearing it. The officers, seeing the ferage on the

Khoja, seized and brought him before the governor, who said to him: "Ho! Khoja, where did you obtain that ferage?" The Khoja responded "As I was taking a walk with my friend Ahmed we saw a fellow lying drunk, whereupon I took off his ferage and went away with it. If it be yours, pray take it." "O no," said the governor, "it does not belong to me."

Even being robbed could not disturb the Khoja's good humour. When he was lying in bed one night a loud noise was heard in the street before his house. Said he to his wife: "Get up and light a candle, and I will go and see what is the matter." "You had much better stay where you are," advised his wife. But the Khoja, without heeding her words, put the counterpane on his shoulders and went out. A fellow, on perceiving him, immediately snatched the counterpane from off the Khoja's shoulders and ran away. Shivering with cold, the Khoja returned into the house, and when his wife asked him the cause of the noise, he said: "It was on account of our counterpane; when they got that, the noise ceased at once."

But in the following story we have a very old acquaintance in a new dress: One day the Khoja's wife, in order to plague him, served up some exceedingly hot broth, and, forgetting what she had done, put a spoonful of it in her mouth, which so scalded her that the tears came into her eyes. "O wife," said the Khoja, "what is the matter with you—is the broth hot?" "Dear Efendi," said she, "my mother, who is now dead, loved broth very much; I thought of that, and wept on her account." The Khoja, thinking that what she said was truth, took a spoonful of the broth, and, it burning his mouth, he began to bellow. "What is the matter with you?" said his wife. "Why do you cry?" Quoth the Khoja: "You cry because your mother is gone, but I cry because her daughter is here."[27]

Many of the Muslim jests, like some our of own, are at the expense of poor preachers. Thus: there was in Baghdád a preacher whom no one attended after hearing him but once. One Friday when he came down from the pulpit he discovered that the only one who remained in the mosque was the muezzin—all his hearers had left him to finish his discourse as, and when, he pleased—and, still worse, his slippers had also disappeared. Accusing the muezzin of having stolen them, "I am rightly served by your suspicion," retorted he, "for being the only one that remained to hear you."—In Gladwin's *Persian Moonshee* we read that whenever a certain learned man preached in the mosque, one of the congregation wept constantly, and the preacher, observing this, concluded that his words made a great impression on the man's heart. One day some of the people said to the man: "That learned man makes no impression on our minds;—what kind of a heart have you, to be thus always in tears?" He answered: "I do not weep at his discourse, O Muslims. But I had a goat of which I was very fond, and when he grew old he died. Now, whenever the learned man speaks and wags his beard I am reminded of my goat, for he had just such a voice and beard."[28] But they are not always represented as mere dullards; for example: A miserly old fellow once sent a Muslim preacher a gold ring without a stone, requesting him to put up a prayer for him from the pulpit. The holy man prayed that he should have in Paradise a golden palace without a roof. When he descended from the pulpit, the man went to him, and, taking him by the hand, said: "O preacher, what manner of prayer is that thou hast made for me?" "If thy ring had had a stone," replied the preacher, "thy palace should also have had a roof."

Apropos of misers, our English facetiæ books furnish many examples of their ingenuity in excusing themselves from granting favours asked of them by their acquaintances; and, human nature being much the same everywhere, the misers in the East are represented as being equally adroit, as well as witty, in parrying such objectionable requests. A Persian who had a very miserly friend went to him one day, and said: "I am going on a journey; give me your ring, which I will constantly wear, and whenever I look on it, I shall remember you." The other answered: "If you wish to remember me, whenever you see your finger *without* my ring upon it, always think of me, that I did not give you my ring." And quite as good is the story of the dervish who said to the miser that he wanted something of him; to which he replied: "If you will consent to a request of mine, I will consent to whatever else you may require"; and when the dervish desired to know what it was, he said: "Never ask me for anything and whatever else you say I will perform."

II

THE TWO DEAF MEN AND THE TRAVELLER—THE
DEAF PERSIAN AND THE HORSEMAN—LAZY
SERVANTS—CHINESE HUMOUR: THE RICH MAN
AND THE SMITHS; HOW TO KEEP PLANTS ALIVE;
CRITICISING A PORTRAIT—THE PERSIAN
COURTIER AND HIS OLD FRIEND—THE SCRIBE—
THE SCHOOLMASTER AND THE WIT—THE PERSIAN
AND HIS CAT—A LIST OF BLOCKHEADS—THE ARAB
AND HIS CAMEL—A WITTY BAGHDÁDÍ—THE
UNLUCKY SLIPPERS

It is well known that deaf men generally dislike having their infirmity alluded to, and even endeavour to conceal it as much as possible. Charles Lamb, or some other noted wit, seeing a deaf acquaintance on the other side of the street one day while walking with a friend, stopped and motioned to him; then opened his mouth as if speaking in a loud tone, but saying not a word. "What are you bawling for?" demanded the deaf one. "D'ye think I can't hear?"—Two Eastern stories I have met with are most diverting examples of this peculiarity of deaf folks. One is related by my friend Pandit Natésa Sastrí in his *Folk-Lore of Southern India*, of which a few copies were recently issued at Bombay.[29] A deaf man was sitting one day where three roads crossed, when a neathered happened to pass that way. He had lately lost a good cow and a calf, and had been seeking them some days. When he saw the deaf man sitting by the way he took him for a soothsayer, and asked him to find out by his knowledge of magic where the cow would likely be found. The herdsman was also very deaf, and the other, without hearing what he had said, abused him, and said he wished to be left undisturbed, at the same time stretching out his hand and pointing at his face. This pointing the herd supposed to indicate the direction where the lost cow and calf should be sought; thus thinking (for he, too, had not heard a word of what the other man had said to him), the herd went off in search, resolving to present the soothsayer with the calf if he found it with the cow. To his joy, and by mere chance, of course, he found them both, and, returning with them to the deaf man (still sitting by the wayside), he pointed to the calf and asked him to accept of it. Now, it so happened that the calf's tail was broken and crooked, and the deaf man

36

supposed that the herdsman was blaming him for having broken it, and by a wave of his hand he denied the charge. This the poor deaf neatherd mistook for a refusal of the calf and a demand for the cow, so he said: "How very greedy you are, to be sure! I promised you the calf, and not the cow." "Never!" exclaimed the deaf man in a rage. "I know nothing of you or your cow and calf. I never broke the calf's tail." While they were thus quarrelling, without understanding each other, a third man happened to pass, and seeing his opportunity to profit by their deafness, he said to the neatherd in a loud voice, yet so as not to be heard by the other deaf man: "Friend, you had better go away with your cow. Those soothsayers are always greedy. Leave the calf with me, and I shall make him accept it." The poor neatherd, highly pleased to have secured his cow, went off, leaving the calf with the traveller. Then said the traveller to the deaf man: "It is, indeed, very unlawful, friend, for that neatherd to charge you with an offence which you did not commit; but never mind, since you have a friend in me. I shall contrive to make clear to him your innocence; leave this matter to me." So saying, he walked away with the calf, and the deaf man went home, well pleased that he had escaped from such a serious accusation.

The other story is of a deaf Persian who was taking home a quantity of wheat, and, coming to a river which he must cross, he saw a horseman approach; so he said to himself: "When that horseman comes up, he will first salute me, 'Peace be with thee'; next he will ask, 'What is the depth of this river?' and after that he will ask, how many *máns* of wheat I have with me." (A *mán* is a Persian weight, which seems to vary in different places.) But the deaf man's surmises were all in vain; for when the horseman came up to him, he cried: "Ho! my man, what is the depth of this river?" The deaf one replied: "Peace be with thee, and the mercy of Allah and his blessing." At this the horseman laughed, and said: "May they cut off thy beard!" The deaf one rejoined: "To my neck and bosom." The horseman said: "Dust be on thy mouth!" The deaf man answered: "Eighty *máns* of it."

The laziness of domestics is a common complaint in this country at the present day, but surely never was there a more lazy servant than the fellow whose exploits are thus recorded: A Persian husbandman one night desired his servant to shut the door, and the man said it was already shut. In the morning his master bade him open the door, and he coolly replied that, foreseeing this request, he had left it open the preceding night. Another night his master bade him rise and see whether it rained. But he called for the dog that lay at the door, and finding his paws dry, answered that the night was fair; then being desired to see whether the fire was extinguished, he called the cat, and finding her paws cold, replied in the affirmative.—This story had gained currency in Europe in the 13th century, and it forms one of the mediæval *Latin Stories* edited, for the Percy Society, by Thos. Wright, where it is entitled, "De Maimundo Armigero."

There is another Persian story of a lazy fellow whose master, being sick, said to him: "Go and get me some medicine." "But," rejoined he, "it may happen that the doctor is not at home." "You will find him at home." "But if I do find him at home he may not give me the medicine," quoth the servant. "Then take this note to him and he will give it to you." "Well," persisted the fellow, "he may give me the medicine, but suppose it does you no good?" "Villain!" exclaimed his master, out of all patience, "will you do as I bid you, instead of sitting there so coolly, raising difficulties?" "Good sir," reasoned this lazy philosopher, "admitting that the medicine should produce some effect, what will be the ultimate result? We must all die some time, and what does it matter whether it be to-day or to-morrow?"

The Chinese seem not a whit behind other peoples in appreciating a good jest, as has been shown by the tales and *bon mots* rendered into French by Stanislas Julien and other eminent *savans*. Here are three specimens of Chinese humour:

A wealthy man lived between the houses of two blacksmiths, and was constantly annoyed by the noise of their hammers, so that he could not get rest, night or day. First he asked them to strike more gently; then he made them great promises if they would remove at once. The two blacksmiths consented, and he, overjoyed to get rid of them, prepared a grand banquet for their entertainment. When the banquet was over, he asked them where they were going to take up their new abodes, and they replied—to the intense dismay of their worthy host, no doubt: "He who lives on the left of your house is going to that on the right; and he who lives on your right is going to the house on your left."

There is a keen satirical hit at the venality of Chinese judges in our next story. A husbandman, who wished to rear a particular kind of vegetable, found that the plants always died. He consulted an experienced gardener as to the best means of preventing the death of plants. The old man replied: "The affair is very simple; with every plant put down a piece of money." His friend asked what effect money could possibly have in a matter of this kind. "It is the case now-a-days," said the old man, "that where there is money *life* is safe, but where there is none death is the consequence."

The tale of Apelles and the shoemaker is familiar to every schoolboy, but the following story of the Chinese painter and his critics will be new to most readers: A gentleman having got his portrait painted, the artist suggested that he should consult the passers-by as to whether it was a good likeness. Accordingly he asked the first that was going past: "Is this portrait like me?" The man said: "The *cap* is very like." When the next was asked, he said: "The *dress* is very like." He was about to ask a third, when the painter stopped him, saying: "The cap and the dress do not matter much; ask the person what he thinks of the face." The third man hesitated a long time, and then said: "The *beard* is very like."

And now we shall revert once more to Persian jests, many of which are, however, also current in India, through the medium of the Persian language. When a man becomes suddenly rich it not unfrequently follows that he becomes as suddenly oblivious of his old friends. Thus, a Persian having obtained a lucrative appointment at court, a friend of his came shortly afterwards to congratulate him thereon. The new courtier asked him: "Who are you? And why do you come here?" The other coolly replied: "Do you not know me, then? I am your old friend, and am come to condole with you, having heard that you had lately lost your sight."—This recalls the clever epigram:

> When Jack was poor, the lad was frank and free;
> Of late he's grown brimful of pride and pelf;
> You wonder that he don't remember me?
> Why, don't you see, Jack has forgot himself!

The humour of the following is—to me, at least—simply exquisite: A man went to a professional scribe and asked him to write a letter for him. The scribe said that he had a pain in his foot. "A pain in your foot!" echoed the man. "I don't want to send you to any place that you should make such an excuse." "Very true," said the scribe; "but, whenever I write a letter for any one, I am always sent for to read it, because no one else can make it out."— And this is a very fair specimen of ready wit: During a season of great drought in Persia, a schoolmaster at the head of his pupils marched out of Shíráz to pray (at the tomb of some saint in the suburbs) for rain, when they were met by a waggish fellow, who inquired where they were going. The preceptor informed him, and added that, no doubt, Allah would listen to the prayers of innocent children. "Friend," quoth the wit, "if that were the case, I fear there would not be a schoolmaster left alive."

The "harmless, necessary cat" has often to bear the blame of depredations in which she had no share—especially the "lodging-house cat"; and, that such is the fact in Persia as well as nearer our own doors, let a story related by the celebrated poet Jámí serve as evidence: A husband gave a *mán* of meat to his wife, bidding her cook it for his dinner. The woman roasted it and ate it all herself, and when her husband asked for the meat she said the cat had stolen it. The husband weighed the cat forthwith, and found that she had not increased in weight by eating so much meat; so, with a hundred perplexing thoughts, he struck his hand on his knee, and, upbraiding his wife, said: "O lady, doubtless the cat, like the meat, weighed one *mán*; the meat would add another *mán* thereto. This point is not clear to me—that two *máns* should become one *mán*. If this is the cat, where is the meat? And if this is the meat, why has it the form of the cat?"

Readers of our early English jest-books will perhaps remember the story of a court-jester being facetiously ordered by the king to make out a list of all the fools in his dominions, who replied that it would be a much easier task to write down a list of all the wise men. I fancy there is some trace of this incident in the following Persian story, though the details are wholly different: Once upon a time a party of merchants exhibited to a king some fine horses, which pleased him so well that he bought them, and gave the merchants besides a large sum of money to pay for more horses which they were to bring from their own country. Some time after this the king, being merry with wine, said to his chief vazír: "Make me out a list of all the blockheads in my kingdom." The vazír replied that he had already made out such a list, and had put his Majesty's name at the top. "Why so?" demanded the king. "Because," said the vazír, "you gave a great sum of money for horses to be brought by merchants for whom no person is surety, nor does any one know to what country they belong; and this is surely a sign of stupidity." "But what if they should bring the horses?" The vazír readily replied: "If they should bring the horses, I should then erase your Majesty's name and put the names of the merchants in its place."[30]

Everybody knows the story of the silly old woman who went to market with a cow and a hen for sale, and asked only five shillings for the cow, but ten pounds for the hen. But no such fool was the Arab who lost his camel, and, after a long and fruitless search, anathematised the errant quadruped and her father and her mother, and swore by the Prophet that, should he find her, he would sell her for a dirham (sixpence). At length his search was successful, and he at once regretted his oath; but such an oath must not be violated, so he tied a cat round the camel's neck, and went about proclaiming: "I will sell this camel for a dirham, and this cat for a hundred dínars (fifty pounds); but I will not sell one without the other." A man who passed by and heard this exclaimed: "What a very desirable bargain that camel would be if she had not such a *collar* round her neck!"[31]

For readiness of wit the Arabs would seem to compare very favourably with any race, European or Asiatic, and many examples of their felicitous repartees are furnished by native historians and grammarians. One of the best is: When a khalíf was addressing the people in a mosque on his accession to the khalífate, and told them, among other things in his own praise, that the plague which had so long raged in Baghdád had ceased immediately he became khalíf; an old fellow present shouted: "Of a truth, Allah was too merciful to give us both *thee* and the plague at the same time."

The story of the Unlucky Slippers in Cardonne's *Mélanges de Littérature Orientale* is a very good specimen of Arabian humour:[32]

In former times there lived in the famous city of Baghdád a miserly old merchant named Abú Kasim. Although very rich, his clothes were mere rags; his turban was of coarse cloth, and exceedingly dirty; but his slippers were perfect curiosities—the soles were studded with great nails, while the upper leathers consisted of as many different pieces as the celebrated ship Argos. He had worn them during ten years, and the art of the ablest cobblers in Baghdád had been exhausted in preventing a total separation of the parts; in short, by frequent accessions of nails and patches they had become so heavy that they passed into a proverb, and anything ponderous was compared to Abú Kasim's slippers. Walking one day in the great bazaar, the purchase of a large quantity of crystal was offered to this merchant, and, thinking it a bargain, he bought it. Not long after this, hearing that a bankrupt perfumer had nothing left to sell but some rose-water, he took advantage of the poor man's misfortune, and purchased it for half the value. These lucky speculations had put him into good humour, but instead of giving an entertainment, according to the custom of merchants when they have made a profitable bargain, Abú Kasim deemed it more expedient to go to the bath, which he had not frequented for some time. As he was undressing, one of his acquaintances told him that his slippers made him the laughing-stock of the whole city, and that he ought to provide himself with a new pair. "I have been thinking about it," he answered; "however, they are not so very much worn but they will serve some time longer." While he was washing himself, the kází of Baghdád came also to bathe. Abú Kasim, coming out before the judge, took up his clothes but could not find his slippers—a new pair being placed in their room. Our miser, persuaded, because he wished it, that the friend who had spoken to him about his old slippers had made him a present, without hesitation put on these fine ones, and left the bath highly delighted. But when the kází had finished bathing, his servants searched in vain for his slippers; none could be found but a wretched pair, which were at once identified as those of Abú Kasim. The officers hastened after the supposed thief, and, bringing him back with the theft on his feet, the kází, after exchanging slippers, committed him to prison. There was no escaping from the claws of justice without money, and, as Abú Kasim was known to be very rich, he was fined in a considerable sum.

On returning home, our merchant, in a fit of indignation, flung his slippers into the Tigris, that ran beneath his window. Some days after they were dragged out in a fisherman's net that came up more heavy than usual. The nails with which the soles were thickly studded had torn the meshes of the net, and the fisherman, exasperated against the miserly Abú Kasim and his slippers—for they were known to everyone—determined to throw them into his house through the window he had left open. The slippers, thrown with great force, reached the jars of rose-water, and smashed them in pieces, to the intense consternation of the owner. "Cursed slippers!" cried he, tearing his beard, "you shall cause me no farther mischief!" So saying, he took a spade and began to dig a hole in his garden to bury them. One of his neighbours, who had long borne him ill-will, perceiving him busied in digging the ground, ran at once to inform the governor that Abú Kasim had discovered some hidden treasure in his garden. Nothing more was needful to rouse the cupidity of the commandant. In vain did our miser protest that he had found no treasure; and that he only meant to bury his old slippers. The governor had counted on the money, so the afflicted man could only preserve his liberty at the expense of a large sum of money. Again heartily cursing the slippers, in order to effectually rid himself of them, he threw them into an aqueduct at some distance from the city, persuaded that he should now hear no more of them. But his evil genius had not yet sufficiently plagued him: the slippers got into the mouth of the pipe and stopped the flow of the water. The keepers of the aqueduct made haste to repair the damage, and, finding the obstruction was caused by Abú Kasim's slippers, complained of this to the governor, and once more was Abú Kasim heavily fined, but the governor considerately returned him the slippers. He now resolved to burn them, but, finding them thoroughly soaked with water, he exposed them to the sun upon the terrace of his house. A neighbour's dog, perceiving the slippers, leaped from the terrace of his master's house upon that of Abú Kasim, and, seizing one of them in his mouth, he let it drop into the street: the fatal slipper fell directly on the head of a woman who was passing at the time, and the fright as well as the violence of the blow caused her to miscarry. Her husband brought his complaint before the kází, and Abú Kasim was again sentenced to pay a fine proportioned to the calamity he was supposed to have occasioned. He then took the slippers in his hand, and, with a vehemence that made the judge laugh, said: "Behold, my lord, the fatal instruments of my misfortune! These cursed slippers have at length reduced me to poverty. Vouchsafe, therefore, to publish an order that no one may any more impute to me the disasters they may yet occasion." The kází could not refuse his request, and thus Abú Kasim learned, to his bitter cost, the danger of wearing his slippers too long.

III

THE YOUNG MERCHANT OF BAGHDÁD; OR, THE WILES OF WOMAN

Too many Eastern stories turn upon the artful devices of women to screen their own profligacy, but there is one, told by Arab Sháh, the celebrated historian, who died A.D. 1450, in a collection entitled *Fakihat al-Khalífa*, or Pastimes of the Khalífs, in which a lady exhibits great ingenuity, without any very objectionable motive. It is to the following effect:

A young merchant in Baghdád had placed over the front of his shop, instead of a sentence from the Kurán, as is customary, these arrogant words: "Verily there is no cunning like unto that of man, seeing it surpasses the cunning of women." It happened one day that a very beautiful young lady, who had been sent by her aunt to purchase some rich stuffs for dresses, noticed this inscription, and at once resolved to compel the despiser of her sex to alter it. Entering the shop, she said to him, after the usual salutations: "You see my person; can anyone presume to say that I am humpbacked?" He had hardly recovered from the astonishment caused by such a question, when the lady drew her veil a little to one side and continued: "Surely my neck is not as that of a raven, or as the ebony idols of Ethiopia?" The young merchant, between surprise and delight, signified his assent. "Nor is my chin double," said she, still farther unveiling her face; "nor my lips thick, like those of a Tartar?" Here the young merchant smiled. "Nor are they to be believed who say that my nose is flat and my cheeks are sunken?" The merchant was about to express his horror at the bare idea of such blasphemy, when the lady wholly removed her veil and allowed her beauty to flash upon the bewildered youth, who instantly became madly in love with her. "Fairest of creatures!" he cried, "to what accident do I owe the view of those charms, which are hidden from the eyes of the less fortunate of my sex?" She replied: "You see in me an unfortunate damsel, and I shall explain the cause of my present conduct. My mother, who was sister to a rich amír of Mecca, died some years ago, leaving my father in possession of an immense fortune and myself as sole heiress. I am now seventeen, my personal endowments are such as you behold, and a very small portion of my mother's fortune would quite suffice to obtain for me a good establishment in marriage. Yet such is the unfeeling avarice of my father, that he absolutely refuses me the least

43

trifle to settle me in life. The only counsellor to whom I could apply for help in this extremity was my kind nurse, and it is by her advice, as well as from the high opinion I have ever heard expressed of your merits, that I have been induced to throw myself upon your goodness in this extraordinary manner." The emotions of the young merchant on hearing this story, may be readily imagined. "Cruel parent!" he exclaimed. "He must be a rock of the desert, not a man, who can condemn so charming a person to perpetual solitude, when the slightest possible sacrifice on his part might prevent it. May I inquire his name?" "He is the chief kází," replied the lady, and disappeared like a vision.

The young merchant lost no time in waiting on the kází at his court of justice, whom he thus addressed: "My lord, I am come to ask your daughter in marriage, of whom I am deeply enamoured." Quoth the judge: "Sir, my daughter is unworthy of the honour you design for her. But be pleased to accompany me to my dwelling, where we can talk over this matter more at leisure." They proceeded thither accordingly, and after partaking of refreshments, the young man repeated his request, giving a true account of his position and prospects, and offering to settle fifteen purses on the young lady. The kází expressed his gratification, but doubted whether the offer was made in all seriousness, but when assured that such was the case, he said: "I no longer doubt your earnestness and sincerity in this affair; it is, however, just possible that your feelings may change after the marriage, and it is but natural that I should now take proper precautions for my daughter's welfare. You will not blame me, therefore, if, in addition to the fifteen purses you have offered, I require that five more be paid down previous to the marriage, to be forfeited in case of a divorce." "Say ten," cried the merchant, and the kází looked more and more astonished, and even ventured to remonstrate with him on his precipitancy, but without effect. To be brief, the kází consented, the ten purses were paid down, the legal witnesses summoned, and the nuptial contract signed that very evening; the consummation of the marriage being, much against the will of our lover, deferred till the following day.

When the wedding guests had dispersed, the young merchant was admitted to the chamber of his bride, whom he discovered to be humpbacked and hideous beyond conception! As soon as it was day, he arose from his sleepless couch and repaired to the public baths, where, after his ablutions, he gave himself up to melancholy reflections. Mingled with grief for his disappointment was mortification at having been the dupe of what now appeared to him a very shallow artifice, which nothing but his own passionate and unthinking precipitation could have rendered plausible. Nor was he without some twinges of conscience for the sarcasms which he had often uttered against women, and for which his present sufferings were no more than a just retribution. Then came meditations of revenge upon the beautiful author of all this mischief; and then his thoughts reverted to the possible means of escape from his difficulties: the forfeiture of the ten purses, to say nothing of the implacable resentment of the kází and his relatives; and he bethought himself how he should become the talk of his neighbourhood—how Malik bin Omar, the jeweller, would sneer at him, and Salih, the barber, talk sententiously of his folly. At length, finding reflection of no avail, he arose and with slow and pensive steps proceeded to his shop.

His marriage with the kází's deformed daughter had already become known to his neighbours, who presently came to rally him upon his choice of such a bride, and scarcely had they left when the young lady who had so artfully tricked him entered with a playful smile on her lips, and a glancing in her dark eye, which speedily put to flight the young merchant's thoughts of revenge. He arose and greeted her courteously. "May this day be propitious to thee!" said she. "May Allah protect and bless thee!" Replied he: "Fairest of earthly creatures, how have I offended thee that thou shouldst make me the subject of thy sport?" "From thee," she said, "I have received no personal injury." "What, then, can have been thy motive for practising so cruel a deception on one who has never harmed thee?" The young lady simply pointed to the inscription over the shop front. The merchant was abashed, but felt somewhat relieved on seeing good humour beaming from her beautiful eyes, and he immediately took down the inscription, and substituted another, which declared that "TRULY THERE IS NO CUNNING LIKE UNTO THE CUNNING OF WOMEN, SEEING IT SURPASSES AND CONFOUNDS EVEN THE CUNNING OF MEN." Then the young lady communicated to him a plan by which he might get rid of his objectionable bride without incurring her father's resentment, which he forthwith put into practice.

Next morning, as the kází and his son-in-law were taking their coffee together, in the house of the former, they heard a strange noise in the street, and, descending to ascertain the cause of the disturbance, found that it proceeded from a crowd of low fellows—mountebanks, and such like gentry, who had assembled with all sorts of musical instruments, with which they kept up a deafening din, at the same time dancing and capering about, and loudly felicitating themselves on the marriage of their pretended kinsman with the kází's daughter. The young merchant acknowledged their compliments by throwing handfuls of money among the crowd, which caused a renewal of the dreadful clamour. When the noise had somewhat subsided, the kází, hitherto dumb from astonishment, turned to his son-in-law, and demanded to know the meaning of such a scene before his mansion. The merchant replied that the leaders of the crowd were his kinsfolk, although his father had abandoned the fraternity and adopted commercial pursuits. He could not, however, disown his kindred, even for the sake of the kází's daughter. On hearing this the judge was beside himself with rage and mortification, exclaiming: "Dog, and son

45

of a dog! what dirt is this you have made me eat?" The merchant reminded him that he was now his son-in-law; that his daughter was his lawful wife; declaring that he would not part with her for untold wealth. But the kází insisted upon a divorce and returned the merchant his ten purses. In the sequel, the young merchant, having ascertained the parentage of the clever damsel, obtained her in marriage, and lived with her for many years in happiness and prosperity.[33]

IV

ASHAAB THE COVETOUS—THE STINGY MERCHANT AND THE HUNGRY BEDOUIN—THE SECT OF SAMRADIANS—THE STORY-TELLER AND THE KING—ROYAL GIFTS TO POETS—THE PERSIAN POET AND THE IMPOSTOR—"STEALING POETRY"— THE RICH MAN AND THE POOR POET

Avaricious and covetous men are always the just objects of derision as well as contempt, and surely covetousness was quite concentrated in the person of Ashaab, a servant of Othman (seventh century), and a native of Medina, whose character has been very amusingly drawn by the scholiast: He never saw a man put his hand into his pocket without hoping and expecting that he would give him something. He never saw a funeral go by, but he was pleased, hoping that the deceased had left him something. He never saw a bride about to be conducted through the streets to the house of the bridegroom but he prepared his own house for her reception, hoping that her friends would bring her to his house by mistake. If he saw a workman making a box, he took care to tell him that he was putting in one or two boards too many, hoping that he would give him what was over, or, at least, something for the suggestion. He is said to have followed a man who was chewing mastic (a sort of gum, chewed, like betel, by Orientals as a pastime) for a whole mile, thinking he was perhaps eating food, intending, if so, to ask him for some. When the youths of the town jeered and taunted him, he told them there was a wedding at such a house, in order to get rid of them (because they would go to get a share of the bonbons distributed there); but, as soon as they were gone, it struck him that possibly what he had told them was true, and that they would not have quitted him had they not been aware of its truth; and he actually followed them himself to see what he could do, though exposing himself thereby to fresh taunts from them. When asked whether he knew anyone more covetous than himself, he said: "Yes; a sheep I once had, that climbed to an upper stage of my house, and, seeing a rainbow, mistook it for a rope of hay, and jumping at it, broke her neck"—whence "Ashaab's sheep" became proverbial among the Arabs for covetousness as well as Ashaab himself.

Hospitality has ever been the characteristic virtue of the Arabs, and a mean, stingy disposition is rarely to be found among them. A droll story of an Arab of the latter description has been rendered into verse by the Persian poet Liwá'í, the substance of which is as follows: An Arab merchant who had been trading between Mecca and Damascus, at length turned his face homeward, and had reached within one stage of his house when he sat down to rest and to refresh himself with the contents of his wallet. While he was eating, a Bedouin, weary and hungry, came up, and, hoping to be invited to share his repast, saluted him, "Peace be with thee!" which the merchant returned, and asked the nomad who he was and whence he came. "I have come from thy house," was the answer. "Then," said the merchant, "how fares my son Ahmed, absence from whom has grieved me sore?" "Thy son grows apace in health and innocence." "Good! and how is his mother?" "She, too, is free from the shadow of sorrow." "And how is my beauteous camel, so strong to bear his load?" "Thy camel is sleek and fat." "My house-dog, too, that guards my gate, pray how is he?" "He is on the mat before thy door, by day, by night, on constant guard." The merchant, having thus his doubts and fears removed, resumed his meal with freshened appetite, but gave nought to the poor nomad, and, having finished, closed his wallet. The Bedouin, seeing his stinginess, writhed with the pangs of hunger. Presently a gazelle passed rapidly by them, at which he sighed heavily, and the merchant inquiring the cause of his sorrow, he said: "The cause is this—had not thy dog died he would not have allowed that gazelle to escape!" "My dog!" exclaimed the merchant. "Is my doggie, then, dead?" "He died from gorging himself with thy camel's blood." "Who hath cast this dust on me?" cried the merchant. "What of my camel?" "Thy camel was slaughtered to furnish the funeral feast of thy wife." "Is my wife, too, dead?" "Her grief for Ahmed's death was such that she dashed her head against a rock." "But, Ahmed," asked the father—"how came he to die?" "The house fell in and crushed him." The merchant heard this tale with full belief, rent his robe, cast sand upon his head, then started swiftly homeward to bewail his wife and son, leaving behind his well-filled wallet, a prey to the starving desert-wanderer.[34]

The Samradian sect of fire-worshippers, who believe only in the "ideal," anticipated Bishop Berkeley's theory, thus referred to by Lord Byron (*Don Juan*, xi, 1):

> When Bishop Berkeley said, "there was no matter,"
> And proved it—'twas no matter what he said;
> They say, his system 'tis in vain to batter,
> Too subtle for the airiest human head.

Some amusing anecdotes regarding this singular sect are given in the Dabistán, a work written in Persian, which furnishes a very impartial account of the principal religions of the world: A Samradian said to his servant: "The world and its inhabitants have no actual existence—they have merely an ideal being." The servant, on hearing this, took the first opportunity to steal his master's horse, and when he was about to ride, brought him an ass with the horse's saddle. When the Samradian asked: "Where is the horse?" he replied: "Thou hast been thinking of an idea; there was no horse in being." The master said: "It is true," and then mounted the ass. Having proceeded some distance, followed by his servant on foot, he suddenly dismounted, and taking the saddle off the back of the ass placed it on the servant's back, drawing the girths tightly, and, having forced the bridle into his mouth, he mounted him, and flogged him along vigorously. The servant having exclaimed in piteous accents: "What is the meaning of this, O master?" the Samradian replied: "There is no such thing as a whip; it is merely ideal. Thou art thinking only of a delusion." It is needless to add that the servant immediately repented and restored the horse.—Another of this sect having obtained in marriage the daughter of a wealthy lawyer, she, on finding out her husband's peculiar creed, purposed to have some amusement at his expense. One day the Samradian brought home a bottle of excellent wine, which during his absence she emptied of its contents and filled again with water. When the time came for taking wine, she poured out the water into a gold cup, which Was her own property. The Samradian remarked: "Thou hast given me water instead of wine." "It is only ideal," she answered; "there was no wine in existence." The husband then said: "Thou hast spoken well; give me the cup that I may go to a neighbour's house and bring it back full of wine." He thereupon took the gold cup and went out and sold it, concealing the money, and, instead of the gold vase, he brought back an earthen vessel filled with wine. The wife, on seeing this, said: "What hast thou done with the golden cup?" He quietly replied: "Thou art surely thinking of an ideal gold cup," on which the lady sorely repented her witticism.[35]

I do not know whether there are any English parallels to these stories, but I have read of a Greek sage who instructed his slave that all that occurred in this world was the decree of Fate. The slave shortly after deliberately committed some offence, upon which his master commenced to soften his ribs with a stout cudgel, and when the slave pleaded that it was no fault of his, it was the decree of Fate, his master grimly replied that it was also decreed that he should have a sound beating.

In *Don Quixote*, it will be remembered by all readers of that delightful work, Sancho begins to tell the knight a long story about a man who had to ferry across a river a large flock of sheep, but he could only take one at a time, as the boat could hold no more. This story Cervantes, in all likelihood, borrowed from the *Disciplina Clericalis* of Petrus Alfonsus, a converted Spanish Jew, who flourished in the 12th century, and who avowedly derived the materials of his work from the Arabian fabulists— probably part of them also from the Talmud.[36] His eleventh tale is of a king who desired his minstrel to tell him a long story that should lull him to sleep. The story-teller accordingly begins to relate how a man had to cross a ferry with 600 sheep, two at a time, and falls asleep in the midst of his narration. The king awakes him, but the story-teller begs that the man be allowed to ferry over the sheep before he resumes the story.³⁷—Possibly the original form of the story is that found in the *Kathá Manjarí*, an ancient Indian story-book: There was a king who used to inquire of all the learned men who came to his court whether they knew any stories, and when they had related all they knew, in order to avoid rewarding them, he abused them for knowing so few, and sent them away. A shrewd and clever man, hearing of this, presented himself before the king, who asked his name. He replied that his name was Ocean of Stories. The king then inquired how many stories he knew, to which he answered that the name of Ocean had been conferred on him because he knew an endless number. On being desired to relate one, he thus began: "O King, there was a tank 36,000 miles in breadth, and 54,000 in length. This was densely filled with lotus plants, and millions upon millions of birds with golden wings [called Hamsa] perched on those flowers. One day a hurricane arose, accompanied with rain, which the birds were not able to endure, and they entered a cave under a rock, which was in the vicinity of the tank." The king asked what happened next, and he replied that one of the birds flew away. The king again inquired what else occurred, and he answered: "Another flew away"; and to every question of the king he continued to give the same answer. At this the king felt ashamed, and, seeing it was impossible to outwit the man, he dismissed him with a handsome present.

A story bearing some resemblance to this is related of a khalíf who was wont to cheat poets of their expected reward when they recited their compositions to him, until he was at length outwitted by the famous Arabian poet Al-Asma'í: It is said that a khalíf, who was very penurious, contrived by a trick to send from his presence without any reward those poets who came and recited their compositions to him. He had himself the faculty of retaining in his memory a poem after hearing it only once; he had a mamlúk (white slave) who could repeat one that he had heard twice; and a slave-girl who could repeat one that she had heard thrice. Whenever a poet came to compliment him with a panegyrical poem, the king used to promise him that if he found his verses to be of his own composition he would give him a sum of money equal in weight to what they were written on. The poet, consenting, would recite his ode, and the king would say: "It is not new, for I have known it some years"; and he would repeat it as he had heard it; after which he would add: "And this mamlúk also retains it in his memory," and order the mamlúk to repeat it, which, having heard it twice, from the poet and the king, he would do. Then the king would say to the poet: "I have also a slave-girl who can repeat it," and, ordering her to do so, stationed behind the curtains, she would repeat what she had thus thrice heard; so the poet would go away empty-handed. The celebrated poet Al-Asma'í, having heard of this device, determined upon outwitting the king, and accordingly composed an ode made up of very difficult

50

words. But this was not the poet's only preparative measure—another will be presently explained; and a third was to assume the dress of a Bedouin, that he might not be known, covering his face, the eyes only excepted, with a *litham* (piece of drapery), as is usual with the Arabs of the desert. Thus disguised, he went to the palace, and having obtained permission, entered and saluted the king, who said to him: "Who art thou, O brother of the Arabs? and what dost thou desire?" The poet answered: "May Allah increase the power of the king! I am a poet of such a tribe, and have composed an ode in praise of our lord the khalíf." "O brother of the Arabs," said the king, "hast thou heard of our condition?" "No," answered the poet; "and what is it, O khalíf of the age?" "It is," replied the king, "that if the ode be not thine, we give thee no reward; and if it be thine, we give thee the weight in money equal to what it is written upon." "How," said the poet, "should I assume to myself that which belongeth to another, and knowing, too, that lying before kings is one of the basest of actions? But I agree to the condition, O our lord the khalíf." So he repeated his ode. The king, perplexed, and unable to remember any of it, made a sign to the mamlúk, but he had retained nothing; then called to the female slave, but she was unable to repeat a word. "O brother of the Arabs," said the king, "thou hast spoken truth; and the ode is thine without doubt. I have never heard it before. Produce, therefore, what it is written upon, and I will give thee its weight in money, as I have promised." "Wilt thou," said the poet, "send one of the attendants to carry it?" "To carry what?" demanded the king. "Is it not upon a paper in thy possession?" "No, O our lord the khalíf. At the time I composed it I could not procure a piece of paper on which to write it, and could find nothing but a fragment of a marble column left me by my father; so I engraved it upon that, and it lies in the courtyard of the palace." He had brought it, wrapped up, on the back of a camel. The king, to fulfil his promise, was obliged to exhaust his treasury; and, to prevent a repetition of this trick, in future rewarded poets according to the custom of kings.

Apropos of royal gifts to poets, it is related that, when the Afghans had possession of Persia, a rude chief of that nation was governor of Shíráz. A poet composed a panegyric on his wisdom, his valour, and his virtues. As he was taking it to the palace he was met by a friend at the outer gate, who inquired where he was going, and he informed him of his purpose. His friend asked him if he was insane, to offer an ode to a barbarian who hardly understood a word of the Persian language. "All that you say may be very true," said the poor poet, "but I am starving, and have no means of livelihood but by making verses. I must, therefore, proceed." He went and stood before the governor with his ode in his hand. "Who is that fellow?" said the Afghan lord. "And what is that paper which he holds?" "I am a poet," answered the man, "and this paper contains some poetry." "What is the use of poetry?" demanded the governor. "To render great men like you immortal," he replied, making at the same time a profound bow. "Let us hear some of it." The poet, on this mandate, began reading his composition

51

aloud, but he had not finished the second stanza when he was interrupted. "Enough!" exclaimed the governor; "I understand it all. Give the poor man some money—*that* is what he wants." As the poet retired he met his friend, who again commented on the folly of carrying odes to a man who did not understand one of them. "Not understand!" he replied. "You are quite mistaken. He has beyond all men the quickest apprehension of a *poet's meaning!*"

The khalífs were frequently lavish of their gifts to poets, but they were fond of having their little jokes with them when in merry mood. One day the Arabian poet Thálebí read before the khalíf Al-Mansúr a poem which he had just composed, and it found acceptance. The khalíf said: "O Thálebí, which wouldst thou rather have—that I give thee 300 gold dínars [about £150], or three wise sayings, each worth 100 dínars?" The poet replied: "Learning, O Commander of the Faithful, is better than transitory treasure." "Well, then," said the khalíf, "the first saying is: When thy garment grows old, sew not a new patch on it, for it hath an ill look." "O woe!" cried the poet, "one hundred dínars are lost!" Mansúr smiled, and proceeded: "The second saying is: When thou anointest thy beard, anoint not the lower part, for that would soil the collar of thy vest." "Alas!" exclaimed Thálebí, "a thousand times, alas! two hundred dínars are lost!" Again the khalíf smiled, and continued: "The third saying"—but before he had spoken it, the poet said: "O khalíf of our prosperity, keep the third maxim in thy treasury, and give me the remaining hundred dínars, for they will be worth a thousand times more to me than the hearing of maxims." At this the khalíf laughed heartily, and commanded his treasurer to give Thálebí five hundred dínars of gold.

A droll story is told of the Persian poet Anwarí: Passing the market-place of Balkh one day, he saw a crowd of people standing in a ring, and going up, he put his head within the circle and found a fellow reciting the poems of Anwarí himself as his own. Anwarí went up to the man, and said: "Sir, whose poems are these you are reciting?" He replied: "They are Anwarí's." "Do you know him, then?" said Anwarí. The man, with cool effrontery, answered: "What do you say? I am Anwarí." On hearing this Anwarí laughed, and remarked: "I have heard of one who stole poetry, but never of one who stole the poet himself!"—Talking of "stealing poetry," Jámí tells us that a man once brought a composition to a critic, every line of which he had plagiarised from different collections of poems, and each rhetorical figure from various authors. Quoth the critic: "For a wonder, thou hast brought a line of camels; but if the string were untied, every one of the herd would run away in different directions."

There is no little humour in the story of the Persian poet who wrote a eulogium on a rich man, but got nothing for his trouble; he then abused the rich man, but he said nothing; he next seated himself at the rich man's gate, who said to him: "You praised me, and I said nothing; you abused me, and I said nothing; and now, why are you sitting here?" The poet answered: "I only wish that when you die I may perform the funeral service."

V

UNLUCKY OMENS—THE OLD MAN'S PRAYER—THE OLD WOMAN IN THE MOSQUE—THE WEEPING TURKMANS—THE TEN FOOLISH PEASANTS—THE WAKEFUL SERVANT—THE THREE DERVISHES—THE OIL-MAN'S PARROT—THE MOGHUL AND HIS PARROT—THE PERSIAN SHOPKEEPER AND THE PRIME MINISTER—HEBREW FACETIAE

Muslims and other Asiatic peoples, like Europeans not so many centuries since, are always on the watch for lucky or unlucky omens. On first going out of a morning, the looks and countenances of those who cross their path are scrutinised, and a smile or a frown is deemed favourable or the reverse. To encounter a person blind of the left eye, or even with one eye, forebodes sorrow and calamity. While Sir John Malcolm was in Persia, as British Ambassador, he was told the following story: When Abbas the Great was hunting, he met one morning as day dawned an uncommonly ugly man, at the sight of whom his horse started. Being nearly dismounted, and deeming it a bad omen, the king called out in a rage to have his head cut off. The poor peasant, whom the attendants had seized and were on the point of executing, prayed that he might be informed of his crime. "Your crime," said the king, "is your unlucky countenance, which is the first object I saw this morning, and which has nearly caused me to fall from my horse." "Alas!" said the man, "by this reckoning what term must I apply to your Majesty's countenance, which was the first object my eyes met this morning, and which is to cause my death?" The king smiled at the wit of the reply, ordered the man to be released, and gave him a present instead of cutting off his head.—Another Persian story is to the same purpose: A man said to his servant: "If you see two crows together early in the morning, apprise me of it, that I may also behold them, as it will be a good omen, whereby I shall pass the day pleasantly." The servant did happen to see two crows sitting in one place, and informed his master, who, however, when he came saw but one, the other having in the meantime flown away.

He was very angry, and began to beat the servant, when a friend sent him a present of game. Upon this the servant exclaimed: "O my lord! you saw only one crow, and have received a fine present; had you seen *two*, you would have met with *my* fare."[38]

It would seem, from the following story, that an old man's prayers are sometimes reversed in response, as dreams are said to "go by contraries": An old Arab left his house one morning, intending to go to a village at some distance, and coming to the foot of a hill which he had to cross he exclaimed: "O Allah! send some one to help me over this hill." Scarcely had he uttered these words when up came a fierce soldier, leading a mare with a very young colt by her side, who compelled the old man, with oaths and threats, to carry the colt. As they trudged along, they met a poor woman with a sick child in her arms. The old man, as he laboured under the weight of the colt, kept groaning, "O Allah! O Allah!" and, supposing him to be a dervish, the woman asked him to pray for the recovery of her child. In compliance, the old man said: "O Allah! I beseech thee to shorten the days of this poor child." "Alas!" cried the mother, "why hast thou made such a cruel prayer?" "Fear nothing," said the old man; "thy child will assuredly enjoy long life. It is my fate to have the reverse of whatever I pray for. I implored Allah for assistance to carry me over this hill, and, by way of help, I suppose, I have had this colt imposed on my shoulders."

Jámí tells this humorous story in the Sixth "Garden" of his *Baháristán*, or Abode of Spring: A man said the prescribed prayers in a mosque and then began his personal supplications. An old woman, who happened to be near him, exclaimed: "O Allah! cause me to share in whatsoever he supplicates for." The man, overhearing her, then prayed: "O Allah! hang me on a gibbet, and cause me to die of scourging." The old trot continued: "O Allah! pardon me, and preserve me from what he has asked for." Upon this the man turned to her and said: "What a very unreasonable partner this is! She desires to share in all that gives rest and pleasure, but she refuses to be my partner in distress and misery."

We have already seen that even the grave and otiose Turk is not devoid of a sense of the ludicrous, and here is another example, from Mr. E. J. W. Gibb's translation of the *History of the Forty Vezírs*: A party of Turkmans left their encampment one day and went into a neighbouring city. Returning home, as they drew near their tents, they felt hungry, and sat down and ate some bread and onions at a spring-head. The juice of the onions went into their eyes and caused them to water. Now the children of those Turkmans had gone out to meet them, and, seeing the tears flow from their eyes, they concluded that one of their number had died in the city, so, without making any inquiry, they ran back, and said to their mothers: "One of ours is dead in the city, and our fathers are coming weeping." Upon this all the women and children of the encampment went

55

forth to meet them, weeping together. The Turkmans who were coming from the city thought that one of theirs had died in the encampment; and thus they were without knowledge one of the other, and they raised a weeping and wailing together such that it cannot be described. At length the elders of the camp stood up in their midst and said: "May ye all remain whole; there is none other help than patience"; and they questioned them. The Turkmans coming from the city asked: "Who is dead in the camp?" The others replied: "No one is dead in the camp; who has died in the city?" Those who were coming from the city, said: "No one has died in the city." The others said: "For whom then are ye wailing and lamenting?" At length they perceived that all this tumult arose from their trusting the words of children.

This last belongs rather to the class of simpleton-stories; and in the following, from the Rev. J. Hinton Knowles' *Folk Tales of Kashmír* (Trübner: 1888), we have a variant of the well-known tale of the twelve men of Gotham who went one day to fish, and, before returning home, miscounted their number, of which several analogues are given in my *Book of Noodles*, pp. 28 ff. (Elliot Stock: 1888): Ten peasants were standing on the side of the road weeping. They thought that one of their number had been lost on the way, as each man had counted the company, and found them nine only. "Ho! you—what's the matter?" shouted a townsman passing by. "O sir," said the peasants, "we were ten men when we left the village, but now we are only nine." The townsman saw at a glance what fools they were: each of them had omitted to count himself in the number. He therefore told them to take off their *topís* (skull-caps) and place them on the ground. This they did, and counted ten of them, whereupon they concluded they were all there, and were comforted. But they could not tell how it was.

That wakefulness is not necessarily watchfulness may seem paradoxical, yet here is a Persian story which goes far to show that they are not always synonymous terms: Once upon a time (to commence in the good old way) there came into a city a merchant on horseback, attended by his servant on foot. Hearing that the city was infested by many bold and expert thieves, in consequence of which property was very insecure, he said to his servant at night: "I will keep watch, and do you sleep; for I cannot trust you to keep awake, and I much fear that my horse may be stolen." But to this arrangement his faithful servant would not consent, and he insisted upon watching all night. So the master went to sleep, and three hours after awoke, when he called to his servant: "What are you doing?" He answered: "I am meditating how Allah has spread the earth upon the water." The master said: "I am afraid lest thieves come, and you know nothing of it." "O my lord, be satisfied; I am on the watch." The merchant again went to sleep, and awaking about midnight cried: "Ho! what are you doing?" The servant replied: "I am considering how Allah has supported the sky without pillars." Quoth the master: "But I am afraid that while you are busy meditating thieves will carry off my horse." "Be not afraid, master, I am fully awake; how, then, can thieves come?" The master replied: "If you wish to sleep, I will keep watch." But the servant would not hear of this; he was not at all sleepy; so his master addressed himself once more to slumber; and when one hour of the night yet remained he awoke, and as usual asked him what he was doing, to which he coolly answered: "I am considering, since the thieves have stolen the horse, whether I shall carry the saddle on my head, or you, sir."

Somewhat akin to the familiar "story" of the man whose eyesight was so extraordinary that he could, standing in the street, perceive a fly on the dome of St. Paul's is the tale of the Three Dervishes who, travelling in company, came to the sea-shore of Syria, and desired the captain of a vessel about to sail for Cyprus to give them a passage. The captain was willing to take them "for a consideration"; but they told him they were dervishes, and therefore without money, but they possessed certain wonderful gifts, which might be of use to him on the voyage. The first dervish said that he could descry any object at the distance of a year's journey; the second could hear at as great a distance as his brother could see. "Well!" exclaimed the captain, "these are truly miraculous gifts; and pray, sir," said he, turning to the third dervish, "what may *your* particular gift be?" "I, sir," replied he, "am an unbeliever." When the captain heard this, he said he could not take such a person on board of his ship; but on the others declaring they must all three go together or remain behind, he at length consented to allow the third dervish a passage with the two highly-gifted ones. In the course of the voyage, it happened one fine day that the captain and the three dervishes were on deck conversing, when suddenly the first dervish exclaimed: "Look, look!—see, there—the daughter of the sultan of India sitting at the window of her palace, working embroidery." "A mischief on your eyes!" cried the second dervish, "for her needle has this moment dropped from her hand, and I hear it sound upon the pavement below her window." "Sir," said the third dervish, addressing the captain, "shall I, or shall I not, be an unbeliever?" Quoth the captain: "Come, friend, come with me into my cabin, and let us cultivate unbelief together!"

A very droll parrot story occurs—where, indeed, we should least expect to meet with such a thing—in the *Masnaví* of Jelálu-'d-Dín er-Rúmí (13th century), a grand mystical poem, or rather series of poems, in six books, written in Persian rhymed couplets, as the title indicates. In the second poem of the First Book we read that an oilman possessed a fine parrot, who amused him with her prattle and watched his shop during his absence. It chanced one day, when the oilman had gone out, that a cat ran into the shop in chase of a mouse, which so frightened the parrot that she flew about from shelf to shelf, upsetting several jars and spilling their contents.

When her master returned and saw the havoc made among his goods he fetched the parrot a blow that knocked out all her head feathers, and from that day she sulked on her perch. The oilman, missing the prattle of his favourite, began to shower his alms on every passing beggar, in hopes that some one would induce the parrot to speak again. At length a bald-headed mendicant came to the shop one day, upon seeing whom, the parrot, breaking her long silence, cried out: "Poor fellow! poor fellow! hast thou, too, upset some oil-jar?"[39]

Somewhat more credible is the tale of the man who taught a parrot to say, "What doubt is there of this?" (*dur ín cheh shuk*) and took it to market for sale, fixing the price at a hundred rupís. A Moghul asked the bird: "Are you really worth a hundred rupís?" to which the bird answered very readily: "What doubt is there of this?" Delighted with the apt reply, he bought the parrot and took it home; but he soon found that, whatever he might say, the bird always made the same answer, so he repented his purchase and exclaimed: "I was certainly a great fool to buy this bird!" The parrot said: "What doubt is there of this?" The Moghul smiled, and gave the bird her liberty.

Sir John Malcolm cites a good example of the ready wit of the citizens of Isfahán, in his entertaining *Sketches of Persia*, as follows: When the celebrated Haji Ibrahím was prime minister of Persia [some sixty years since], his brother was governor of Isfahán, while other members of his family held several of the first offices of the kingdom. A shop-keeper one day went to the governor to represent that he was unable to pay certain taxes. "You must pay them," replied the governor, "or leave the city." "Where can I go to?" asked the Isfahání. "To Shíráz or Kashan." "Your nephew rules in one city and your brother in the other." "Go to the Sháh, and complain if you like." "Your brother the Haji is prime minister." "Then go to Satan," said the enraged governor. "Haji Merhúm, your father, the pious pilgrim, is dead," rejoined the undaunted Isfahání. "My friend," said the governor, bursting into laughter, "I will pay your taxes, even myself, since you declare that my family keep you from all redress, both in this world and the next."

The Hebrew Rabbis who compiled the Talmud were, some of them, witty as well as wise—indeed I have always held that wisdom and wit are cousins german, if not full brothers—and our specimens of Oriental Wit and Humour may be fittingly concluded with a few Jewish jests from a scarce little book, entitled, *Hebrew Tales*, by Hyman Hurwitz: An Athenian, walking about in the streets of Jerusalem one day, called to a little Hebrew boy, and, giving him a *pruta* (a small coin of less value than a farthing), said: "Here is a pruta, my lad, bring me something for it, of which I may eat enough, leave some for my host, and carry some home to my family." The boy went, and presently returned with a quantity of salt, which he

58

handed to the jester. "Salt!" he exclaimed, "I did not ask thee to buy me salt." "True," said the urchin; "but didst thou not tell me to bring thee something of which thou mightest eat, leave, and take home? Of this salt there is surely enough for all three purposes."[40]

Another Athenian desired a boy to buy him some cheese and eggs. Having done so, "Now, my lad," said the stranger, "tell me which of these cheese were made of the milk of white goats and which of black goats?" The little Hebrew answered: "Since thou art older than I, and more experienced, first do thou tell me which of these eggs came from white and which from black hens."

Once more did a Hebrew urchin prove his superiority in wit over an Athenian: "Here, boy," said he, "here is some money; bring us some figs and grapes." The lad went and bought the fruit, kept half of it for himself, and gave the other half to the Athenian. "How!" cried the man, "is it the custom of this city for a messenger to take half of what he is sent to purchase?" "No," replied the boy; "but it is our custom to speak what we mean, and to do what we are desired." "Well, then, I did not desire thee to take half of the fruit." "Why, what else could you mean," rejoined the little casuist, "by saying, 'Bring *us*?' Does not that word include the hearer as well as the speaker?" The stranger, not knowing how to answer such reasoning, smiled and went his way, leaving the shrewd lad to eat his share of the fruit in peace.

"There is no rule without some exception," as the following tale demonstrates: Rabbi Eliezar, who was as much distinguished by his greatness of mind as by the extraordinary size of his body, once paid a friendly visit to Rabbi Simon. The learned Simon received him most cordially, and filling a cup with wine handed it to him. Eliezar took it and drank it off at a draught. Another was poured out—it shared the same fate. "Brother Eliezar," said Simon, jestingly, "rememberest thou not what the wise men have said on this subject?" "I well remember," replied his corpulent friend, "the saying of our instructors, that people ought not to take a cup at one draught. But the wise men have not so defined their rule as to admit of no exception; and in this instance there are not less than three—the *cup* is small, the *receiver* is large, and your WINE, brother Simon, is DELICIOUS!"

TALES OF A PARROT

I

GENERAL PLAN OF EASTERN ROMANCES— THE "TÚTÍ NÁMA," OR PARROT-BOOK—THE FRAME-STORY—TALES: THE STOLEN IMAGES—THE WOMAN CARVED OUT OF WOOD—THE MAN WHOSE MARE WAS KICKED BY A MERCHANT'S HORSE

Oriental romances are usually constructed on the plan of a number of tales connected by a general or leading story running throughout, like the slender thread that holds a necklace of pearls together—a familiar example of which is the *Book of the Thousand and One Nights*, commonly known amongst us under the title of *Arabian Nights Entertainments*. In some the subordinate tales are represented as being told by one or more individuals to serve a particular object, by the moral, or warning, which they are supposed to convey; as in the case of the *Book of Sindibád*, in which a prince is falsely accused by one of his father's ladies, and defended by the king's seven vazírs, or counsellors, who each in turn relate to the king two stories, the purport of which being to warn him to put no faith in the accusations of women, to which the lady replies by stories representing the wickedness and perfidy of men; and that of the *Bakhtyár Náma*, in which a youth, falsely accused of having violated the royal harem, obtains for himself a respite from death during ten days by relating to the king each day a story designed to caution him against precipitation in matters of importance. In others supernatural beings are the narrators of the subordinate tales, as in the Indian romances, *Vetála Panchavinsati*, or Twenty-five Tales of a Demon, and the *Sinhásana Dwatrinsati*, or Tales of the Thirty-two Speaking Statues—literally, Thirty-two (Tales) of a Throne. In others, again, the relators are birds, as in the Indian work entitled *Hamsa Vinsati*, or Twenty Tales of a Goose.

Of this last class is the popular Persian work, *Túti Náma*, (Tales of a Parrot, or Parrot-Book), of which I purpose furnishing some account, as it has not yet been completely translated into English. This work was composed, according to Pertsch, in A.D. 1329, by a Persian named Nakhshabí, after an older Persian version, now lost, which was made from a Sanskrit work, also no longer extant, but of which the modern representative is the *Suka Saptati*, or Seventy Tales of a Parrot.[41] The frame, or leading story, of the Persian Parrot-Book is to the following effect:

A merchant who had a very beautiful wife informs her one day that he has resolved to travel into foreign countries in order to increase his wealth by trade. His wife endeavours to persuade him to remain at home in peace and security instead of imperiling his life among strangers. But he expatiates on the evils of poverty and the advantages of wealth: "A man without riches is fatherless, and a home without money is deserted. He that is in want of cash is a nonentity, and wanders in the land unknown. It is, therefore, everybody's duty to procure as much money as possible; for gold is the delight of our lives—it is the bright live-coal of our hearts—the yellow links which fasten the coat of mail—the gentle stimulative of the world—the complete coining die of the globe—the traveller who speaks all languages, and is welcome in every city—the splendid bride unveiled—the defender, register, and mirror of jehandars. The man who has dirhams [*Scottice*, 'siller'—*Fr.* 'l'argent'] is handsome; the sun never shines on the inauspicious man without money."[42] Before leaving home the merchant purchased at great cost in the bazaar a wonderful parrot, that could discourse eloquently and intelligently, and also a sharak, a species of nightingale, which, according to Gerrans, "imitates the human voice in so surprising a manner that, if you do not see the bird, you cannot help being deceived"; and, having put them into the same cage, he charged his spouse that whenever she had any matter of importance to transact she should first obtain the sanction of both birds.

The merchant having protracted his absence many months (Vatsyayana, in his *Káma Sutra*, says that the man who is given to much travelling does not deserve to be married), and, his wife chancing to be on the roof of her house one day when a young foreign prince of handsome appearance passed by with his attendants, she immediately fell in love with him—"the battle-axe of prudence dropped from her hand; the vessel of continence became a sport to the waves of confusion; while the avenues leading to the fortress of reason remained unguarded, the sugar-cane of incontinence triumphantly raised its head above the rose-tree of patience." The prince had also observed the lady, as she stood on the terrace of her house, and was instantly enamoured of her. He sends an old woman (always the obliging—"for a consideration"—go-between of Eastern lovers) to solicit an interview with the lady at his own palace in the evening, and, after much persuasion, she consents. Arraying her beauteous person in the finest apparel, she proceeds to the cage, and first consults the sharak as to the propriety of her purpose. The sharak forbids her to go, and is at once rewarded by having her head wrung off. She then represents her case to the parrot, who, having witnessed the fate of his companion, prudently resolves to temporise with the amorous dame; so he "quenched the fire of her indignation with the water of flattery, and began a tale conformable to her temperament, which he took care to protract till the morning." In this manner does the prudent parrot prevent the lady's intended intrigue by relating, night after night, till the merchant returns home from his travels, one or more fascinating tales, which he does not bring to an end till it is too late for the assignation.[43]

The order of the parrot's tales is not the same in all texts; in Kádirí's abridgment there are few of the Nights which correspond with those of the India Office MS. No. 2573, which may, perhaps, be partly accounted for by the circumstance that Kádirí has given only 35 of the 52 tales that are in the original text. For the general reader, however, the sequence of the tales is a minor consideration; and I shall content myself with giving abstracts of some of the best stories, irrespective of their order in any text, and complete translations of two or three others. It so happens that the Third Night is the same in Kádirí and the India Office MS. No. 2573, which comprises the complete text; and the story the eloquent bird relates on that night may be entitled

The Stolen Images

A goldsmith and a carpenter, travelling in company, steal from a Hindú temple some golden images, which, when they arrive in the neighbourhood of their own city, they bury beneath a tree. The goldsmith goes secretly one night and carries away the images, and next morning, when both go together to share the spoil, the goldsmith accuses the carpenter of having played him false. But the carpenter was a shrewd fellow, and so he makes a figure resembling the goldsmith, dresses it in clothes similar to what he usually wore, and procures a couple of bear's cubs, which he teaches to take their food from the skirts and sleeves of the effigy. Thus the cubs conceived a great affection for the figure of the goldsmith. He then contrives to steal the goldsmith's two sons, and, when the father comes to seek them at his house, he pretends they have been changed into young bears. The goldsmith brings his case before the kází; the cubs are brought into court, and no sooner do they discover the goldsmith than they run up and fondle him. Upon this the judge decides in favour of the carpenter, to whom the goldsmith confesses his guilt, and offers to give up all the gold if he restore his children, which he does accordingly.[44]

The Sixth Tale of the Parrot, according to the India Office MS., relates to

The Woman Carved out of Wood

Four men—a goldsmith, a carpenter, a tailor, and a dervish—travelling together, one night halted in a desert place, and it was agreed they should watch turn about until daybreak. The carpenter takes the first watch, and to amuse himself he carves the figure of a woman out of a log of wood. When it came to the goldsmith's turn to watch, finding the beautiful female figure, he resolved also to exhibit his art, and accordingly made a set of ornaments of gold and silver, which he placed on the neck, arms, and ankles. During the third watch the tailor made a suit of clothes becoming a bride, and put them on the figure. Lastly, the dervish, when it came to his turn to watch, beholding the captivating female form, prayed that it might be endowed with life, and immediately the effigy became animated. In the morning all four fell in love with the charming damsel, each claiming her for himself; the carpenter, because he had carved her with his own hands; the goldsmith, because he had adorned her with gems; the tailor, because he had suitably clothed her; and the dervish, because he had, by his intercession, endowed her with life. While they were thus disputing, a man came to the spot, to whom they referred the case. On seeing the woman, he exclaimed: "This is my own wife, whom you have stolen from me," and compelled them to come before the kutwal, who, on viewing her beauty, in his turn claimed her as the wife of his brother, who had been waylaid and murdered in the desert. The kutwal took them all, with the woman, before the kází, who declared that she was his slave, who had absconded from his house with a large sum of money. An old man who was present suggested that they should all seven appeal to the Tree of Decision, and thither they went accordingly; but no sooner had they stated their several claims than the trunk of the tree split open, the woman ran into the cleft, and on its reuniting she was no more to be seen. A voice proceeded from the tree, saying: "Everything returns to its first principles"; and the seven suitors of the woman were overwhelmed with shame.[45]

I am strongly of opinion that the foregoing story is of Buddhistic extraction; but however this may be, it is not a bad specimen of Eastern humour, nor is the following, which the eloquent bird tells the lady another night:

Of the Man whose Mare was kicked by a Merchant's Horse

A merchant had a vicious horse that kicked a mare, which he had warned the owner not to tie near his animal. The man carried the merchant before the kází, and stated his complaint. The kází inquired of the merchant what he had to say in his own defence; but he pretended to be dumb, answering not a word to the judge's interrogatives. Upon this the kází remarked to the plaintiff that since the merchant was dumb he could not be to blame for the accident. "How do you know he is dumb?" said the owner of the mare.

"At the time I wished to fasten my mare near his horse he said, 'Don't!' yet now he feigns himself dumb." The kází observed that if he was duly warned against the accident he had himself to blame, and so dismissed the case.

II

THE EMPEROR'S DREAM—THE GOLDEN APPARITION—THE FOUR TREASURE-SEEKERS

We are not without instances in European popular fictions of two young persons dreaming of each other and falling in love, although they had never met or known of each other's existence. A notable example is the story of the Two Dreams in the famous *History of the Seven Wise Masters*. Incidents of this kind are very common in Oriental stories: the romance of *Kámarupa* (of Indian origin, but now chiefly known through the Persian version) is based upon a dream which the hero has of a certain beautiful princess, with whom he falls in love, and he sets forth with his companions to find her, should it be at the uttermost ends of the earth. It so happens that the damsel also dreams of him, and, when they do meet, they need no introduction to each other. The Indian romance of *Vasayadatta* has a similar plot. But the royal dreamer and lover in the following story, told by the Parrot on the 39th Night, according to the India Office MS. No. 2573, adopted a plan for the discovery of the beauteous object of his vision more conformable to his own ease:

The Emperor's Dream

An emperor of China dreamt of a very beautiful damsel whom he had never seen or heard of, and, being sorely pierced with the darts of love for the creature of his dreaming fancy, he could find no peace of mind. One of his vazírs, who was an excellent portrait painter, receiving from the emperor a minute description of the lady's features, drew the face, and the imperial lover acknowledged the likeness to be very exact. The vazír then went abroad with the portrait, to see whether any one could identify it with the fair original. After many disappointments he met with an old hermit, who at once recognised it as the portrait of the princess of Rúm,[46] who, he informed the vazír, had an unconquerable aversion against men ever since she beheld, in her garden, a peacock basely desert his mate and their young ones, when the tree on which their nest was built had been struck by lightning. She believed that all men were quite as selfish as that peacock, and was resolved never to marry. Returning to his imperial master with

65

these most interesting particulars regarding the object of his affection, he next undertakes to conquer the strange and unnatural aversion of the princess. Taking with him the emperor's portrait and other pictures, he procures access to the princess of Rúm; shows her, first, the portrait of the emperor of China, and then pictures of animals in the royal menagerie, among others that of a deer, concerning which he relates a story to the effect that the emperor, sitting one day in his summer-house, saw a deer, his doe, and their fawn on the bank of the river, when suddenly the waters overflowed the banks, and the doe, in terror for her life, fled away, while the deer bravely remained with the fawn and was drowned. This story, so closely resembling her own, struck the fair princess with wonder and admiration, and she at once gave her consent to be united to the emperor of China; and we may suppose that "they continued together in joy and happiness until they were overtaken by the terminater of delights and the separator of companions."

There can be little or no doubt, I think, that in this tale we find the original of the frame, or leading story, of the Persian Tales, ascribed to a dervish named Mukhlis, of Isfahán, and written after the *Arabian Nights*, as it is believed, in which the nurse of the Princess has to relate almost as many stories to overcome her aversion against men (the result of an incident similar to that witnessed by the Lady of Rúm) as the renowned Sheherazade had to tell her lord, who entertained—for a very different reason—a bitter dislike of women.

I now present a story unabridged, translated by Gerrans in the latter part of the last century. It is assuredly of Buddhistic origin:

The Golden Apparition

In the extreme boundaries of Khurasán there once lived, according to general report, a merchant named Abdal-Malik, whose warehouses were crowded with rich merchandise, and whose coffers overflowed with money. The scions of genius ripened into maturity under the sunshine of his liberality; the sons of indigence fattened on the bread of his hospitality; and the parched traveller amply slaked his thirst in the river of his generosity. One day, as he meditated on the favours which his Creator had so luxuriantly showered upon him, he testified his gratitude by the following resolution: "Long have I traded in the theatre of the world, much have I received, and little have I bestowed. This wealth was entrusted to my care, with no other design or intention but to enable me to assist the unfortunate and indigent. Before, therefore, the Angel of Death shall come to demand the spoil of my mortality, it is my last wish and sole intention to expiate my sins and follies by voluntary oblations of this she-camel [alluding to the Muslim Feast of the Camel] in the last month of her pregnancy, and to proclaim to all men, by this late breakfasting [alluding

66

to the Feast of Ramadan, when food is only permitted after sunset], my past mortification."

In the tranquil hour of midnight an apparition stood before him, in the habit of a fakír. The merchant cried: "What art thou?" It answered: "I am the apparition of thy good fortune and the genius of thy future happiness. When thou, with such unbounded generosity, didst bequeath all thy wealth to the poor, I determined not to pass by thy door unnoticed, but to endow thee with an inexhaustible treasure, conformable to the greatness of thy capacious soul. To accomplish which I will, every morning, in this shape, appear to thee; thou shalt strike me a few blows on the head, when I shall instantly fall low at thy feet, transformed into an image of gold. From this freely take as much as thou shalt have occasion for; and every member or joint that shall be separated from the image shall be instantly replaced by another of the same precious metal."[47]

At daybreak the demon of avarice had conducted Hajm, the covetous, to the durbar of Abdal-Malik, the generous. Soon after his arrival the apparition presented itself. Abdal-Malik immediately arose, and after striking it several blows on the head it fell down before him, and was changed into an image of gold. As much as sufficed for the necessities of the day he took for himself, and gave a much larger portion to his visitor. Hajm was overjoyed at the present, and concluded from what he had seen that he or any other person who should treat a fakír in the same manner could convert him into gold, and consequently that by beating a number he might multiply his golden images. Heated with this fond imagination, he quickly returned to his house and gave the necessary orders for a most sumptuous entertainment, to which he invited all the fakírs in the province.

When the keen appetite was assuaged, and the exhilarating sherbet began to enliven the convivial meeting, Hajm seized a ponderous club, and with it regaled his guests till he broke their heads, and the crimson torrent stained the carpet of hospitality. The fakírs elevating the shriek of sore distress, the kutwal's guard came to their assistance, and soon a multitude of people assembled, who, after binding the offender with the strong cord of captivity, carried him, together with the fakírs, before the governor of the city. He demanded to know the reason why he had so inhospitably and cruelly behaved to these harmless people. The confounded Hajm replied: "As I was yesterday in the house of Abdal-Malik, a fakír suddenly appeared. The merchant struck him some blows on the head, and he fell prostrate before him, transformed into a golden image. Imagining that any other person could, by a similar behaviour, force any fakír to undergo the like metamorphosis, I invited these men to a banquet, and regaled them with some blows of my cudgel to compel them to a similar transformation;

but the demon of avarice has deceived me, and the fascinating temptation of gold has involved me in a labyrinth of ills."

The governor at once sent for Abdal-Malik, and, demanding a solution of Hajm's mysterious tale, was thus answered by the charitable merchant: "The unfortunate Hajm is my neighbour. Some days ago he began to exhibit symptoms of a disordered imagination and distracted brain, and during these violent paroxysms of insanity he related some ridiculous fable of me and the rest of my neighbours. No better specimen can be adduced than the extravagant action of which he now stands accused, and the absurd tale by which he attempts to apologise for the commission of it. That madness may no longer usurp the palace of reason, to revel upon the ruins of his mind, deliver him to the sons of ingenuity, the preservers and restorers of health; let them purify his blood by sparing diet, abridge him of his daily potations, and by the force of medicinal beverage recall him from the precipice of ruin." This advice was warmly applauded by the governor, who, after Hajm had been compelled to ask pardon of the fakírs for the ill-treatment they had received, was soundly bastinadoed before the tribunal, and carried to the hospital for madness.

That each man has his "genius" of good or evil fortune is an essentially Buddhistic idea. The same story occurs, in a different form, in the *Hitopadesa*, or Friendly Counsel, an ancient Sanskrit collection of apologues, and an abridgment of the *Panchatantra*, or Five Chapters, where it forms Fable 10 of Book III: In the city of Ayodhya (Oude) there was a soldier named Churamani, who, being anxious for money, for a long time with pain of body worshipped the deity, the jewel of whose diadem is the lunar crescent. Being at length purified from his sins, in his sleep he had a vision in which, through the favour of the deity, he was directed by the lord of the Yakshas [Kuvera, the god of wealth] to do as follows: "Early in the morning, having been shaved, thou must stand, club in hand, concealed behind the door of the house; and the beggar whom thou seest come into the court thou wilt put to death without mercy by blows of thy staff. Instantly the beggar will become a pot full of gold, by which thou wilt be comfortable for the rest of thy life." These instructions being followed, it came to pass accordingly; but the barber who had been brought to shave him, having witnessed it all, said to himself, "O is this the mode of gaining a treasure? Why, then, may not I also do the same?" From that day forward the barber in like manner, with club in hand, day after day awaited the coming of the beggar. One day a beggar being so caught was attacked by him and killed with the stick, for which offence the barber himself was beaten by the king's officers, and died.—In the *Panchatantra*, in place of a soldier, a banker who had lost all his wealth determines to put an end to his life, when he dreams that the personification of Kuvera, the god of riches, appears before him in the form of a Jaina mendicant—a conclusive proof of the Buddhistic origin of the story.—A trunkless head performs the

68

same part in the Russian folk-tale of the Stepmother's Daughter, on which Mr. Ralston remarks that, "according to Buddhist belief the treasure which has belonged to anyone in a former existence may come to him in the form of a man, who, when killed, is turned to gold."[48]

There is an analogous story to this of the Golden Apparition in an entertaining little book entitled, *The Orientalist; or, Letters of a Rabbi*, by James Noble, published at Edinburgh in 1831, of which the following is the outline:

An old Dervish falls ill in the house of a poor widow, who tends him with great care, and when he recovers his health he offers to take charge of her only son, Abdallah. The good woman gladly consents, and the Dervish sets out accompanied by his young ward, having intimated to his mother that they must perform a journey which would last about two years. One day they arrived at a solitary place, and the Dervish said to Abdallah: "My son, we are now at the end of our journey. I shall employ my prayers to obtain from Allah that the earth shall open and make an entrance wide enough to permit thee to descend into a place where thou shalt find one of the greatest treasures that the earth contains. Hast thou courage to descend into the vault?" Abdallah assured him that he might depend on his fidelity; and then the Dervish lighted a small fire, into which he cast a perfume: he read and prayed for some minutes, after which the earth opened, and he said to the young man: "Thou mayest now enter. Remember that it is in thy power to do me a great service; and that this is perhaps the only opportunity thou shalt ever have of testifying to me that thou art not ungrateful. Do not let thyself be dazzled by the riches that thou shalt find there: think only of seizing upon an iron candlestick with twelve branches, which thou shalt find close to the door. That is absolutely necessary to me: come up with it at once." Abdallah descended, and, neglecting the advice of the Dervish, filled his vest and sleeves with the gold and jewels which he found heaped up in the vault, whereupon the opening by which he had entered closed of itself. He had, however, sufficient presence of mind to seize the iron candlestick, and endeavoured to find some other means of escape from the vault. At length he discovers a narrow passage, which he follows until he reaches the surface of the earth, and looking for the Dervish saw him not, but to his surprise found that he was close to his mother's house. On showing his wealth to his mother, it all suddenly vanished. But the candlestick remained. He lighted one of the branches, upon which a dervish appeared, and after turning round an hour he threw down an asper (about three farthings in value) and vanished. Next night he put a lighted candle in each of the branches, when twelve dervishes appeared, and having continued their gyrations for an hour each threw down an asper and vanished. In this way did Abdallah and his mother contrive to live for a time, till at length he resolved to carry the candlestick to the good Dervish, hoping to obtain from him the treasure which he had seen in the vault. He remembered his name and city, and on reaching his dwelling found the Dervish living in a magnificent palace, with fifty porters at the gate. The Dervish thus addressed Abdallah: "Thou art an ungrateful wretch! Hadst thou known the value of the candlestick thou wouldst never have brought it to me. I will show thee its true use." Then the Dervish placed a light in each branch, whereupon twelve dervishes appeared and began to whirl, but on his giving each a blow with a stick, in an instant they were changed into twelve heaps of sequins, diamonds, and other precious stones. Ungrateful as Abdallah had shown himself, yet the Dervish gave him two camels laden with gold, and a slave, telling him that he must depart the next morning. During the night Abdallah stole the candlestick and placed it at the bottom of his sacks. At daybreak he took leave of the generous Dervish and set off. When about half a day's journey from his own city he sold the slave, that there should be no witness to his former poverty, and bought another in his stead. Arriving home, he carefully placed his loads of treasure in a private chamber, and then put a light in each branch of the candlestick; and when the twelve dervishes appeared, he dealt each of them a blow with a stick. But he had not observed that the good Dervish employed his left hand, and he had naturally used his right, in consequence of which the twelve dervishes drew each from under their robes a heavy club and beat him till he was nearly dead, and then vanished, as did also the treasure, the camels, the slave, and the wonder-working candlestick![49]

A warning against avarice is intended to be conveyed in the tale, or rather apologue, or perhaps we should consider it as a sort of allegory, related by the sagacious bird on the 47th Night, according to the India Office MS., but the 16th Night of Kádirí's abridgment. It is to the following effect, and may be entitled

The Four Treasure-Seekers

Once on a time four intimate friends, who made a common fund of all their possessions, and had long enjoyed the wealth of their industrious ancestors, at length lost all their goods and money, and, barely saving their lives, quitted together the place of their nativity. In the course of their travels they meet a wise Bráhman, to whom they relate the history of their misfortunes. He gives each of them a pearl, which he places on their heads, telling them, whenever the pearl drops from the head of any of them, to examine the spot, and share equally what they find there. After walking some distance the pearl drops from the head of one of the companions, and on examining the place he discovers a copper mine, the produce of which he offers to share with the others, but they refuse, and, leaving him, continue their journey. By-and-by the pearl drops from the head of another of the friends, and a silver mine is found; but the two others, believing that better things were in store farther on, left him to his treasure, and proceeded on their way till the pearl of the third companion dropped, and they found in the place a rich gold mine. In vain does he endeavour to persuade his companion to be content with the wealth here obtainable: he disdainfully refuses, saying that, since copper, silver, and gold had been found, fortune had evidently reserved something infinitely better for him; and so he quitted his friend and went on, till he reached a narrow valley destitute of water; the air like that of Jehennan;⁵⁰ the surface of the earth like infernal fire; no animal or bird was to be seen; and chilling blasts alternated with sulphurous exhalations. Here the fourth pearl dropped and the owner discovered a mine of diamonds and other gems, but the ground was covered with snakes, cockatrices, and the most venomous serpents. On seeing this he determines to return and share the produce of the third companion's gold mine; but when he comes to the spot he can find no trace of the mine or of the owner. Proceeding next to the silver mine, he finds it is exhausted, and his friend who owned it has gone; so he will now content himself with copper; but, alas! his first friend had died the day before his arrival, and strangers were now in possession of the mine, who laughed at his pretensions, and even beat him for his impertinence. Sad at heart, he journeys on to where he and his companions had met the Bráhman, but he had long since departed to a far distant country; and thus, through his obstinacy and avarice, he was overwhelmed with poverty and disgrace—without money and without friends.

This story of the Four Treasure-seekers forms the third of Book V of the *Panchatantra*, where the fourth companion, instead of finding a diamond mine guarded by serpents, etc., discovers a man with a wheel upon his head, and on his asking this man where he could procure water, who he was, and why he stood with the wheel on his head, straightway the wheel is transferred to his own head, as had been the case of the former victim who had asked the same questions of his predecessor. The third man, who had found the gold mine, wondering that his companion tarried so long, sets off in search of him, and, finding him with the wheel on his head, asks why he stood thus. The fourth acquaints him of the property of the wheel, and then relates a number of stories to show that those who want common sense will surely come to grief.

It is more than probable that several of the tales and apologues in the *Panchatantra* were derived from Buddhist sources; and the incident of a man with a wheel on his head is found in the Chinese-Sanskrit work entitled *Fu-pen-hing-tsi-king*, which Wassiljew translates 'Biography of Sákyamuni and his Companions,' and of which Dr. Beal has published an abridged English translation under the title of the *Romantic History of Buddha*. In this work (p. 342 ff.) a merchant, who had struck his mother because she would not sanction his going on a trading voyage, in the course of his wanderings discovers a man "on whose head there was placed an iron wheel, this wheel was red with heat, and glowing as from a furnace, terrible to behold. Seeing this terrible sight, Máitri exclaimed: 'Who are you? Why do you carry that terrible wheel on your head?' On this the wretched man replied: 'Dear sir, is it possible you know me not? I am a merchant chief called Gorinda.' Then Máitri asked him and said: 'Pray, then, tell me, what dreadful crime have you committed in former days that you are constrained to wear that fiery wheel on your head.' Then Gorinda answered: 'In former days I was angry with and struck my mother as she lay on the ground, and for this reason I am condemned to wear this fiery iron wheel around my head.' At this time Máitri, self-accused, began to cry out and lament; he was filled with remorse on recollection of his own conduct, and exclaimed in agony: 'Now am I caught like a deer in the snare.' Then a certain Yaksha, who kept guard over that city, whose name was Viruka, suddenly came to the spot, and removing the fiery wheel from off the head of Gorinda, he placed it on the head of Máitri. Then the wretched man cried out in his agony and said: 'O what have I done to merit this torment?' to which the Yaksha replied: 'You, wretched man, dared to strike your mother on the head as she lay on the ground; now, therefore, on your head you shall wear this fiery wheel; through 60,000 years your punishment shall last: be assured of this, through all these years you shall wear this wheel.'"

III

THE SINGING ASS: THE FOOLISH THIEVES: THE FAGGOT-MAKER AND THE MAGIC BOWL

Some of the Parrot's recitals have other tales sphered within them, so to say—a plan which must be familiar to all readers of the *Arabian Nights*. In the following amusing tale, which is perhaps the best of the whole series (it is the 41st of the India Office MS. No. 2573, and the 31st in Kadiri's version), there are two subordinate stories:

The Singing Ass

At a certain period of time, as ancient historians inform us, an ass and an elk were so fond of each other's company that they were never seen separate. If the plains were deficient in pasture, they repaired to the meadows; or, if famine pervaded the valleys, they overleaped the garden-fence, and, like friends, divided the spoil.

One night, during the season of verdure, about the gay termination of spring, after they had rioted in the cup of plenty, and lay rolling on a green carpet of spinach, the cup of the silly ass began to overflow with the froth of conceit, and he thus expressed his unseasonable intentions:

"O comrade of the branching antlers, what a mirth-inspiring night is this! How joyous are the heart-attracting moments of spring! Fragrance distils from every tree; the garden breathes otto of roses, and the whole atmosphere is pregnant with musk. In the umbrageous gloom of the waving cypress the turtles are exchanging their vows, and the bird of a thousand songs [*i.e.*, the nightingale] sips nectar from the lips of the rose: nothing is wanting to complete the joys of spring but one of my melodious songs. When the warm blood of youth shall cease to give animation to these elegant limbs of mine, what relish shall I have for pleasure? And when the lamp of my life is extinguished, the spring will return in vain."

Nakhshabí, music at every season is delightful, and a song sweetly murmured captivates the senses.

The musician who charms our ears will most assuredly find the road of success to our hearts.[51]

The elk answered: "Sagacious, long-eared associate, what an unseasonable proposal is this? Rather let us converse together about pack-saddles and sacks; tell me a story about straw, beans, or hay-lofts, unmerciful drivers, and heavy burdens."

What business has the Ass to meddle with music?

What occasion has Long-ears to attempt to sing?

"You ought also to recollect," continued the elk, "that we are thieves, and that we came into this garden to plunder. Consider what an enormous quantity of beets, lettuces, parsley, and radishes we have eaten, and what a fine bed of spinach we are spoiling! 'Nothing can be more disgusting than a bird that sings out of season' is a proverb which is as current among the sons of wisdom as a bill of exchange among merchants, and as valuable as an unpierced pearl. If you are so infatuated as to permit the enchanting melody of your voice to draw you into this inextricable labyrinth, the gardener will instantly awake, rouse his whole caravan of workmen, hasten to this garden and convert our music into mourning; so that our history will be like that of the house-breakers."

The Prince of Folly, expressing a wish to know how that was, received the following information:

The Foolish Thieves

In one of the cities of Hindústán some thieves broke into a house, and after collecting the most valuable movables sat down in a corner to bind them up. In this corner was a large two-eared earthen vessel, brimful of the wine of seduction, which sublime to their mouths they advanced and long-breathed potations exhausted, crying: "Everything is good in its turn; the hours of business are past—come on with the gift which fortune bestows; let us mitigate the toils of the night and smooth the forehead of care." As they approached the bottom of the flagon, the vanguard of intoxication began to storm the castle of reason; wild uproar, tumult, and their auxiliaries commanded by a sirdar of nonsense, soon after scaled the walls, and the songs of folly vociferously proclaimed that the sultan of discretion was driven from his post, and confusion had taken possession of the garrison. The noise awakened the master of the mansion, who was first overwhelmed with surprise, but soon recollecting himself, he seized his trusty scimitar, and expeditiously roused his servants, who forthwith attacked the sons of disorder, and with very little pains or risk extended them on the pavement of death.

Nakhshabí, everything is good in its season.

Let each perform his part in the world, that the world may go round.

He who drinks at an unseasonable hour ought not to complain of the vintner.

Here Long-ears superciliously answered: "Pusillanimous companion, I am the blossom of the city and the luminary of the people; my presence gives life to the plains, and my harmony cultivates the desert. If, when in vulgar prose I express the unpremeditated idea, every ear is filled with delight, and the fleeting soul, through ecstacy, flutters on the trembling lips—what must be the effect of my songs?"

The elk rejoined: "The ear must be deprived of sensation, the heart void of blood, and formed of the coarsest clay must be he who can attend your lays with indifference. But condescend, for once, to listen to advice, and postpone this music, in which you are so great a proficient, and suppress not only the song, but the sweet murmuring in your throat, prelusive to your singing, and shrink not up your graceful nostrils, nor extent the extremities of your jaws, lest you should have as much reason to repent of your singing as the faggot-maker had of his dancing." The ass demanding how that came to pass, the elk made answer as follows:

The Faggot-maker and the Magic Bowl

As a faggot-maker was one day at work in a wood, he saw four perís [or fairies] sitting near him, with a magnificent bowl before them, which supplied them with all they wanted. If they had occasion for food of the choicest taste, wines of the most delicious flavour, garments the most valuable and convenient, or perfumes of the most odoriferous exhalation— in short, whatever necessity could require, luxury demand, or avarice wish for—they had nothing more to do but put their hands into the bowl and pull out whatever they desired. The day following, the poor faggot-maker being at work in the same place, the perís again appeared, and invited him to be one of their party. The proposal was cheerfully accepted, and impressing his wife and children with the seal of forgetfulness, he remained some days in their company. Recollecting himself, however, at last, he thus addressed his white-robed entertainers:

"I am a poor faggot-maker, father of a numerous family; to drive famine from my cot, I every evening return with my faggots; but my cares for my wife and fireside have been for some time past obliterated by the cup of your generosity. If my petition gain admission to the durbar of your enlightened auditory, I will return to give them the salaam of health, and inquire into the situation of their affairs."

The perís graciously nodded acquiescence, adding: "The favours you have received from us are trifling, and we cannot dismiss you empty-handed. Make choice, therefore, of whatever you please, and the fervour of your most unbounded desire shall be slaked in the stream of our munificence."

The wood-cutter replied: "I have but one wish to gratify, and that is so unjust and so unreasonable that I dread the very thought of naming it, since nothing but the bowl before us will satisfy my ambitious heart."

The perís, bursting into laughter, answered: "We shall suffer not the least inconvenience by the loss of it, for, by virtue of a talisman which we possess, we could make a thousand in a twinkling. But, in order to make it as great a treasure to you as it has been to us, guard it with the utmost care, for it will break by the most trifling blow, and be sure never to make use of it but when you really want it."

The faggot-maker, overcome with joy, said: "I will pay the most profound attention to this inexhaustible treasure; and to preserve it from breaking I will exert every faculty of my soul." Upon saying this he received the bowl, with which he returned on the wings of rapture, and for some days enjoyed his good fortune better than might be expected. The necessaries and comforts of life were provided for his family, his creditors were paid, alms distributed to the poor, the brittle bowl of plenty was guarded with discretion, and everything around him was arranged for the reception of his friends, who assembled in such crowds that his cottage overflowed. The faggot-maker, who was one of those choice elevated spirits whose money never rusts in their possession, finding his habitation inadequate for the entertainment of his guests, built another, more spacious and magnificent, to which he invited the whole city, and placed the magic bowl in the middle of the grand saloon, and every time he made a dip pulled out whatever was wished for. Though the views of his visitors were various, contentment was visibly inscribed on every forehead: the hungry were filled with the bread of plenty; the aqueducts overflowed with the wine of Shíráz; the effeminate were satiated with musky odours, and the thirst of avarice was quenched by the bowl of abundance. The wondering spectators exclaimed: "This is no bowl, but a boundless ocean of mystery! It is not what it appears to be, a piece of furniture, but an inexhaustible magazine of treasure!"

After the faggot-maker had thus paraded his good fortune and circulated the wine-cup with very great rapidity, he stood up and began to dance, and, to show his dexterity in the art, placed the brittle bowl on his left shoulder, which every time he turned round he struck with his hand, crying: "O soul-exhilarating goblet, thou art the origin of my ease and affluence—the spring of my pomp and equipage—the engineer who has lifted me from the dust of indigence to the towering battlements of glory! Thou art the nimble berid [running foot-man] of my winged wishes, and the regulator of all my actions! To thee am I indebted for all the splendour that surrounds me! Thou art the source of my currency, and art the author of our present festival!"

With these and similar foolish tales he entertained his company, as the genius of nonsense dictated, making the most ridiculous grimaces, rolling his eyes like a fakír in a fit of devotion, and capering like one distracted, till the bowl, by a sudden slip of his foot, fell from his shoulder on the pavement of ruin, and was broken into a hundred pieces. At the same instant, all that he had in the house, and whatever he had circulated in the city, suddenly vanished;—the banquet of exultation was quickly converted into mourning, and he who a little before danced for joy now beat his breast for sorrow, blamed to no purpose the rigour of his inauspicious fortune, and execrated the hour of his birth. Thus a jewel fell into the hands of an unworthy person, who was unacquainted with its value; and an inestimable gem was entrusted to an indigent wretch, who, by his ignorance and ostentation, converted it to his own destruction.

"Melodious bulbul of the long-eared race," continued the elk, "as the wood-cutter's dancing was an unpardonable folly which met with the chastisement it deserved, so I fearfully anticipate that your unseasonable singing will become your exemplary punishment."

His ass-ship listened thus far with reluctance to the admonition of his friend, without intending to profit by it; but arose from the carpet of spinach, eyed his companion with a mortifying glance of contempt, pricked up his long snaky ears, and began to put himself into a musical posture. The nimble, small-hoofed elk, perceiving this, said to himself: "Since he has stretched out his neck and prepared his pitch-pipe, he will not remain long without singing." So he left the vegetable banquet, leaped over the garden wall, and fled to a place of security. The ass was no sooner alone than he commenced a most loud and horrible braying, which instantly awoke the gardeners, who, with the noose of an insidious halter, to the trunk of a tree fast bound the affrighted musician, where they belaboured him with their cudgels till they broke every bone in his body, and converted his skin to a book, in which, in letters of gold, a múnshí [learned man] of luminous pen, with the choicest flowers of the garden of rhetoric, and for the benefit of the numerous fraternity of asses, inscribed this instructive history.

Magical articles such as the wonderful wishing-bowl of our unlucky friend the Faggot-maker figure very frequently in the folk-tales of almost every country, assuming many different forms: a table-cloth, a pair of saddle-bags, a purse, a flask, etc.; but since a comprehensive account of those highly-gifted objects—alas, that they should no longer exist!—is furnished in the early chapters of my *Popular Tales and Fictions*, I presume I need not go over the same wide field again.—In the *Kathá Sarit Ságara* (Ocean of the Streams of Story), a very large collection of tales and apologues, composed, in Sanskrit, by Somadeva, in the 12th century, after a much older work, the *Vrihat Kathá* (or Great Story), the tale of the Faggot-maker occurs as a separate recital. It is there an inexhaustible pitcher which he receives from four yakshas—supernatural beings, who correspond to some extent with the perís of Muslim mythology—and he is duly warned that should it be broken it departs at once. For a time he concealed the secret from his relations until one day, when he was intoxicated, they asked him how it came about that he had given up carrying burdens, and had abundance of all kinds of dainties, eatable and drinkable. "He was too much puffed up with pride to tell them plainly, but, taking the wish-granting pitcher on his shoulder, he began to dance; and, as he was dancing, the inexhaustible pitcher slipped from his shoulder, as his feet tripped with over-abundance of intoxication, and, falling on the ground, was broken in pieces. And immediately it was mended again, and reverted to its original possessor; but Subadatta was reduced to his former condition, and filled with despondency." In a note to this story, Mr. Tawney remarks that in Bartsch's Meklenburg Tales a man possesses himself of an inexhaustible beer-can, but as soon as he tells how he got it the beer disappears.—The story of the Foolish Thieves noisily carousing in the house they had just plundered occurs also in Saádí's *Gulistán* and several other Eastern story-books.

In Kádíri's abridgment of the Parrot-Book, the Elk is taken prisoner as well as his companion the Ass, and the two subordinate stories, of the Foolish Thieves and of the Faggot-maker, are omitted. They are also omitted in the version of the Singing Ass found in the *Panchatantra* (B. v, F. 7), where a jackal, not an elk, is the companion of the ass, and when he perceives the latter about to "sing" he says: "Let me get to the door of the garden, where I may see the gardener as he approaches, and then sing away as long as you please." The gardener beats the ass till he is weary, and then fastens a clog to the animal's leg and ties him to a post. After great exertion, the ass contrives to get free from the post and hobbles away with the clog still on his leg. The jackal meets his old comrade and exclaims: "Bravo, uncle! You would sing your song, though I did all I could to dissuade you, and now see what a fine ornament you have received as recompense for your performance." This form of the story reappears in the *Tantrákhyána*, a collection of tales, in Sanskrit, discovered by Prof. Cecil Bendall in 1884, of which he has given an interesting account in the *Journal of the Royal Asiatic Society*, vol. xx, pp. 465-501, including the original text of a number of the stories.—In Ralston's *Tibetan Tales*, translated from Schiefner's German rendering of stories from the *Kah-gyur* (No. xxxii), the story is also found, with a bull in place of a jackal. An ass meets the bull one evening and proposes they should go together and feast themselves to their hearts' content in the king's bean-field, to which the bull replies: "O nephew, as you are wont to let your voice resound, we should run great risk." Said the ass: "O uncle, let us go; I will not raise my voice." Having entered the bean-field together, the ass uttered no sound until he had eaten his fill. Then quoth he: "Uncle, shall I not sing a little?" The bull responded: "Wait an instant until I have gone away, and then do just as you please." So the bull runs away, and the ass lifts up his melodious voice, upon which the king's servants came and seized him, cut off his long ears, fastened a pestle on his neck, and drove him out of the field.—There can be no question, I think, as to the superiority, in point of humour, of Nakhshabí's version in *Túti Náma*, as given above.

IV

THE COVETOUS GOLDSMITH—THE KING WHO DIED OF LOVE—THE DISCOVERY OF MUSIC—THE SEVEN REQUISITES OF A PERFECT WOMAN

To quit, for the present at least, the regions of fable and magic, and return to tales of common life: the 30th recital in Kádíri's abridged text is of

The Goldsmith who lost his Life through his Covetousness

A soldier finds a purse of gold on the highway, and entrusts it to the keeping of a goldsmith (how frequently do goldsmiths figure in these stories—and never to the credit of the craft!), but when he comes to demand it back the other denies all knowledge of it. The soldier cites him before the kází, but he still persists in denying that he had ever received any money from the complainant. The kází was, however, convinced of the truth of the soldier's story, so he goes to the house of the goldsmith, and privately causes two of his own attendants to be locked up in a large chest that was in one of the rooms. He then confines the goldsmith and his wife in the same room. During the night the concealed men hear the goldsmith inform his wife where he had hidden the soldier's money; and next morning, when the kází comes again and is told by his men what they had heard the goldsmith say to his wife about the money, he causes search to be made, and, finding it, hangs the goldsmith on the spot.

Kázís are often represented in Persian stories as being very shrewd and ingenious in convicting the most expert rogues, but this device for discovering the goldsmith's criminality is certainly one of the cleverest examples.

On the 36th Night of MS. (26th of Kádiri) the loquacious bird relates the story of

The King who died of Love for a Merchant's beautiful Daughter

A merchant had a daughter, the fame of whose beauty drew many suitors for her hand, but he rejected them all; and when she was of proper age he wrote a letter to the king, describing her charms and accomplishments, and respectfully offering her to him in marriage. The king, already in love with the damsel from this account of her beauty, sends his four vazírs to the merchant's house to ascertain whether she was really as charming as her father had represented her to be. They find that she far surpassed the power of words to describe; but, considering amongst themselves that should the king take this bewitching girl to wife, he would become so entangled in the meshes of love as totally to neglect the affairs of the state, they underrate her beauty to the king, who then gives up all thought of her. But it chanced one day that the king himself beheld the damsel on the terrace of her house, and, perceiving that his vazírs had deceived him, he sternly reprimanded them, at the same time expressing his fixed resolution of marrying the girl. The vazírs frankly confessed that their reason for misrepresenting the merchant's daughter to him was their fear lest, possessing such a charming bride, he should forget his duty to the state; upon which the king, struck with their anxiety for his true interests, resolved to deny himself the happiness of marrying the girl. But he could not suppress his affection for her: he fell sick, and soon after died, the victim of love.

This story forms the 17th of the Twenty-five Tales of a Demon (*Vetála Panchavinsati*), according to the Sanskrit version found in the *Kathá Sarit Ságara*; but its great antiquity is proved by the circumstance that it is found in a Buddhistic work dating probably 200 years before our era— namely, Buddhaghosha's Parables. "Dying for love," says Richardson, "is considered amongst us as a mere poetical figure, and we can certainly support the reality by few examples; but in Eastern countries it seems to be something more, many words in the Arabic and Persian languages which express love implying also melancholy; madness, and death." Shakspeare affirms that "men have died, and worms have eaten them, but not for love." There is, however, one notable instance of this on record, in the story (as related by Warton, in his *History of English Poetry*) of the gallant troubadour Geoffrey Rudel, who died for love—and love, too, from hearsay description of the beauty of the Countess of Tripoli.

On the 14th Night the Parrot entertains the Lady with a very curious account of

The Discovery of Music

Some attribute, says the learned and eloquent feathered sage (according to Gerrans), the discovery to the sounds made by a large stone against the frame of an oil-press; and others to the noise of meat when roasting; but the sages of Hind [India] are of opinion that it originated from the following accident: As a learned Bráhman was travelling to the court of an illustrious rájá he rested about the middle of the day under the shade of a mulberry tree, on the top of which he beheld a mischievous monkey climbing from bough to bough, till, by a sudden slip, he fell upon a sharp-pointed shoot, which instantly ripped up his belly and left his entrails suspended in the tree, while the unlucky animal fell, breathless, on the dust of death. Some time after this, as the Bráhman was returning, he accidentally sat down in the same place, and, recollecting the circumstance, looked up, and saw that the entrails were dried, and yielded a harmonious sound every time the wind gently impelled them against the branches. Charmed at the singularity of the adventure, he took them down, and after binding them to the two ends of his walking-stick, touched them with a small twig, by which he discovered that the sound was much improved. When he got home he fastened the staff to another piece of wood, which was hollow, and by the addition of a bow, strung with part of his own beard, converted it to a complete instrument. In succeeding ages the science received considerable improvements. After the addition of a bridge, purer notes were extracted; and the different students, pursuing the bent of their inclinations, constructed instruments of various forms, according to their individual fancies; and to this whimsical accident we are indebted for the tuneful ney and the heart-exhilarating rabáb, and, in short, all the other instruments of wind and strings.

Having thus discoursed upon the discovery of music, the Parrot proceeds to detail

The Seven Requisites of a Perfect Woman

1. She ought not to be always merry.
2. She ought not to be always sad.
3. She ought not to be always talking.
4. She ought not to be always thinking.
5. She ought not to be constantly dressing.
6. She ought not to be always unadorned.
7. She is a perfect woman who, at all times, possesses herself; can be cheerful without levity, grave without austerity; knows when to elevate the tongue of persuasion, and when to impress her lips with the signet of silence; never converts trifling ceremonies into intolerable burdens; always dresses becoming to her rank and age; is modest without prudery, religious without an alloy of superstition; can hear the one sex praised without envy, and converse with the other without permitting the torch of inconstancy to kindle the unhallowed fire in her breast; considers her husband as the most accomplished of mortals, and thinks all the sons of Adam besides unworthy of a transient glance from the corner of her half-shut eyes.

Such are the requisites of a perfect woman, and how thankful we should be that we have so many in this highly-favoured land who possess them all! These maxims are assuredly of Indian origin—no Persian could ever have conceived such virtues as being attainable by women.

V

THE PRINCESS OF ROME AND HER SON—
THE KING AND HIS SEVEN VAZIRS

The story told by the Parrot on the 50th Night is very singular, and presents, no doubt, a faithful picture of Oriental manners and customs. In the original text it is entitled

Story of the Daughter of the Kaysar of Rome, and her trouble by reason of her Son

In former times there was a great king, whose army was numerous and whose treasury was full to overflowing; but, having no enemy to contend with, he neglected to pay his soldiers, in consequence of which they were in a state of destitution and discontent. At length one day the soldiers went to the prime vazír and made their condition known to him. The vazír promised that he would speedily devise a plan by which they should have employment and money. Next morning he presented himself before the king, and said that it was widely reported that the kaysar of Rome had a daughter unsurpassed for beauty—one who was fit only for such a great monarch as his Majesty—and suggested that it would be advantageous if an alliance were formed between two such potentates. The notion pleased the king well, and he forthwith despatched to Rome an ambassador with rich gifts, and requested the kaysar to grant him his daughter in marriage. But the kaysar waxed wroth at this, and refused to give his daughter to the king. When the ambassador returned thus unsuccessful, the king, enraged at being made of no account, resolved to make war upon the kaysar, and, opening the doors of his treasury, he distributed much money among his troops, and then, "with a woe-bringing lust, and a blood-drinking army, he trampled Rome and the Romans in the dust." And when the kaysar was become powerless, he sent his daughter to the king, who married her according to the law of Islám.

Now that princess had a son by a former husband, and the kaysar had said to her before she departed: "Beware that thou mention not thy son, for my love for his society is great, and I cannot part with him." But the princess was sick at heart for the absence of her son, and she was ever pondering how she should speak to the king about him, and in what manner she might contrive to bring him to her. It happened one day the king gave her a string of pearls and a casket of jewels. She said: "With my father is a slave well skilled in the science of jewels." The king replied: "If I should ask that slave of thy father, would he give him to me?" "Nay," said she; "for he holds him in the place of a son. But, if the king desire him, I will send a merchant to Rome, and I myself will give him a token, and with pleasant wiles and fair speeches will bring him hither." Then the king sent for a clever merchant who knew Arabic eloquently and the language of Rome, and gave him goods for trading, and sent him to Rome with the object of procuring that slave. But the daughter of the kaysar said privately to the merchant: "That slave is my son; I have, for a good reason, said to the king that he is a slave; so thou must bring him as a slave, and let it be thy duty to take care of him." In due course the merchant brought the youth to the king's service; and when the king saw his fair face, and discovered in him many pleasing and varied accomplishments, he treated him with distinction and favour, and conferred on the merchant a robe of honour and gifts. His mother saw him from afar, and was pleased with receiving a salutation from him.

One day (the text proceeds) the king had gone to the chase, and the palace remained void of rivals; so the mother called in her son, kissed his fair face, and told him the tale of her great sorrow. A chamberlain became aware of the secret, and another suspicion fell upon him, and he said to himself: "The harem of the king is the sanctuary of security and the palace of protection. If I speak not of this, I shall be guilty of treachery, and shall have wrought unfaithfulness." When the king returned from the chase, the chamberlain related to him what he had seen, and the king was angry and said: "This woman has deceived me with words and deeds, and has brought hither her desire by craft and cunning. This conjecture must be true, else why did she play such a trick, and why did she hatch such a plot, and why did she send the merchant?" The king, enraged, went into the harem. The queen saw from his countenance that the occurrence of the night before had become known to him, and she said: "Be it not that I see the king angry." He said: "How should I not be angry? Thou, by craft, and trickery, and intrigue, and plotting, hast brought thy desire from Rome—what wantonness is this that thou hast done?" Then he thought to slay her, but he forbore, because of his great love for her. But he ordered the chamberlain to carry the youth to some obscure place, and straightway sever his head from his body. When the poor mother saw this she well-nigh fell on her face, and her soul was near leaving her body. But she knew that sorrow would not avail, and she restrained herself.

And when the chamberlain took the youth into his own house, he said to him: "O youth, know you not that the harem of the king is the sanctuary of security? What great treachery is this that thou hast perpetrated?" The youth replied: "That queen is my mother, and I am her true son. Because of her natural delicacy, she said not to the king that she had a son by another husband. And when yearning came over her, she contrived to bring me here from Rome; and while the king was engaged in the chase maternal love stirred, and she called me to her and embraced me." On hearing this, the chamberlain said to himself: "What is passing in his mother's breast? What I have not done I can yet do, and it were better that I preserve this youth some days, for such a rose may not be wounded through idle words, and such a bough may not be broken by a single breath. For some day the truth of this matter will be disclosed, and it will become known to the king, when repentance may be of no avail." Another day he went before the king, and said: "That which was commanded have I fulfilled." On hearing this the king's wrath was to some extent removed, but his trust in the kaysar's daughter was departed; while she, poor creature, was grieved and dazed at the loss of her son.

Now in the palace harem there was an old woman, who said to the queen: "How is it that I find thee sorrowful?" And the queen told the whole story, concealing nothing. The old woman was a heroine in the field of craft, and she answered: "Keep thy mind at ease: I will devise a stratagem by which the heart of the king will be pleased with thee, and every grief he has will vanish from his heart." The queen said, that if she did so she should be amply rewarded. One day the old woman, seeing the king alone, said to him: "Why is thy former aspect altered, and why are traces of care and anxiety visible on thy countenance?" The king then told her all. The old woman said: "I have an amulet of the charms of Solomon, in the Syriac language, in the the writing of the jinn [genii]. When the queen is asleep do thou place it on her breast, and, whatever it may be, she will tell all the truth of it. But take care, fall thou not asleep, but listen well to what she says." The king wondered at this, and said: "Give me that amulet, that the truth of this matter may be learned." So the old woman gave him the amulet, and then went to the queen and explained what she had done, and said: "Do thou feign to be asleep, and relate the whole of the story faithfully."

When a watch of the night was past, the king laid the amulet upon his wife's breast, and she thus began: "By a former husband I had a son, and when my father gave me to this king, I was ashamed to say I had a tall son. When my yearning passed all bounds, I brought him here by an artifice. One day that the king was gone to the chase, I called him into the house, when, after the way of mothers, I took him in my arms and kissed him. This reached the king's ears, and he unwittingly gave it another construction, and cut off the head of that innocent boy, and withdrew from me his own heart. Alike is my son lost to me and the king angry." When the king heard these words he kissed her and exclaimed: "O my life, what an error is this thou hast committed? Thou hast brought calumny upon thyself, and hast given such a son to the winds, and hast made me ashamed!" Straightway he called the chamberlain and said: "That boy whom thou hast killed is the son of my beloved and the darling of my beauty! Where is his grave, that we may make there a guest-house?" The chamberlain said: "That youth is yet alive. When the king commanded his death I was about to kill him, but he said: 'That queen is my mother; through modesty before the king she revealed not the secret that she had a tall son. Kill me not; it may be that some day the truth will become known, and repentance profits not, and regret is useless.'" The king commanded them to bring the youth, so they brought him straightway. And when the mother saw the face of her son, she thanked God and praised the Most High, and became one of the Muslims, and from the sect of unbelievers came into the faith of Islám. And the king favoured the chamberlain in the highest degree, and they passed the rest of their lives in comfort and ease.

This tale is also found in the Persian *Bakhtyár Náma* (or the Ten Vazírs), the precise date of which has not been ascertained, but a MS. Túrkí (Uygúr) version of it, preserved in the Bodleian Library, Oxford, bears to have been written in 1434; the Persian text must therefore have been composed before that date. In the text translated by Sir William Ouseley, in place of the daughter of the kaysar of Rome it is the daughter of the king of Irák whom the king of Abyssinia marries, after subduing the power of her father; and, so far from a present of jewels to her being the occasion of her mentioning her son, in the condition of a slave, it is said that one day the king behaved harshly to her, and spoke disrespectfully of her father, upon which she boasted that her father had in his service a youth of great beauty and possessed of every accomplishment, which excited the king's desire to have him brought to his court; and the merchant smuggled the youth out of the country of Irák concealed in a chest, placed on the back of a camel. In Lescallier's French translation it is said that the youth was the fruit of a *liaison* of the princess, unknown to her father; that his education was secretly entrusted to certain servants; and that the princess afterwards contrived to introduce the boy to her father, who was so charmed with his beauty, grace of manner, and accomplishments, that he at once took him into his service. Thus widely do manuscripts of the same Eastern work vary!

The King and his Seven Vazírs

On the Eighth Night the Parrot relates, in a very abridged form, the story of the prince who was falsely accused by one of his father's women of having made love to her, and who was saved by the tales which the royal counsellors related to the king in turn during seven consecutive days. The original of this romance is the *Book of Sindibád*, so named after the prince's tutor, Sindibád the sage: the Arabic version is known under the title of the *Seven Vazírs*; the Hebrew, *Mishlé Sandabar*; the Greek, *Syntipas*; and the Syriac, *Sindbán*; and its European modifications, the

87

Seven Wise Masters. In the Parrot-Book the first to the sixth vazírs each relate one story only, and the damsel has no stories (all other Eastern versions give two to each of the seven, and six to the queen); the seventh vazír simply appears on the seventh day and makes clear the innocence of the prince. This version, however, though imperfect, is yet of some value in making a comparative study of the several texts.

VI

THE TREE OF LIFE—LEGEND OF RÁJÁ RASÁLÚ—CONCLUSION

Many others of the Parrot's stories might be cited, but we shall merely glance at one more, as it calls up a very ancient and wide-spread legend:

The Tree of Life

A prince, who is very ill, sends a parrot of great sagacity to procure him some of the fruit of the Tree of Life. When at length the parrot returns with the life-giving fruit, the prince scruples to eat it, upon which the wise bird relates the legend of Solomon and the Water of Immortality: how that monarch declined to purchase immunity from death on consideration that he should survive all his friends and female favourites. The prince, however, having suspicions regarding the genuineness of the fruit, sends some trusty messengers to "bring the first apple that fell from the Tree of Existence." But it happened that a black serpent had poisoned it by seizing it in his mouth and then letting it drop again. When the messengers return with the fruit, the prince tries its effect on an old pír (holy man), who at once falls down dead. Upon seeing this the prince doomed the parrot to death, but the sagacious bird suggested that,before the prince should execute him for treason, he should himself go to the Tree of Life, and make another experiment with its fruit. He does so, and on returning home gives part of the fruit to an old woman, "who, from age and infirmity had not stirred abroad for many years," and she had no sooner tasted it than she was changed into a blooming beauty of eighteen!—Happy, happy old woman!

A different version of the legend occurs in a Canarese collection, entitled *Kathá Manjarí*, which is worthy of reproduction, since it may possibly be an earlier form than that in the Persian Parrot-Book: A certain king had a magpie that flew one day to heaven with another magpie. When it was there it took away some mango-seed, and, having returned, gave it into the hands of the king, saying: "If you cause this to be planted and grow, whoever eats of its fruit old age will forsake him and youth return." The king was much pleased, and caused it to be sown in his favourite garden, and carefully watched it. After some time, buds having shown themselves

89

in it became flowers, then young fruit, then it was grown; and when it was full of ripe fruit, the king ordered it to be cut and brought, and that he might test it gave it to an old man. But on that fruit there had fallen poison from a serpent, as it was carried through the air by a kite, therefore he immediately withered and died. The king, having seen this, was much afraid, and exclaimed: "Is not this bird attempting to kill me?" Having said this, with anger he seized the magpie, and swung it round and killed it. Afterwards in that village the tree had the name of the Poisonous Mango. While things were thus, a washerman, taking the part of his wife in a quarrel with his aged mother, struck the latter, who was so angry at her son that she resolved to die [in order that the blame of her death should fall on him]; and having gone to the poisonous mango-tree in the garden, she cut off a fruit and ate it; and immediately she was more blooming than a girl of sixteen. This wonder she published everywhere. The king became acquainted with it, and having called her and seen her, caused the fruit to be given to other old people. Having seen what was thus done by the wonderful virtue of the mango, the king exclaimed: "Alas! is the affectionate magpie killed which gave me this divine tree? How guilty am I!" and he pierced himself with his sword and died. Therefore (moralises the story-teller) those who do anything without thought are easily ruined.[52]

The incident of fruit or food being poisoned by a serpent is of frequent occurrence in Eastern stories; thus, in the *Book of Sindibád* a man sends his slave-girl to fetch milk, with which to feast some guests. As she was returning with it in an open vessel a stork flew over her, carrying a snake in its beak; the snake dropped some of its poison into the milk, and all the guests who partook of it immediately fell down and died.—The Water of Life and the Tree of Life are the subjects of many European as well as Asiatic folk-tales. Muslims have a tradition that Alexander the Great despatched the prophet Al-Khizar (who is often confounded with Moses and Elias in legends) to procure him some of the Water of Life. The prophet, after a long and perilous journey, at length reached this Spring of Everlasting Youth, and, having taken a hearty draught of its waters, the stream suddenly disappeared—and has, we may suppose, never been rediscovered. Al-Khizar, they say, still lives, and occasionally appears to persons whom he desires especially to favour, and always clothed in a green robe, the emblem of perennial youth. In Arabic, Khizar signifies *green*.

The faithful and sagacious Parrot having entertained the lady during fifty-two successive nights, and thereby prevented her from prosecuting her intended intrigue, on the following day the merchant returned, and, missing the sharak from the cage, inquired its fate of the Parrot, who straight-way acquainted him of all that had taken place in his absence, and, according to Kádiri's abridged text, he put his wife to death, which was certainly very unjust, since the lady's offence was only in *design*, not in *fact*.⁵³

It will be observed that the frame of the *Túti Náma* somewhat resembles the story, in the *Arabian Nights*, of the Merchant, his Wife, and the Parrot, which properly belongs to, and occurs in, all the versions of the *Book of Sindibád*, and also in the *Seven Wise Masters*; in the latter a magpie takes the place of the parrot. In my *Popular Tales and Fictions* I have pointed out the close analogy which the frame of the Parrot-Book bears to a Panjábí legend of the renowned hero Rájá Rasálú. In the *Túti Náma* the merchant leaves a parrot and a sharak to watch over his wife's conduct in his absence, charging her to obtain their consent before she enters upon any undertaking of moment; and on her consulting the sharak as to the propriety of her assignation with the young prince, the bird refuses consent, whereupon the enraged dame kills it on the spot; but the parrot, by pursuing a middle course, saves his life and his master's honour. In the Panjábí legend Rájá Rasálú, who was very frequently from home on hunting excursions, left behind him a parrot and a maina (hill starling), to act as spies upon his young wife, the Rání Kokla. One day while Rasálú was from home she was visited by the handsome Rájá Hodí, who climbed to her balcony by a rope (this incident is the subject of many paintings in fresco on the panels of palaces and temples in India), when the maina exclaimed, "What wickedness is this?" upon which the rájá went to the cage, took out the maina, and dashed it to the ground, so that it died. But the parrot, taking warning, said, "The steed of Rasálú is swift, what if he should surprise you? Let me out of my cage, and I will fly over the palace, and will inform you the instant he appears in sight"; and so she released the parrot. In the sequel, the parrot betrays the rání, and Rasálú kills Rájá Hodí and causes his heart to be served to the rání for supper.⁵⁴

The parrot is a very favourite character in Indian fictions, a circumstance originating, very possibly, in the Hindú belief in metempsychosis, or transmigration of souls after death into other animal forms, and also from the remarkable facility with which that bird imitates the human voice. In the *Kathá Sarit Ságara* stories of wise parrots are of frequent occurrence; sometimes they figure as mere birds, but at other times as men who had been re-born in that form. In the third of the Twenty-Five Tales of a Demon (Sanskrit version), a king has a parrot, "possessed of god-like intellect, knowing all the *shastras*, having been born in that condition owing to a curse"; and his queen has a hen-maina "remarkable for knowledge." They are placed in the same cage; and "one day the parrot became enamoured of the maina, and said to her: 'Marry me, fair one, as we sleep, perch, and feed in the same cage.' But the maina answered him: 'I do not desire intimate union with a male, for all males are wicked and ungrateful.' The parrot answered: 'It is not true that males are wicked, but females are wicked and cruel-hearted.' And so a dispute arose between them. The two birds then made a bargain that, if the parrot won, he should have the maina for wife, and if the maina won, the parrot should be her slave, and they came before the prince to get a true judgment." Each relates a story—the one to show that men are all wicked and ungrateful, the other, that women are wicked and cruel-hearted.

It must be confessed that the frame of the *Túti Náma* is of a very flimsy description: nothing could be more absurd, surely, than to represent the lady as decorating herself fifty-two nights in succession in order to have an interview with a young prince, and being detained each night by the Parrot's tales, which, moreover, have none of them the least bearing upon the condition and purpose of the lady; unlike the Telúgú story-book, having a somewhat similar frame (see *ante*, p. 127, *note 43*), in which the tales related by the bird are about chaste wives. But the frames of all Eastern story-books are more or less slight and of small account. The value of the *Túti Náma* consists in the aid which the subordinate tales furnish in tracing the genealogy of popular fictions, and in this respect the importance of the work can hardly be over-rated.

ADDITIONAL NOTE

In our tale of the Faggot-maker, the fairies warn him to guard the Magic Bowl with the utmost care, "for it will break by the most trifling blow," and he is to use it only when absolutely necessary; and in the notes of variants appended, reference is made (p. 158) to a Meklenburg story where the beer in an inexhaustible can disappears the moment its possessor reveals the secret. The gifts made by fairies and other superhuman beings have indeed generally some condition attached (most commonly, perhaps, that they are not to be examined until the recipients have reached home), as is shown pretty conclusively by my friend Mr. E. Sidney Hartland in a most interesting paper on "Fairy Births and Human Midwives," which enriches the pages of the *Archæological Review* for December, 1889, and at the close of which he cites, from Poestion's *Lappländische Märchen*, p. 119, a curious example, which may be fairly regarded as an analogue of the tale of the Poor Faggot-maker—"far cry" though it be from India to Swedish Lappmark:

"A peasant who had one day been unlucky at the chase was returning disgusted, when he met a fine gentleman, who begged him to come and cure his wife. The peasant protested in vain that he was no doctor. The other would take no denial, insisting that it was no matter, for if he would only put his hands on the lady she would be healed. Accordingly, the stranger led him to the very top of a mountain where was perched a castle he had never seen before. On entering, he found the walls were mirrors, the roof overhead of silver, the carpets of gold-embroidered silk, and the furniture of the purest gold and jewels. The stranger took him into a room where lay the loveliest of princesses on a golden bed, screaming with pain. As soon as she saw the peasant, she begged him to come and put his hands upon her. Almost stupified with astonishment, he hesitated to lay his coarse hands upon so fair a dame. But at length he yielded, and in a moment her pain ceased, and she was made whole. She stood up and thanked him, begging him to tarry awhile and eat with them. This, however, he declined to do, for he feared that if he tasted the food which was offered him he must remain there.

"The stranger whom he had followed then took a leathern purse, filled it with small round pieces of wood, and gave it to the peasant with these words: 'So long as thou art in possession of this purse, money will never fail thee. But if thou shouldst ever see me again, beware of speaking to me; for if thou speak thy luck will depart.' When the man got home he found the purse filled with dollars; and by virtue of its magical property he became the richest man in the parish. As soon as he found the purse always full, whatever he took out of it, he began to live in a spendthrift manner, and frequented the alehouse. One evening as he sat there he beheld the stranger, with a bottle in his hand, going round and gathering the drops which the guests shook from time to time out of their glasses. The rich peasant was surprised that one who had given him so much did not seem able to buy himself a single dram, but was reduced to this means of getting a drink. Thereupon he went up to him and said: 'Thou hast shown me more kindness than any other man ever did, and willingly I will treat thee to a little.' The words were scarce out of his mouth when he received such a blow on his head that he fell stunned to the ground; and when again he came to himself the stranger and his purse were both gone. From that day forward he became poorer and poorer, until he was reduced to absolute beggary."

Among other examples adduced by Mr. Hartland is a Bohemian legend in which "the Frau von Hahnen receives for her services to a water-nix three pieces of gold, with the injunction to take care of them, and never to let them go out of the hands of her own lineage, else the whole family would fall into poverty. She bequeathed the treasures to her three sons; but the youngest son took a wife who with a light heart gave the fairy gold away. Misery, of course, resulted from her folly, and the race of Hahnen speedily came to an end."—But those who are interested in the study of comparative folk-lore would do well to read for themselves the whole paper, which is assuredly by far the most (if not indeed the only) comprehensive attempt that has yet been made in our language to treat scientifically the subject of fairy gifts to human beings.

RABBINICAL LEGENDS, TALES, FABLES, AND APHORISMS

I

INTRODUCTORY

In the Talmud are embodied those rules and institutions—interpretations of the civil and canonical laws contained in the Old Testament—which were transmitted orally to succeeding generations of the Jewish priesthood until the general dispersion of the Hebrew race. According to the Rabbis, Moses received the oral as well as the written law at Mount Sinai, and it was by him communicated to Joshua, from whom it was transmitted through forty successive Receivers. So long as the Temple stood, it was deemed not only unnecessary, but absolutely unlawful, to commit these ancient and carefully-preserved traditions to writing; but after the second destruction of Jerusalem, under Hadrian, when the Jewish people were scattered over the world, the system of oral transmission of these traditions from generation to generation became impracticable, and, to prevent their being lost, they were formed into a permanent record about A.D. 190, by Rabbi Jehudah the Holy, who called his work *Mishna*, or the Secondary Laws. About a hundred years later a commentary on it was written by Rabbi Jochonan, called *Gemara*, or the Completion, and these two works joined together are known as the (Jerusalem) *Talmud*, or Directory. But this commentary being written in an obscure style, and omitting many traditions known farther east, another was begun by Rabbi Asche, who died A.D. 427, and completed by his disciples and followers about the year 500, which together with the Mishna formed the Babylonian Talmud. Both versions were first printed at Venice in the 16th century—the Jerusalem Talmud, in one folio volume, about the year 1523; and the Babylonian Talmud, in twelve folio volumes, 1520-30. In the 12th century Moses Maimonides, a Spanish Rabbi, made an epitome, or digest, of all the laws and institutions of the Talmud. Such, in brief, is the origin and history of this famed compilation, which has been aptly described as an extraordinary monument of human industry, human wisdom, and human folly.

By far the greater portion of the Talmud is devoted to the ceremonial law, as preserved by oral tradition in the manner above explained; but it also comprises innumerable sayings or aphorisms of celebrated Rabbis, together with narratives of the most varied character—legends regarding Biblical personages, moral tales, fables, parables, and facetious stories. Of the rabbinical legends, many are extremely puerile and absurd, and may rank with the extravagant and incredible monkish legends of mediæval times; some, however, are characterised by a richness of humour which one would hardly expect to meet with in such a work; while not a few of the parables, fables, and tales are strikingly beautiful, and will favourably compare with the same class of fictions composed by the ancient sages of Hindústán.

It is a singular circumstance, and significant as well as singular, that while the Hebrew Talmud was, as Dr. Barclay remarks, "periodically banned and often publicly burned, from the age of the Emperor Justinian till the time of Pope Clement VIII," several of the best stories in the *Gesta Romanorum*, a collection of moral tales (or tales "moralised") which were read in Christian churches throughout Europe during the Middle Ages, are derived mediately or immediately from this great storehouse of rabbinical learning.[55]

The traducers of the Talmud, among other false assertions, have represented the Rabbis as holding their own work as more important than even the Old Testament itself, and as fostering among the Jewish people a spirit of intolerance towards all persons outside the pale of the Hebrew religion. In proof of the first assertion they cite the following passage from the Talmud: "The Bible is like water, the Mishna, like wine, the Gemara, spiced wine; the Law, like salt, the Mishna, pepper, the Gemara, balmy spice." But surely only a very shallow mind could conceive from these similitudes that the Rabbis rated the importance of the Bible as less than that of the Talmud; yet an English Church clergyman, in an article published in a popular periodical a few years since, reproduced this passage in proof of rabbinical presumption—evidently in ignorance of the peculiar style of Oriental metaphor. What is actually taught by the Rabbis in the passage in question, regarding the comparative merits of the Bible and the Talmud, is this: The Bible is like water, the Law is like salt; now, water and salt are indispensable to mankind. The Mishna is like wine and pepper—luxuries, not necessaries of life; while the Gemara is like spiced wine and balmy spices—still more refined luxuries, but not necessaries, like water and salt.

With regard to the accusation of intolerance brought against the Rabbis, it is worse than a misconception of words or phrases; it is a gross calumny, the more reprehensible if preferred by those who are acquainted with the teachings of the Talmud, since they are thus guilty of wilfully suppressing the truth. In the following passages a broad, humane spirit of toleration is clearly inculcated:

"It is our duty to maintain the heathen poor along with those of our own nation."

"We must visit their sick, and administer to their relief, bury their dead," and so forth.

"The heathens that dwell out of the land of Israel ought not to be considered as idolators, since they only follow the customs of their fathers."

"The pious men of the heathen will have their portion in the next world."

"It is unlawful to deceive or over-reach any one, not even a heathen."

"Be circumspect in the fear of the Lord, soft in speech, slow in wrath, kind and friendly to all, even to the heathen."

Alluding to the laws inimical to the heathen, Rabbi Mosha says: "What wise men have said in this respect was directed against the ancient idolators, who believed neither in a creation nor in a deliverance from Egypt; but the nations among whom we live, whose protection we enjoy, must not be considered in this light, since they believe in a creation, the divine origin of the law, and many other fundamental doctrines of our religion. It is, therefore, not only our duty to shelter them against actual danger, but to pray for their welfare and the prosperity of their respective governments."[56]

Let the impartial reader compare these teachings of the Rabbis with the intolerant doctrines and practices of Christian pastors, even in modern times as well as during the Middle Ages: when they taught that out of the pale of the Church there could be no salvation; that no faith should be kept with heretics, or infidels: when Catholics persecuted Protestants, and Protestants retaliated upon Catholics:

> Christians have burned each other, quite persuaded
> That all the Apostles would have done as they did!

It will probably occur to most readers, in connection with the rabbinical doctrine, that it is unlawful to over-reach any one, that the Jews appear to have long ignored such maxims of morality. But it should be remembered that if they have earned for themselves, by their chicanery in mercantile transactions, an evil reputation, their ancestors in the bad old times were goaded into the practice of over-reaching by cunning those Christian sovereigns and nobles who robbed them of their property by force and cruel tortures. Moreover, where are the people to be found whose daily actions are in accordance with the religion they profess? At least, the Rabbis, unlike the spiritual teachers of mediæval Europe, did not openly inculcate immoral doctrines.

II

LEGENDS OF SOME BIBLICAL CHARACTERS

There is, no doubt, very much in the Talmud that possesses a recondite, spiritual meaning; but it would likely puzzle the most ingenious and learned modern Rabbis to construe into mystical allegories such absurd legends regarding Biblical personages as the following:

Adam and Eve

Adam's body, according to the Jewish Fathers, was formed of the earth of Babylon, his head of the land of Israel, and his other members of other parts of the world. Originally his stature reached the firmament, but after his fall the Creator, laying his hand upon him, lessened him very considerably.[57] Mr Hershon, in his *Talmudic Miscellany*, says there is a notion among the Rabbis that Adam was at first possessed of a bi-sexual organisation, and this conclusion they draw from Genesis i, 27, where it is said: "God created man in his own image, male-female created he him."[58] These two natures it was thought lay side by side; according to some, the male on the right and the female on the left; according to others, back to back; while there were those who maintained that Adam was created with a *tail*, and that it was from this appendage that Eve was fashioned![59] Other Jewish traditions (continues Mr. Hershon) inform us that Eve was made from the thirteenth rib of the right side, and that she was not drawn out by the head, lest she should be vain; nor by the eyes, lest she should be wanton; nor by the mouth, lest she should be given to garrulity; nor by the ears, lest she should be an eavesdropper; nor by the hands, lest she should be intermeddling; nor by the feet, lest she should be a gadder; nor by the heart, lest she should be jealous;—but she was taken out from the side: yet, in spite of all these precautions, she had every one of the faults so carefully guarded against!

Adam's excuse for eating of the forbidden fruit, "She gave me of the tree and I did eat," is said to be thus ingeniously explained by the learned Rabbis: By giving him of the *tree* is meant that Eve took a stout crab-tree cudgel, and gave her husband (in plain English) a sound rib-roasting, until he complied with her will!—The lifetime of Adam, according to the Book of

98

Genesis, ch. v, 5, was nine hundred and thirty years, for which the following legend (reproduced by the Muslim traditionists) satisfactorily accounts: The Lord showed to Adam every future generation, with their heads, sages, and scribes.[60] He saw that David was destined to live only three hours, and said: "Lord and Creator of the world, is this unalterably fixed?" The Lord answered: "It was my original design." "How many years shall I live?" "One thousand." "Are grants known in heaven?" "Certainly." "I grant then seventy years of my life to David." What did Adam therefore do? He gave a written grant, set his seal to it, and the same was done by the Lord and Metatron.

The body of Adam was taken into the ark by Noah, and when at last it grounded on the summit of Mount Ararat [which it certainly never did!], Noah and his three sons removed the body, "and they followed an angel, who led them to a place where the First Father was to lie. Shem (or Melchizidek, for they are one), being consecrated by God to the priesthood, performed the religious rites, and buried Adam at the centre of the earth, which is Jerusalem. But some say he was buried by Shem, along with Eve in the cave of Machpelah in Hebron; others relate that Noah on leaving the ark distributed the bones of Adam among his sons, and that he gave the head to Shem, who buried it in Jerusalem."[61]

Cain and Abel

The Hebrew commentators are not agreed regarding the cause of Cain's enmity towards his brother Abel. According to one tradition, Cain and Abel divided the whole world between them, one taking the moveable and the other the immoveable possessions. One day Cain said to his brother: "The earth on which thou standest is mine; therefore betake thyself to the air." Abel rejoined: "The garment which thou dost wear is mine; therefore take it off." From this there arose a conflict between them, which resulted in Abel's death. Rabbi Huna teaches, however, that they contended for a twin sister of Abel; the latter claimed her because she was born along with him, while Cain pleaded his right of primogeniture. After Adam's first-born had taken his brother's life, the sheep-dog of Abel faithfully guarded his master's corpse from the attacks of beasts and birds of prey. Adam and Eve also sat near the body of their pious son, weeping bitterly, and not knowing how to dispose of his lifeless clay. At length a raven, whose mate had lately died, said to itself: "I will go and show to Adam what he must do with his son's body," and accordingly scooped a hole in the ground and laid the dead raven therein, and covered it with earth. This having been observed by Adam, he likewise buried the body of Abel. For this service rendered to our great progenitor, we are told, the Deity rewarded the raven, and no one is allowed to injure its young: "they have food in abundance, and their cry for rain is always heard."[62]

The Planting of the Vine

When Noah planted the vine, say the Rabbis, Satan slew a sheep, a lion, an ape, and a sow, and buried the carcases under it; and hence the four stages from sobriety to absolute drunkenness: Before a man begins to drink, he is meek and innocent as a lamb, and as a sheep in the hand of the shearer is dumb; when he has drank enough, he is fearless as a lion, and says there is no one like him in the world; in the next stage, he is like an ape, and dances, jests, and talks nonsense, knowing not what he is doing and saying; when thoroughly drunken, he wallows in the mire like a sow.[63] To this legend Chaucer evidently alludes in the Prologue to the Maniciple's Tale:

> I trow that ye have dronken *wine of ape*,
> And that is when men plaien at a strawe.

Luminous Jewels

Readers of that most fascinating collection of Eastern tales, commonly but improperly called the *Arabian Nights' Entertainments*, must be familiar with the remarkable property there ascribed to certain gems, of furnishing light in the absence of the sun. Possibly the Arabians adopted this notion from the Rabbis, in whose legends jewels are frequently represented as possessing the light-giving property. For example, we learn that Noah and his family, while in the ark, had no light besides what was obtained from diamonds and other precious stones. And Abraham, who, it appears, was extremely jealous of his wives, built for them an enchanted city, of which the walls were so high as to shut out the light of the sun; an inconvenience which he easily remedied by means of a large basin full of rubies and other jewels, which shed forth a flood of light equal in brilliancy to that of the sun itself.[64]

Abraham's Arrival in Egypt

When Abraham journeyed to Egypt he had among his *impedimenta* a large chest. On reaching the gates of the capital the customs officials demanded the usual duties. Abraham begged them to name the sum without troubling themselves to open the chest. They demanded to be paid the duty on clothes. "I will pay for clothes," said the patriarch, with an alacrity which aroused the suspicions of the officials, who then insisted upon being paid the duty on silk. "I will pay for silk," said Abraham. Hereupon the officials demanded the duty on gold, and Abraham readily offered to pay the amount. Then they surmised that the chest contained jewels, but Abraham was quite as willing to pay the higher duty on gems, and now the curiosity of the officials could be no longer restrained. They broke open the chest, when, lo, their eyes were dazzled with the lustrous beauty of Sarah! Abraham, it seems, had adopted this plan for smuggling his lovely wife into the Egyptian dominions.

The Infamous Citizens of Sodom

Some of the rabbinical legends descriptive of the singular customs of the infamous citizens of Sodom are exceedingly amusing—or amazing. The judges of that city are represented as notorious liars and mockers of justice. When a man had cut off the ear of his neighbour's ass, the judge said to the owner: "Let him have the ass till the ear is grown again, that it may be returned to thee as thou wishest." The hospitality shown by the citizens to strangers within their gates was of a very peculiar kind. They had a particular bed for the weary traveller who entered their city and desired shelter for the night. If he was found to be too long for the bed, they reduced him to the proper size by chopping off so much of his legs; and if he was shorter than the bed, he was stretched to the requisite length.65 To preserve their reputation for hospitality, when a stranger arrived each citizen was required to give him a coin with his name written on it, after which the unfortunate traveller was refused food, and as soon as he had died of hunger every man took back his own money. It was a capital offence for any one to supply the stranger with food, in proof of which it is recorded that a poor man, having arrived in Sodom, was presented with money and refused food by all to whom he made his wants known. It chanced that, as he lay by the roadside almost starved to death, he was observed by one of Lot's daughters, who had compassion on him, and supplied him with food for many days, as she went to draw water for her father's household. The citizens, marvelling at the man's tenacity of life, set a person to watch him, and Lot's daughter being discovered bringing him bread, she was condemned to death by burning. Another kind-hearted maiden who had in like manner relieved the wants of a stranger, was punished in a still more dreadful manner, being smeared over with honey, and stung to death by bees.

It may be naturally supposed that travellers who were acquainted with the peculiar ways of the citizens of Sodom would either pass by that city without entering its inhospitable gates, or, if compelled by business to go into the town, would previously provide themselves with food; but even this last precaution did not avail them against the wiles of those wicked people: A man from Elam, journeying to a place beyond Sodom, reached the infamous city about sunset. The stranger had with him an ass, bearing a valuable saddle to which was strapped a large bale of merchandise. Being refused a lodging by each citizen of whom he asked the favour, our traveller made a virtue of necessity, and determined to pass the night, along with his animal and his goods, as best he might, in the streets. His preparations with this view were observed by a cunning and treacherous citizen, named Hidud, who came up, and, accosting him courteously, desired to know whence he had come and whither he was bound. The stranger answered that he had come from Hebron, and was journeying to such a place; that, being refused shelter by everybody, he was preparing to pass the night in the streets; and that he was provided with bread for his own use and with fodder for his beast. Upon this Hidud invited the stranger to his house, assuring him that his lodging should cost him nothing, while the wants of his beast should not be forgotten. The stranger accepted of Hidud's proffered hospitality, and when they came to his house the citizen relieved the ass of the saddle and merchandise, and carefully placed them for security in his private closet. He then led the ass into his stable and amply supplied him with provender; and returning to the house, he set food before his guest, who, having supped, retired to rest. Early in the morning the stranger arose, intending to resume his journey, but his host first pressed him to partake of breakfast, and afterwards persuaded him to remain at his house for two days. On the morning of the third day our traveller would no longer delay his departure, and Hidud therefore brought out his beast, saying kindly to his guest: "Fare thee well." "Hold!" said the traveller. "Where is my beautiful saddle of many colours and the strings attached thereto, together with my bale of rich merchandise?" "What sayest thou?" exclaimed Hidud, in a tone of surprise. The stranger repeated his demand for his saddle and goods. "Ah," said Hidud, affably, "I will interpret thy dream: the strings that thou hast dreamt of indicate length of days to thee; and the many-coloured saddle of thy dream signifies that thou shalt become the owner of a beauteous garden of odorous flowers and rich fruit trees." "Nay," returned the stranger, "I certainly entrusted to thy care a saddle and merchandise, and thou hast concealed them in thy house." "Well," said Hidud, "I have told thee the meaning of thy dream. My usual fee for interpreting a dream is four pieces of silver, but, as thou hast been my guest, I will only ask three pieces of thee." On hearing this very unjust demand the stranger was naturally enraged, and he accused Hidud in the court of Sodom of stealing his property. After each had stated his case, the judge decreed that the stranger must pay Hidud's fee, since he was well known as a professional interpreter of dreams. Hidud then said to the stranger: "As thou hast proved thyself such a liar, I must not only be paid my usual fee of four pieces of silver, but also the value of the two days' food with which I provided thee in my house." "I will cheerfully pay thee for the food," rejoined the traveller, "on condition that thou restore my saddle and merchandise." Upon this the litigants began to abuse each other and were thrust into the street, where the citizens, siding with Hidud, soundly beat the unlucky stranger, and then expelled him from the city.

Abraham once sent his servant Eliezer to Sodom with his compliments to Lot and his family, and to inquire concerning their welfare. As Eliezer entered Sodom he saw a citizen beating a stranger, whom he had robbed of his property. "Shame upon thee!" exclaimed Eliezer to the citizen. "Is this the way you act towards strangers?" To this remonstrance the man replied by picking up a stone and striking Eliezer with it on the forehead with such force as to cause the blood to flow down his face. On seeing the blood the citizen caught hold of Eliezer and demanded to be paid his fee for having freed him of impure blood. "What!" said Eliezer, "am I to pay thee for wounding me?" "Such is our law," returned the citizen. Eliezer refused to pay, and the man brought him before the judge, to whom he made his complaint. The judge then decreed: "Thou must pay this man his fee, since he has let thy blood; such is our law." "There, then," said Eliezer, striking the judge with a stone, and causing him to bleed, "pay my fee to this man, I want it not," and then departed from the court.[66]

Abraham and Ishmael's Wife

Hagar, the handmaid of Sarah, was given as a slave to Abraham, by her father, Pharaoh, king of Egypt, who said: "My daughter had better be a slave in the house of Abraham than mistress in any other house." Her son Ishmael, it is said, took unto himself a wife of the daughters of Moab. Three years afterwards Abraham set out to visit his son, having solemnly promised Sarah (who, it thus appears, was still jealous of her former handmaid) that he would not alight from his camel. He reached Ishmael's house about noontide, and found his wife alone. "Where is Ishmael?" inquired the patriarch. "He is gone into the wilderness with his mother to gather dates and other fruits." "Give me, I pray thee, a little bread and water, for I am fatigued with travelling." "I have neither bread nor water," rejoined the inhospitable matron. "Well," said the patriarch, "tell Ishmael when he comes home that an old man came to see him, and recommends him to change the door-post of his house, for it is not worthy of him." On Ishmael's return she gave him the message, from which he at once understood that the stranger was his father, and that he did not approve of his wife. Accordingly he sent her back to her own people, and Hagar procured him a wife from her father's house. Her name was Fatima.

Another period of three years having elapsed, Abraham again resolved to visit his son; and having, as before, pledged his word to Sarah that he would not alight at Ishmael's house, he began his journey. When he arrived at his son's domicile he found Fatima alone, Ishmael being abroad, as on the occasion of his previous visit. But from Fatima he received every attention, albeit she knew not that he was her husband's father. Highly gratified with Fatima's hospitality, the patriarch called down blessings upon Ishmael, and returned home. Fatima duly informed Ishmael of what had happened in his absence, and then he knew that Abraham still loved him as his son.

This is one of the few rabbinical legends regarding Biblical characters which do not exceed the limits of probability; and I confess I can see no reason why these interesting incidents should be considered as purely imaginary. As a rule, however, the Talmudic legends of this kind must be taken not only *cum grano salis*, but with a whole bushel of that most necessary commodity, particularly such marvellous relations as that of Rabbi Jehoshua, when he informs us that the "ram caught in a thicket," which served as a substitute for sacrifice when Abraham was prepared to offer up his son Isaac, was brought by an angel out of Paradise, where it pastured under the Tree of Life and drank from the brook which flows beneath it. This creature, the Rabbi adds, diffused its perfume throughout the world.[67]

Joseph and Potiphar's Wife

The story of Joseph and Potiphar's wife, as related in the Book of Genesis, finds parallels in the popular tales and legends of many countries: the vengeance of "woman whose love is scorned," says a Hindú writer, "is worse than poison"! But the rabbinical version is quite unique in representing the wife of Potiphar as having aiders and abettors in carrying out her scheme of revenge: For some days after the pious young Israelite had declined her amorous overtures, she looked so ill that her female friends inquired of her the cause, and having told them of her adventure with Joseph, they said: "Accuse him before thy husband, that he may be cast into prison." She desired them to accuse him likewise to their husbands, which they did accordingly; and their husbands went before Pharaoh and complained of Joseph's misconduct towards their wives.[68]

Joseph and his Brethren

Wonderful stories are related of Joseph and his brethren. Simeon, if we may credit the Talmudists, must have been quite a Hercules in strength. The Biblical narrative of Simeon's detention by his brother Joseph is brief but most expressive: "And he turned himself about from them and wept; and returned to them again, and communed with them, and took from them Simeon, and bound him before their eyes."[69] The Talmudists condescend more minutely regarding this interesting incident: When Joseph ordered seventy valiant men to put Simeon in chains, they had no sooner approached him than he roared so loud that all the seventy fell down at his feet and broke their teeth! Joseph then said to his son Manasseh: "Chain thou him"; whereupon Manasseh dealt Simeon a single blow and immediately overpowered him; upon which Simeon exclaimed: "Surely this was the blow of a kinsman!"—When Joseph sent Benjamin to prison, Judah cried so loud that Chushim, the son of Dan, heard him in Canaan and responded. Joseph feared for his life, for Judah was so enraged that he wept blood. Some say that Judah wore five garments, one over the other; but when he was angry his heart swelled so much that his five garments burst open. Joseph cried so terribly that one of the pillars of his house fell in and was changed into sand. Then Judah said: "He is valiant, like one of us."

Jacob's Sorrow

But like a gem, among a heap of rubbish is the touching little story of how the news of Joseph's being alive and the viceroy of Egypt was conveyed to the aged and sorrow-stricken Jacob. When the brethren had returned to the land of Canaan, after their second expedition, they were perplexed how to communicate to their father the joyful intelligence that his long-lamented son still lived, fearing it might have a fatal effect on the old man if suddenly told to him. At length Serach, the daughter of Asher, proposed that she should convey the tidings to her grandfather in a song. Accordingly she took her harp, and sang to Jacob the whole story of Joseph's life and his present greatness, and her music soothed his spirit; and when he fully realised that his son was yet alive, he fervently blessed her, and she was taken into Paradise, without tasting of death.[70]

Moses and Pharaoh

The slaughter of the Hebrew male children by the cruel command of the "Pharoah who knew not Joseph" was a precaution adopted, we are informed by the Rabbis, in consequence of a dream which that monarch had, of an aged man who held a balance in his right hand; in one scale he placed all the sages and nobles of Egypt, and in the other a little lamb, which weighed down them all. In the morning Pharaoh told his strange dream to his counsellors, who were greatly terrified, and Bi'lam, the son of Beor, the magician, said: "This dream, O King, forebodes great affliction, which one of the children of Israel will bring upon Egypt." The king asked the soothsayer whether this threatened evil might not be avoided. "There is but one way of averting the calamity—cause every male child of Hebrew parents to be slain at birth." Pharaoh approved of this advice, and issued an edict accordingly. The Egyptian monarch's kind-hearted daughter (whose name, by the way, was Bathia), who rescued the infant Moses from the common fate of the Hebrew male children, was a leper, and consequently was not permitted to use the warm baths. But no sooner had she stretched forth her hand to the crying infant than she was healed of her leprosy, and, moreover, afterwards admitted bodily into Paradise.[71]

Of the childhood of Moses a curious story is told to account for his being in after life "slow of speech and slow of tongue": Pharaoh was one day seated in his banqueting hall, with his queen at his right hand and Bathia at his left, and around him were his two sons, Bi'lam, the chief soothsayer, and other dignitaries of his court, when he took little Moses (then three years old) upon his knee, and began to fondle him. The Hebrew urchin stretched forth his hand and took the kingly crown from Pharaoh's brow and deliberately placed it upon his own head. To the monarch and his courtiers this action of the child was ominous, and Pharaoh inquired of his counsellors how, in their judgment, the audacious little Hebrew should be punished. Bi'lam, the sooth-sayer, answered: "Do not suppose, O King, that this is necessarily the thoughtless action of a child; recollect thy dream which I did interpret for thee. But let us prove whether this child is possessed of understanding beyond his years, in this manner: let two plates, one containing fire, the other gold, be placed before the child; and if he grasp the gold, then is he of superior understanding, and should therefore be put to death." The plates, as proposed by the soothsayer, were placed before the child Moses, who immediately seized upon the fire, and put it into his mouth, which caused him henceforward to stammer in his speech.

It was no easy matter for Moses and his brother to gain access to Pharaoh, for his palace had 400 gates, 100 on each side; and before each gate stood no fewer than 60,000 tried warriors. Therefore the angel Gabriel introduced them by another way, and when Pharaoh beheld Moses and Aaron he demanded to know who had admitted them. He summoned the guards, and ordered some of them to be beaten and others to be put to death. But next day Moses and Aaron returned, and the guards, when called in, exclaimed: "These men are sorcerers, for they cannot have come in through any of the gates." There were, however, much more formidable guardians of the royal palace: the 400 gates were guarded by bears, lions, and other ferocious beasts, who suffered no one to pass unless they were fed with flesh. But when Moses and Aaron came, they gathered about them, and licked the feet of the prophets, accompanying them to Pharaoh.—Readers who are familiar with the *Thousand and One Nights* and other Asiatic story-books will recollect many tales in which palaces are similarly guarded. In the spurious "Canterbury" *Tale of Beryn* (taken from the first part of the old French romance of the Chevalier Berinus), which has been re-edited for the Chaucer Society, the palace-garden of Duke Isope is guarded by eight necromancers who look like "abominabill wormys, enough to frighte the hertiest man on erth," also by a white lion that had eaten five hundred men.

III

LEGENDS OF DAVID AND SOLOMON, ETC.

Muhammed, the great Arabian lawgiver, drew very largely from the rabbinical legends in his composition of the Kurán, every verse of which is considered by pious Muslims as a miracle, or wonder (*ayet*). The well-known story of the spider weaving its web over the mouth of the cave in which Muhammed and Abú Bekr had concealed themselves in their flight from Mecca to Medina was evidently borrowed from the Talmudic legend of David's flight from the malevolence of Saul: Immediately after David had entered the cave of Adullam, a spider spun its web across the opening. His pursuers presently passing that way were about to search the cave; but perceiving the spider's web, they naturally concluded that no one could have recently entered there, and thus was the future king of Israel preserved from Saul's vengeance.

King David once had a narrow escape from death at the hands of Goliath's brother Ishbi. The king was hunting one morning when Satan appeared before him in the form of a deer.[72] David drew his bow, but missed him, and the feigned deer ran off at the top of his speed. The king, with true sportsman's instinct, pursued the deer, even into the land of the Philistines—which, doubtless, was Satan's object in assuming that form. It unluckily happened that Ishbi, the brother of Goliath, recognised in the person of the royal hunter the slayer of the champion of Gath, and he immediately seized David, bound him neck and heels together, and laid him beneath his wine-press, designing to crush him to death. But, lo, the earth became soft, and the Philistine was baffled. Meanwhile, in the land of Israel a dove with silver wings was seen by the courtiers of King David fluttering about, apparently in great distress, which signified to the wise men that their royal master was in danger of his life. Abishai, one of David's counsellors, at once determined to go and succour his sovereign, and accordingly mounted the king's horse, and in a few minutes was in the land of the Philistines. On arriving at Ishbi's house, he discovered that gentleman's venerable mother spinning at the door. The old lady threw her distaff at the Israelite, and, missing him, desired him to bring it back to her. Abishai returned it in such a manner that she never afterwards required a distaff. This little incident was witnessed by Ishbi, who, resolving to rid himself of one of his enemies forthwith, took David from beneath the wine-press, and threw him high into the air, expecting that he would fall upon his spear, which he had previously fixed into the ground. But Abishai pronounced the Great Name (often referred to in the Talmud), and David, in consequence, remained suspended between earth and sky. In the sequel they both unite against Ishbi, and put him to death.[73]

Of Solomon the Wise there are, of course, many curious rabbinical legends. His reputation for superior sagacity extended over all the world, and the wisest men of other nations came humbly to him as pupils. It would appear that this great monarch was not less willing to afford the poorest of his subjects the benefit of his advice when they applied to him than able to solve the knottiest problem which the most keen-witted casuist could propound. One morning a man, whose life was embittered by a froward, shrewish wife, left his house to seek the advice of Solomon. On the road he overtook another man, with whom he entered into conversation, and presently learned that he was also going to the king's palace. "Pray, friend," said he, "what might be your business with the king? I am going to ask him how I should manage a wife who has long been froward." "Why," said the other, "I employ a great many people, and have a great deal of capital invested in my business; yet I find I am losing more and more every year, instead of gaining; and I want to know the cause, and how it may be remedied." By-and-by they overtook a third man, who informed them that he was a physician whose practice had fallen off considerably, and he was proceeding to ask King Solomon's advice as to how it might be increased. At length they reached the palace, and it was arranged among them that the man who had the shrewish wife should first present himself before the king. In a short time he rejoined his companions with a rather puzzled expression of countenance, and the others inquiring how he had sped, he answered: "I can see no wisdom in the king's advice; he simply advised me to *go to a mill*." The second man then went in, and returned quite as much perplexed as the first, saying: "Of a truth, Solomon is not so wise as he is reported to be; would you believe it?—all he said to me when I had told him my grievance was, *get up early in the morning*." The third man, somewhat discouraged by these apparently idle answers, entered the presence-chamber, and on coming out told his companions that the king had simply advised him to *be proud*. Equally disappointed, the trio returned homeward together. They had not gone far when one of them said to the first man: "Here is a mill; did not the king advise you to go into one?" The man entered, and presently ran out, exclaiming: "I've got it! I've got it! I am to beat my wife!" He went home and gave his spouse a sound thrashing, and she was ever afterwards a very obedient wife.[74] The second man got up very early the next morning, and discovered a number of his servants idling about, and others loading a cart with goods from his warehouse, which they were stealing. He now understood the meaning of Solomon's advice, and henceforward always rose early every morning, looked after his servants, and ultimately became very wealthy. The third man, on reaching home, told his wife to get him a splendid robe, and to instruct all the servants to admit no one into his presence without first obtaining his permission. Next day, as he sat in his private chamber, arrayed in his magnificent gown, a lady sent her servant to demand his attendance, and he was about to enter the physician's chamber, as usual, without ceremony, when he was stopped, and told that the doctor's permission must be first obtained. After some delay the lady's servant was admitted, and found the great doctor seated among his books. On being desired to visit the lady, the doctor told the servant that he could not do so without first receiving his fee. In short, by this professional pride, the physician's practice rapidly increased, and in a few years he acquired a large fortune. And thus in each case Solomon's advice proved successful.[25]

We learn from the Old Testament that the Queen of Sheba (or Sába, whom the Arabians identify with Bilkís, queen of El-Yemen) "came to prove the wisdom of Solomon with hard questions," and that he answered them all. What were the questions—or riddles—the solution of which so much astonished the Queen of Sheba we are not told; but the Rabbis inform us that, after she had exhausted her budget of riddles, she one day presented herself at the foot of Solomon's throne, holding in one hand a bouquet of natural flowers and in the other a bouquet of artificial flowers, desiring the king to say which was the product of nature. Now, the artificial flowers were so exactly modelled in imitation of the others that it was thought impossible for him to answer the question, from the distance at which she held the bouquets. But Solomon was not to be baffled by a woman with scraps of painted paper: he caused a window in the audience-chamber to be opened, when a cluster of bees immediately flew in and alighted upon one of the bouquets, while not one of the insects fixed upon the other. By this device Solomon was enabled to distinguish between the natural and the artificial flowers.

Again the Queen of Sheba endeavoured to outwit the sagacious monarch. She brought before him a number of boys and girls, apparelled all alike, and desired him to distinguish those of one sex from those of the other, as they stood before him. Solomon caused a large basin full of water to be fetched in, and ordered them all to wash their hands. By this expedient he discovered the males from the females; since the boys merely washed their hands, while the girls washed also their arms.[26]

The Arabians and Persians, who have many traditions regarding Solomon, invariably represent him as adept in necromancy, and as being intimately acquainted with the language of beasts and birds. Josephus, the great Jewish historian, distinctly states that Solomon possessed the art of expelling demons, that he composed such incantations also by which distempers are alleviated, and that he left behind him the manner of using exorcisms, by which they drive out demons, never to return. Of course, Josephus merely reproduces rabbinical traditions, and there can be no doubt but the Arabian stories regarding Solomon's magical powers are derived from the same source. It appears that Solomon's signet-ring was the chief instrument with which he performed his numerous magical exploits.[27] By its wondrous power he imprisoned Ashmedai, the prince of devils; and on one occasion the king's curiosity to increase his store of magical knowledge cost him very dear—no less than the loss of his kingdom for a time. Solomon was in the habit of daily plying Ashmedai with questions, to all of which the fiend returned answers, furnishing the desired information, until one day the king asked him a particular question which the captive evil spirit flatly refused to answer, except on condition that Solomon should lend him his signet-ring. The king's passion for magical knowledge overcame his prudence, and he handed his ring to the fiend, thereby depriving himself of all power over his captive, who immediately swallowed the monarch, and stretching out his wings, flew up into the air, and shot out his "inside passenger" four hundred leagues distant from Jerusalem! Ashmedai then assumed the form of Solomon, and sat on his throne. Meanwhile Solomon was become a wanderer on the face of the earth, and it was then that he said (as it is written in the book of Ecclesiasticus i, 3): "This is the reward of all my labour"; which word *this*, one learned Rabbi affirms to have reference to Solomon's walking-staff, and another commentator, to his ragged coat; for the poor monarch went begging from door to door, and in every town he entered he always cried aloud: "I, the Preacher, was king over Israel in Jerusalem!" But the people all thought him insane. At length, in the course of his wanderings, he reached Jerusalem, where he cried, as usual: "I, the Preacher, was king over Israel in Jerusalem!" and as he never varied in his recital, certain wise counsellors, reflecting that a fool is not constant in his tale, resolved to ascertain, if possible, whether the poor beggar was really King Solomon. With this object they assembled, and taking the mendicant with them, they gave him the magical ring and led him into the throne-room.[28] Ashmedai no sooner caught sight of his old master than he shrieked wildly and flew away; and Solomon resumed his mild and beneficent rule over the people of Israel. The Rabbis add, that ever afterwards, even to his dying day, Solomon was afraid of the prince of devils, and could not go to sleep without having his bed surrounded by an armed guard, as it is written in the Book of Canticles, iii, 7, 8.

Another account informs us that the demon, having cajoled Solomon out of possession of his magic ring, at once flung it into the sea and cast the king 400 miles away. Solomon came to a place called Mash Kerim, where he was made chief cook in the palace of the king of Ammon, whose daughter, called Naama, became enamoured of him, and they eloped to a far distant country. As Naama was one day preparing a fish for broiling, she found Solomon's ring in its stomach, which, of course, enabled him to recover his kingdom and to imprison the demon in a copper vessel, which he cast into the Lake of Tiberias.[79]

It may appear strange to some readers that the Rabbis should represent the sagacious Solomon in the character of a practitioner of the Black Art. But the circumstance simply indicates that Solomon's acquirements in scientific knowledge were considerably beyond those of most men of his age; and, as in the case of our own Friar Bacon, his superior attainments were popularly attributed to magical arts. Nature, it need hardly be remarked, is the only school of magic, and men of science are the true magicians.

Unheard-of Monsters

The marvellous creatures which are described by Pliny, and by our own old English writers, Sir John Mandeville and Geoffrey of Monmouth, are common-place in comparison with some of those mentioned in the Talmud. Even the monstrous *roc* of the *Arabian Nights* must have been a mere tom-tit compared with the bird which Rabbi bar Chama says he once saw. It was so tall that its head reached the sky, while its feet rested on the bottom of the ocean; and he affords us some slight notion of the depth of the sea by informing us that a carpenter's axe, which had accidentally fallen in, had not reached the bottom in seven years. The same Rabbi saw "a frog as large as a village containing sixty houses." Huge as this frog was, the snake that swallowed it must have been the very identical serpent of Scandinavian mythology, which encircled the earth; yet a crow gobbled up this serpent, and then flew to the top of a cedar, which was as broad as sixteen waggons placed side by side.—Sailors' "yarns," as they are spun to marvel-loving old ladies in our jest-books, are as nothing to the rabbinical accounts of "strange fish," some with eyes like the moon, others horned, and 300 miles in length. Not less wonderful are some four-footed creatures. The effigy of the unicorn, familiar to every schoolboy, on the royal arms of Great Britain, affords no adequate idea of the actual dimensions of that remarkable animal. Since a unicorn one day old is as large as Mount Tabor, it may readily be supposed that Noah could not possibly have got a full-grown one into the ark; he therefore secured it by its horn to the side, and thus the creature was saved alive. (The Talmudist had forgot that the animals saved from the Flood were in pairs.)[80] The celebrated Og, king of Bashan, it seems, was one of the antediluvians, and was saved by riding on the back of the unicorn. The dwellers in Brobdignag were pigmies compared with the renowned King Og, since his footsteps were forty miles apart, and Abraham's ivory bed was made of one of his teeth. Moses, the Rabbis tell us, was ten cubits high[81] and his walking-stick ten cubits more, with the top of which, after jumping ten cubits from the ground, he contrived to touch the heel of King Og; from which it has been concluded that that monarch was from two to three thousand cubits in height. But (remarks an English writer) a certain Jewish traveller has shown the fallacy of this mensuration, by meeting with the end of one of the leg-bones of the said King Og, and travelling four hours before he came to the other end. Supposing this Rabbi to have been a fair walker, the bone was sixteen miles long!

IV

MORAL AND ENTERTAINING TALES

If most of the rabbinical legends cited in the preceding sections have served simply to amuse the general reader—though to those of a philosophical turn they must have been suggestive of the depths of imbecility to which the human mind may descend—the stories, apologues, and parables contained in the Talmud, of which specimens are now to be presented, are calculated to furnish wholesome moral instruction as well as entertainment to readers of all ranks and ages. In the art of conveying impressive moral lessons, by means of ingenious fictions, the Hebrew sages have never been excelled, and perhaps they are rivalled only by the ancient philosophers of India. The significant circumstance has already been noticed (in the introductory section) that several of the most striking tales in European mediæval collections—particularly the *Disciplina Clericalis* of Petrus Alfonsus and the famous *Gesta Romanorum*—are traceable to Talmudic sources. Little did the priest-ridden, ignorant, marvel-loving laity of European countries imagine that the moral fictions which their spiritual directors recited every Sunday for their edification were derived from the wise men of the despised Hebrew race! But, indeed, there is reason to believe that few mere casual readers even at the present day have any notion of the extent to which the popular fictions of Europe are indebted to the old Jewish Rabbis.

Like the sages of India, the Hebrew Fathers in their teachings strongly inculcate the duty of active benevolence—the liberal giving of alms to the poor and needy; and, indeed, the wealthy Jews are distinguished at the present day by their open-handed liberality in support of the public charitable institutions of the several countries of which they are subjects. "What you increase bestow on good works," says the Hindú sage. "Charity is to money what salt is to meat," says the Hebrew philosopher: if the wealthy are not charitable their riches will perish. In illustration of this maxim is the story of

Rabbi Jochonan and the Poor Woman

One day Rabbi Jochonan was riding outside the city of Jerusalem, followed by his disciples, when he observed a poor woman laboriously gathering the

113

grain that dropped from the mouths of the horses of the Arabs as they were feeding. Looking up and recognising Jochonan, she cried: "O Rabbi, assist me!" "Who art thou?" demanded Jochonan. "I am the daughter of Nakdimon, the son of Guryon." "Why, what has become of thy father's money—the dowry thou receivedst on thy wedding day?" "Ah, Rabbi, is there not a saying in Jerusalem, 'the salt was wanting to the money?'" "But thy husband's money?" "That followed the other: I have lost them both." The good Rabbi wept for the poor woman and helped her. Then said he to his disciples, as they continued on their way: "I remember that when I signed that woman's marriage contract her father gave her as a dowry one million of gold dínars, and her husband was a man of considerable wealth besides."

The ill-fated riches of Nakdimon are referred to in another tale, as a lesson to those who are not charitable according to their means:

A Safe Investment

Rabbi Taraphon, though a very wealthy man, was exceedingly avaricious, and seldom gave help to the poor. Once, however, he involuntarily bestowed a considerable sum in relieving the distressed. Rabbi Akiba came to him one day, and told him that he knew of certain real estate, which would be a very profitable investment. Rabbi Taraphon handed him 4000 dínars in gold to be so invested, and Rabbi Akiba forthwith distributed the whole among the poor. By-and-by, Rabbi Taraphon, happening to meet his friend, desired to know where the real estate was in which his money had been invested. Rabbi Akiba took him to the college, where he caused one of the boys to read aloud the 112th Psalm, and on his reaching the 9th verse, "He distributeth, he giveth to the needy, his righteousness endureth for ever"—"There," said he, "thou seest where thy money is invested." "And why hast thou done this?" demanded Rabbi Taraphon. "Hast thou forgotten," answered his friend, "how Nakdimon, the son of Guryon, was punished because he gave not according to his means?" "But why didst thou not tell me of thy purpose? I could myself have bestowed my money on the poor." "Nay," rejoined Rabbi Akiba, "it is a greater virtue to cause another to give than to give one's self."

Resignation to the divine will under sore family bereavements has, perhaps, never been more beautifully illustrated than by the incident related of the Rabbi Meir. This little tale, as follows, is one of three Talmudic narratives which the poet Coleridge has translated:[82]

The Jewels

The celebrated teacher Rabbi Meir sat during the whole of the Sabbath day

114

in the public school instructing the people. During his absence from the house his two sons died, both of them of uncommon beauty, and enlightened in the law. His wife bore them to her bed-chamber, laid them upon the marriage-bed, and spread a white covering over their bodies. In the evening the Rabbi Meir came home. "Where are my two sons," he asked, "that I may give them my blessing? I repeatedly looked round the school, and I did not see them there." She reached him a goblet. He praised the Lord at the going out of the Sabbath, drank, and again asked: "Where are my sons, that they too may drink of the cup of blessing?" "They will not be afar off," she said, and placed food before him that he might eat. He was in a gladsome and genial mood, and when he had said grace after the meal, she thus addressed him: "Rabbi, with thy permission, I would fain propose to thee one question." "Ask it then, my love," he replied. "A few days ago a person entrusted some jewels into my custody, and now he demands them of me; should I give them back again?" "This is a question," said the Rabbi, "which my wife should not have thought it necessary to ask. What! wouldst thou hesitate or be reluctant to restore to every one his own?" "No," she replied; "but yet I thought it best not to restore them without acquainting you therewith." She then led him to the chamber, and, stepping to the bed, took the white covering from the dead bodies. "Ah, my sons—my sons!" thus loudly lamented the father. "My sons! the light of my eyes, and the light of my understanding! I was your father, but ye were my teachers in the law." The mother turned away and wept bitterly. At length she took her husband by the hand, and said: "Rabbi, didst thou not teach me that we must not be reluctant to restore that which was entrusted to our keeping? See—'the Lord gave, the Lord hath taken away; blessed be the name of the Lord!'"[83] "Blessed be the name of the Lord!" echoed Rabbi Meir. "And blessed be his name for thy sake too, for well is it written: 'Whoso hath found a virtuous wife, hath a greater prize than rubies; she openeth her mouth with wisdom, and in her tongue is the law of kindness.'"[84]

The originals of not a few of the early Italian tales are found in the Talmud—the author of the *Cento Novelle Antiche*, Boccaccio, Sacchetti, and other novelists having derived the groundwork of many of their fictions from the *Gesta Romanorum* and the *Disciplina Clericalis* of Peter Alfonsus, which are largely composed of tales drawn from Eastern sources. The 123rd novel of Sacchetti, in which a young man carves a capon in a whimsical fashion, finds its original in the following Talmudic story:

The Capon-Carver

It happened that a citizen of Jerusalem, while on a distant provincial journey on business, was suddenly taken ill, and, feeling himself to be at the point of death, he sent for the master of the house, and desired him to take charge of his property until his son should arrive to claim it; but, in order to make sure that the claimant was really the son, he was not to deliver up the property until the applicant had proved his wisdom by performing three ingenious actions. Shortly after having given his friend these injunctions the merchant died, and the melancholy intelligence was duly transmitted to his son, who in the course of a few weeks left Jerusalem to claim his property. On reaching the town where his father's friend resided, he began to inquire of the people where his house was situated, and, finding no one who could, or would, give him this necessary information, the youth was in sore perplexity how to proceed in his quest, when he observed a man carrying a heavy load of firewood. "How much for that wood?" he cried. The man readily named his price. "Thou shalt have it," said the stranger. "Carry it to the house of —— [naming his father's friend], and I will follow thee." Well satisfied to have found a purchaser on his own terms, the man at once proceeded as he was desired, and on arriving at the house he threw down his load before the door. "What is all this?" demanded the master. "I have not ordered any wood." "Perhaps not," said the man; "but the person behind me has bought it, and desired me to bring it hither." The stranger had now come up, and, saluting the master of the house, told him who he was, and explained that, since he could not ascertain where his house was situated by inquiries of people in the streets, he had adopted this expedient, which had succeeded. The master praised the young man's ingenuity, and led him into the house.

When the several members of the family, together with the stranger, were assembled round the dinner-table, the master of the house, in order to test the stranger's ingenuity, desired his guest to carve a dish containing five chickens, and to distribute a portion to each of the persons who were present—namely, the master and mistress, their two daughters and two sons, and himself. The young stranger acquitted himself of the duty in this manner: One of the chickens he divided between the master and the mistress; another between the two daughters; the third between the two sons; and the remaining two he took for his own share. "This visitor of mine," thought the master, "is a curious carver; but I will try him once more at supper."

Various amusements made the afternoon pass very agreeably to the stranger, until supper-time, when a fine capon was placed upon the table, which the master desired his guest to carve for the company. The young man took the capon, and began to carve and distribute it thus: To the master of the house he gave the head; to the mistress, the inward part; to the two daughters, each a wing; to the two sons, each a leg; and the remainder he took for himself. After supper the master of the house thus addressed his visitor: "Friend, I thought thy carving at dinner somewhat peculiar, but thy distribution of the capon this evening seems to me extremely whimsical. Give me leave to ask, do the citizens of Jerusalem usually carve their capons in this fashion?"

"Master," said the youth, "I will gladly explain my system of carving, which does appear to you so strange. At dinner I was requested to divide five chickens among seven persons. This I could not do otherwise than arithmetically; therefore, I adopted the perfect number *three* as my guide—thou, thy wife, and one chicken made *three*; thy two daughters and one chicken made *three*; thy two sons and one chicken made *three*; and I had to take the remaining chickens for my own share, as two chickens and myself made *three*." "Very ingenious, I must confess," said the master. "But how dost thou explain thy carving of the capon?" "That, master, I performed according to what appeared to me the fitness of things. I gave the head of the capon to thee, because thou art the head of this house; I gave the inward part to the mistress, as typical of her fruitfulness; thy daughters are both of marriageable years, and, as it is natural to wish them well settled in life, I gave each of them a wing, to indicate that they should soon fly abroad; thy two sons are the pillars of thy house, and to them I gave the legs, which are the supporters of the animal; while to myself I took that part of the capon which most resembles a boat, in which I came hither, and in which I intend to return." From these proofs of his ingenuity the master was now fully convinced that the stranger was the true son of his late friend the merchant, and next morning he delivered to him his father's property.[85]

V

MORAL TALES, FABLES, AND PARABLES

Reverence for parents, which is still a marked characteristic of Eastern races, has ever been strongly inculcated by the Jewish Fathers; and the noble conduct of Damah, the son of Nethuna, towards both his father and mother, is adduced in the Talmud as an example for all times and every condition of life:

A Dutiful Son

The mother of Damah was unfortunately insane, and would frequently not only abuse him but strike him in the presence of his companions; yet would not this dutiful son suffer an ill word to escape his lips, and all he used to say on such occasions was: "Enough, dear mother, enough." One of the precious stones attached to the high priest's sacerdotal garments was once, by some means or other, lost. Informed that the son of Nethuna had one like it, the priests went to him and offered him a very large price for it. He consented to take the sum offered, and went into an adjoining room to fetch the jewel. On entering he found his father asleep, his foot resting on the chest wherein the gem was deposited. Without disturbing his father, he went back to the priests and told them that he must for the present forego the large profit he could make, as his father was asleep. The case being urgent, and the priests thinking that he only said so to obtain a larger price, offered him more money. "No," said he; "I would not even for a moment disturb my father's rest for all the treasures in the world." The priests waited till the father awoke, when Damah brought them the jewel. They gave him the sum they had offered him the second time, but the good man refused to take it. "I will not," said he, "barter for gold the satisfaction of having done my duty. Give me what you offered at first, and I shall be satisfied." This they did, and left him with a blessing.

An Ingenious Will

One of the best rabbinical stories of common life is of a wise man who, residing at some distance from Jerusalem, had sent his son to the Holy City in order to complete his education, and, dying during his son's absence, bequeathed the whole of his estate to one of his own slaves, on the condition that he should allow his son to select any one article which pleased him for an inheritance. Surprised, and naturally angry, at such gross injustice on the part of his father in preferring a slave for his heir in place of himself, the young man sought counsel of his teacher, who, after considering the terms of the will, thus explained its meaning and effect: "By this action thy father has simply secured thy inheritance to thee: to prevent his slaves from plundering the estate before thou couldst formally claim it, he left it to one of them, who, believing himself to be the owner, would take care of the property. Now, what a slave possesses belongs to his master. Choose, therefore, the slave for thy portion, and then possess all that was thy father's." The young man followed his teacher's advice, took possession of the slave, and thus of his father's wealth, and then gave the slave his freedom, together with a considerable sum of money.[86]

And now we proceed to cite one or two of the rabbinical fables, in the proper signification of the term—namely, moral narratives in which beasts or birds are the characters. Although it is generally allowed that Fable was the earliest form adopted for conveying moral truths, yet it is by no means agreed among the learned in what country of remote antiquity it originated. Dr. Landsberger, in his erudite introduction to *Panchatantra* (1859), contends that the Jews were the first to employ fables for purposes of moral instruction, and that the oldest fable extant is Jotham's apologue of the trees desiring a king (Book of Judges, ix. 8-15).[87] According to Dr. Landsberger, the sages of India were indebted to the Hebrews for the idea of teaching by means of fables, probably during the reign of Solomon, who is believed to have had commerce with the western shores of India.[88] We are told by Josephus that Solomon "composed of parables and similitudes three thousand; for he spoke a parable upon every sort of tree, from the hyssop to the cedar; and, in like manner, also about beasts, about all sorts of living creatures, whether upon earth, or in the seas, or in the air; for he was not unacquainted with any of their natures, nor omitted inquiring about them, but described them all like a philosopher, and demonstrated his exquisite knowledge of their several properties." These fables of Solomon, if they were ever committed to writing, had perished long before the time of the great Jewish historian; but there seems no reason to doubt the fact that the wise king of Israel composed many works besides those ascribed to him in the Old Testament. The general opinion among European orientalists is that Fable had its origin in India; and the Hindús themselves claim the honour of inventing our present system of numerals (which came into Europe through the Arabians, who derived it from the Hindús), the game of chess, and the Fables of Vishnusarman (the *Panchatantra* and its abridgment, the *Hitopadesa*).

It is said that Rabbi Meir knew upwards of three hundred fables relating to the fox alone; but of these only three fragments have been preserved, and this is one of them, according to Mr. Polano's translation:

The Fox and the Bear

A Fox said to a Bear: "Come, let us go into this kitchen; they are making preparations for the Sabbath, and we shall be able to find food." The Bear followed the Fox, but, being bulky, he was captured and punished. Angry thereat, he designed to tear the Fox to pieces, under the pretence that the forefathers of the Fox had once stolen his food, wherein occurs the saying, "the fathers have eaten sour grapes, and the children's teeth are set on edge."[89] "Nay," said the Fox, "come with me, my good friend; let us not quarrel. I will lead thee to another place where we shall surely find food." The Fox then led the Bear to a deep well, where two buckets were fastened together by a rope, like a balance. It was night, and the Fox pointed to the moon reflected in the water, saying: "Here is a fine cheese; let us descend and partake of it." The Fox entered his bucket first, but being too light to balance the weight of the Bear, he took with him a stone. As soon as the Bear had got into the other bucket, however, the Fox threw the stone away, and consequently the bear descended to the bottom and was drowned.

The reader will doubtless recognise in this fable the original of many modern popular tales having a similar catastrophe. It will also be observed that the vulgar saying of the moon being "a fine cheese" is of very considerable antiquity.[90]

And here is another rabbinical fable of a Fox—a very common character in the apologues of most countries; although the "moral" appended to this one by the pious fabulist is much more striking than is sometimes the case of those deduced from beast-fables:

The Fox in the Garden

A Fox once came near a very fine garden, where he beheld lofty trees laden with fruit that charmed the eye. Such a beautiful sight, added to his natural greediness, excited in him the desire of possession. He fain would taste the forbidden fruit; but a high wall stood between him and the object of his wishes. He went about in search of an entrance, and at last found an opening in the wall, but it was too small to admit his body. Unable to penetrate, he had recourse to his usual cunning. He fasted three days, and became sufficiently reduced in bulk to crawl through the small aperture. Having effected an entrance, he carelessly roved about in this delightful region, making free with its exquisite produce and feasting on its more rare and delicious fruits. He remained for some time, and glutted his appetite, when a thought occurred to him that it was possible he might be observed, and in that case he should pay dearly for his feast. He therefore retired to the place where he had entered, and attempted to get out, but to his great consternation he found his endeavours vain. He had by indulgence grown so fat and plump that the same space would no more admit him. "I am in a fine predicament," said he to himself. "Suppose the master of the garden were now to come and call me to account, what would become of me? I see my only chance of escape is to fast and half starve myself." He did so with great reluctance, and after suffering hunger for three days, he with difficulty made his escape. As soon as he was out of danger, he took a farewell view of the scene of his late pleasure, and said: "O garden! thou art indeed charming, and delightful are thy fruits—delicious and exquisite; but of what benefit art thou to me? What have I now for all my labour and cunning? Am I not as lean as I was before?"—It is even so with man, remarks the Talmudist. Naked he comes into the world—naked must he go out of it, and of all his toils and labour he can carry nothing with him save the fruits of his righteousness.

From fables to parables the transition is easy; and many of those found in the Talmud are exceedingly beautiful, and are calculated to cause even the most thoughtless to reflect upon his way of life. Let us first take the parable of the Desolate Island, one of those adapted by the monkish compilers of European mediæval tales, to which reference has been made in the preceding sections:

The Desolate Island

A very wealthy man, who was of a kind, benevolent disposition, desired to make his slave happy. He therefore gave him his freedom, and presented him with a shipload of merchandise. "Go," said he, "sail to different countries; dispose of these goods, and that which thou mayest receive for them shall be thy own." The slave sailed away upon the broad ocean, but before he had been long on his voyage a storm overtook him, his ship was driven on a rock and went to pieces; all on board were lost—all save this slave, who swam to an island near by. Sad, despondent, with nothing in this world, he traversed this island until he approached a large and beautiful city, and many people approached him, joyously shouting: "Welcome! welcome! Long live the king!" They brought a rich carriage, and, placing him therein, escorted him to a magnificent palace, where many servants gathered about him—clothing him in royal garments, and addressing him as their sovereign, and expressing their obedience to his will. The slave was amazed and dazzled, believing that he was dreaming, and that all he saw, heard, and experienced was mere passing fantasy. Becoming convinced of the reality of his condition, he said to some men about him, for whom he entertained a friendly feeling: "How is this? I cannot understand it. That you should thus elevate and honour a man whom you know not—a poor, naked wanderer, whom you have never seen before—making him your ruler—causes me more wonder than I can readily express." "Sire," they replied, "this island is inhabited by spirits. Long since they prayed to God to send them yearly a son of man to reign over them, and he has answered their prayers. Yearly he sends them a son of man, whom they receive with honour and elevate to the throne; but his dignity and power end with the year. With its close the royal garments are taken from him, he is placed on board a ship, and carried to a vast and desolate island, where, unless he has previously been wise and prepared for the day, he will find neither friend nor subject, and be obliged to pass a weary, lonely, miserable life. Then a new king is selected here, and so year follows year. The kings who preceded thee were careless and indifferent, enjoying their power to the full, and thinking not of the day when it should end. Be wise, then. Let our words find rest within thy heart." The newly-made king listened attentively to all this, and felt grieved that he should have lost even the time he had already spent for making preparations for his loss of power. He addressed the wise man who had spoken, saying: "Advise me, O spirit of wisdom, how I may prepare for the days which will come upon me in the future." "Naked thou camest to us," replied the other, "and naked thou wilt be sent to the desolate island, of which I have told thee. At present thou art king, and mayest do as pleaseth thee; therefore, send workmen to this island, let them build houses, till the ground, and beautify the surroundings. The barren soil will be changed into fruitful fields, people will journey thither to live, and thou wilt have established a new kingdom for thyself, with subjects to welcome thee in gladness when thou shalt have lost thy power here. The year is short, the work is long; therefore be earnest and energetic." The king followed this advice. He sent workmen and materials to the desolate island, and before the close of his temporary power it had become a blooming, pleasant, and attractive spot. The rulers who had preceded him had anticipated the close of their power with dread, or smothered all thought of it in revelry; but he looked forward to it as a day of joy, when he should enter upon a career of permanent peace and happiness. The day came; the freed slave who had been made a king was deprived of his authority; with his power he lost his royal garments; naked he was placed upon a ship, and its sails were set for the desolate island. When he approached its shores, however, the people whom he had sent there came to meet him with music, song, and great joy. They made him a prince among them, and he lived ever after in pleasantness and peace.

The Talmudist thus explains this beautiful parable of the Desolate Island: The wealthy man of kindly disposition is God, and the slave to whom he gave freedom is the soul which he gives to man. The island at which the slave arrives is the world: naked and weeping he appears to his parents, who are the inhabitants that greet him warmly and make him their king. The friends who tell him of the ways of the country are his good inclinations. The year of his reign is his span of life, and the desolate island is the future world, which he must beautify by good deeds—the workmen and materials—or else live lonely and desolate for ever.[91]

Closely allied to the foregoing is the characteristic Jewish parable of

The Man and his Three Friends

A certain man had three friends, two of whom he loved dearly, but the other he lightly esteemed. It happened one day that the king commanded his presence at court, at which he was greatly alarmed, and wished to procure an advocate. Accordingly he went to the two friends whom he loved: one flatly refused to accompany him, the other offered to go with him as far as the king's gate, but no farther. In his extremity he called upon the third friend, whom he least esteemed, and he not only went willingly with him, but so ably defended him before the king that he was acquitted. In like manner, says the Talmudist, every man has three friends when Death summons him to appear before his Creator. His first friend, whom he loves most, namely, his *money*, cannot go with him a single step; his second, *relations* and *neighbours*, can only accompany him to the grave, but cannot defend him before the Judge; while his third friend, whom he does not highly esteem, the *law* and his *good works*, goes with him before the king, and obtains his acquittal.[92]

Another striking and impressive parable akin to the two immediately preceding is this of

The Garments

A king distributed amongst his servants various costly garments. Now some of these servants were wise and some were foolish. And those that were wise said to themselves: "The king may call again for the garments; let us therefore take care they do not get soiled." But the fools took no manner of care of theirs, and did all sorts of work in them, so that they became full of spots and grease. Some time afterwards the king called for the garments. The wise servants brought theirs clean and neat, but the foolish servants brought theirs in a sad state, ragged and unclean. The king was pleased with the first, and said: "Let the clean garments be placed in the treasury, and let their keepers depart in peace. As for the unclean garments, they must be washed and purified, and their foolish keepers must be cast into prison."—This parable is designed to illustrate the passage in Eccles., xii, 7, "Then shall the dust return to the earth as it was, and the spirit shall return unto God, who gave it"; which words "teach us to remember that God gave us the soul in a state of innocence and purity, and that it is therefore our duty to return it unto him in the same state as he gave it unto us—pure and undefiled."

Solomon's Choice

of Wisdom, in preference to all other precious things, is thus finely illustrated: A certain king had an officer whom he fondly loved. One day he desired his favourite to choose anything that he could give, and it would at once be granted him. The officer considered that if he asked the king for gold and silver and precious stones, these would be given him in abundance; then he thought that if he had a more exalted station it would be granted; at last he resolved to ask the king for his daughter, since with such a bride both riches and honours would also be his. In like manner did Solomon pray, "Give thy servant an understanding heart," when the Lord said to him, "What shall I give thee?" (1st Kings, iii, 5, 9.)

But perhaps the most beautiful and touching of all the Talmudic parables is the following (Polano's version), in which Israel is likened to a bride, waiting sadly, yet hopefully, for the coming of her spouse:

Bride and Bridegroom

There was once a man who pledged his dearest faith to a maiden beautiful and true. For a time all passed pleasantly, and the maiden lived in happiness. But then the man was called from her side, and he left her. Long she waited, but still he did not return. Friends pitied her, and rivals mocked her; tauntingly they pointed to her and said: "He has left thee, and will never come back." The maiden sought her chamber, and read in secret the letters which her lover had written to her—the letters in which he promised to be ever faithful, ever true. Weeping, she read them, but they brought comfort to her heart; she dried her eyes and doubted not. A joyous day dawned for her: the man she loved returned, and when he learned that others had doubted, while she had not, he asked her how she had preserved her faith; and she showed his letters to him, declaring her eternal trust. [In like manner] Israel, in misery and captivity, was mocked by the nations; her hopes of redemption were made a laughing-stock; her sages scoffed at; her holy men derided. Into her synagogues, into her schools, went Israel. She read the letters which her God had written, and believed in the holy promises which they contained. God will in time redeem her; and when he says: "How could you alone be faithful of all the mocking nations?" she will point to the law and answer: "Had not thy law been my delight, I should long since have perished in my affliction."[93]

In the account of the Call of Abraham given in the Book of Genesis, xii, 1-3, we are not told that his people were all idolaters; but in the Book of Joshua, xxiv, 1-2, it is said that the great successor of Moses, when he had "waxed old and was stricken with age," assembled the tribes of Israel, at Shechem, and said to the people: "Your fathers dwelt on the other side of the flood in old time, even Terah, the father of Abraham and the father of Nachor; and they served other gods." The sacred narrative does not state the circumstances which induced Abraham to turn away from the worship of false deities, but the information is furnished by the Talmudists— possibly from ancient oral tradition—in this interesting tale of

124

Abraham and the Idols

Abraham's father Terah, who dwelt in Ur of the Chaldees, was not only an idolater, but a maker of idols. Having occasion to go a journey of some distance, he instructed Abraham how to conduct the business of idol-selling during his absence. The future founder of the Hebrew nation, however, had already obtained a knowledge of the true and living God, and consequently held the practice of idolatry in the utmost abhorrence. Accordingly, whenever any one came to buy an idol Abraham inquired his age, and upon his answering, "I am fifty (or sixty) years old," he would exclaim, "Woe to the man of fifty who would worship the work of man's hands!" and his father's customers went away shamefaced at the rebuke. But, not content with this mode of showing his contempt for idolatry, Abraham resolved to bring matters to a crisis before his father returned home; and an opportunity was presented for his purpose one day when a woman came to Terah's house with a bowl of fine flour, which she desired Abraham to place as a votive offering before the idols. Instead of doing this, however, Abraham took a hammer and broke all the idols into fragments excepting the largest, into whose hands he then placed the hammer. On Terah's return he discovered the destruction of his idols, and angrily demanded of Abraham, who had done the mischief. "There came hither a woman," replied Abraham, "with a bowl of fine flour, which, as she desired, I set before the gods, whereupon they disputed among themselves who should eat first, and the tallest god broke all the rest into pieces with the hammer." "What fable is this thou art telling me?" exclaimed Terah. "As for the god thou speakest of, is he not the work of my own hands?' Did I not carve him out of the timber of the tree which I cut down in the wilderness? How, then, could he have done this evil? Verily *thou* hast broken my idols!" "Consider, my father," said Abraham, "what it is thou sayest—that I am capable of destroying the gods which thou dost worship!" Then Terah took and delivered him to Nimrod, who said to Abraham: "Let us worship the fire." To which Abraham replied: "Rather the water that quenches the fire." "Well, the water." "Rather the cloud which carries the water." "Well, the cloud." "Rather the wind that scatters the cloud." "Well, the wind." "Rather man, for he endures the wind." "Thou art a babbler!" exclaimed Nimrod. "I worship the fire, and will cast thee into it. Perchance the God whom thou dost adore will deliver thee from thence." Abraham was accordingly thrown into a heated furnace, but God saved him.[94]

Alexander the Great is said to have wept because there were no more worlds for him to conquer; and truly says the sage Hebrew King, "The grave and destruction can never have enough, nor are the eyes of man ever satisfied" (Prov. xxvii, 20), a sentiment which the following tale, or parable, is designed to exemplify:

The Vanity of Ambition

Pursuing his journey through dreary deserts and uncultivated ground, Alexander came at last to a small rivulet, whose waters glided peacefully along their shelving banks. Its smooth, unruffled surface was the image of contentment, and seemed in its silence to say, "This is the abode of tranquility." All was still: not a sound was heard save soft murmuring tones which seemed to whisper in the ear of the weary traveller, "Come, and partake of nature's bounty," and to complain that such an offer should be made in vain. To a contemplative mind, such a scene might have suggested a thousand delightful reflections. But what charms could it have for the soul of Alexander, whose breast was filled with schemes of ambition and conquest; whose eye was familiarised with rapine and slaughter; and whose ears were accustomed to the clash of arms—to the groans of the wounded and the dying? Onward, therefore, he marched. Yet, overcome by fatigue and hunger, he was soon obliged to halt. He seated himself on the bank of the river, took a draught of the water, which he found of a very fine flavour and most refreshing. He then ordered some salt fish, with which he was well provided, to be brought to him. These he caused to be dipped in the stream, in order to take off the briny taste, and was greatly surprised to find them emit a fine fragrance. "Surely," said he, "this river, which possesses such uncommon qualities, must flow from some very rich and happy country."

Following the course of the river, he at length arrived at the gates of Paradise. The gates were shut. He knocked, and, with his usual impetuosity, demanded admittance. "Thou canst not be admitted here," exclaimed a voice from within; "this gate is the Lord's." "I am the Lord— the Lord of the earth," rejoined the impatient chief. "I am Alexander the Conqueror. Will you not admit *me*?" "No," was the answer; "here we know of no conquerors, save such as conquer their passions: *None but the just can enter here.*" Alexander endeavoured in vain to enter the abode of the blessed—neither entreaties nor menaces availed. Seeing all his attempts fruitless, he addressed himself to the guardian of Paradise, and said: "You know I am a great king, who has received the homage of nations. Since you will not admit me, give me at least some token that I may show an astonished world that I have been where no mortal has ever been before me." "Here, madman," said the guardian of Paradise—"here is something for thee. It may cure the maladies of thy distempered soul. One glance at it may teach thee more wisdom than thou hast hitherto derived from all thy former instructors. Now go thy ways."

Alexander took the present with avidity, and repaired to his tent. But what was his confusion and surprise to find, on examining his present, that it was nothing but a fragment of a human skull. "And is this," exclaimed he, "the mighty gift that they bestow on kings and heroes? Is this the fruit of so much toil and danger and care?" Enraged and disappointed, he threw it on the ground. "Great king," said one of the learned men who were present, "do not despise this gift. Contemptible as it may appear in thine eyes, it yet possesses some extraordinary qualities, of which thou mayest soon be convinced, if thou wilt but cause it to be weighed against gold or silver." Alexander ordered this to be done. A pair of scales were brought. The skull was placed in one, a quantity of gold in the other; when, to the astonishment of the beholders, the skull over-balanced the gold. More gold was added, yet still the skull preponderated. In short, the more gold there was put in the one scale the lower sank that which contained the skull. "Strange," exclaimed Alexander, "that so small a portion of matter should outweigh so large a mass of gold! Is there nothing that will counterpoise it?" "Yes," answered the philosophers, "a very little matter will do it." They then took some earth and covered the skull with it, when immediately down went the gold, and the opposite scale ascended. "This is very extraordinary," said Alexander, astonished. "Can you explain this phenomenon?" "Great king," said the sages, "this fragment is the socket of a human eye, which, though small in compass, is yet unbounded in its desires. The more it has, the more it craves. Neither gold nor silver nor any other earthly possession can ever satisfy it. But when it is once laid in the grave and covered with a little earth, there is an end to its lust and ambition."

Shakspeare's well-known masterly description of the Seven Ages of Man, which he puts into the mouth of the melancholy Jaques (*As You Like It*, ii, 7), was anticipated by Rabbi Simon, the son of Eliezer, in this Talmudic description of

The Seven Stages of Human Life

Seven times in one verse did the author of Ecclesiastes make use of the word *vanity*, in allusion to the seven stages of human life.[95]

The first commences in the first year of human existence, when the *infant* lies like a king on a soft couch, with numerous attendants about him, all ready to serve him, and eager to testify their love and attachment by kisses and embraces.

The second commences about the age of two or three years, when the darling *child* is permitted to crawl on the ground, and, like an unclean animal, delights in dirt and filth.

Then at the age of ten, the thoughtless *boy*, without reflecting on the past or caring for the future, jumps and skips about like a young kid on the enamelled green, contented to enjoy the present moment.

The fourth stage begins about the age of twenty, when the *young man*, full of vanity and pride, begins to set off his person by dress; and, like a young unbroken horse, prances and gallops about in search of a wife.

Then comes the *matrimonial state*, when the poor *man*, like a patient ass, is obliged, however reluctantly, to toil and labour for a living.

Behold him now in the *parental state*, when surrounded by helpless children craving his support and looking to him for bread. He is as bold, as vigilant, and as fawning, too, as the faithful dog; guarding his little flock, and snatching at everything that comes in his way, in order to provide for his offspring.

At last comes the final stage, when the decrepit *old man*, like the unwieldy though most sagacious elephant, becomes grave, sedate, and distrustful. He then also begins to hang down his head towards the ground, as if surveying the place where all his vast schemes must terminate, and where ambition and vanity are finally humbled to the dust.

But the Talmudist, in his turn, was forestalled by Bhartrihari, an ancient Hindú sage, one of whose three hundred apothegms has been thus rendered into English by Sir Monier Williams:

> Now for a little while a child; and now
> An amorous youth; then for a season turned
> Into a wealthy householder; then, stripped
> Of all his riches, with decrepit limbs
> And wrinkled frame, man creeps towards the end
> Of life's erratic course; and, like an actor,
> Passes behind Death's curtain out of view.

Here, however, the Indian philosopher describes human life as consisting of only four scenes; but, like our own Shakspeare, he compares the world to a stage and man to a player. An epigram preserved in the *Anthologia* also likens the world to a theatre and human life to a drama:

> This life a theatre we well may call,
>   Where every actor must perform with art;
> Or laugh it through, and make a farce of all,
>   Or learn to bear with grace a tragic part.

It is surely both instructive and interesting thus to discover resemblances in thought and expression in the writings of men of comprehensive intellect, who lived in countries and in times far apart.

VI

WISE SAYINGS OF THE RABBIS

"Concise sentences," says Bacon, "like darts, fly abroad and make impressions, while long discourses are flat things, and not regarded." And Seneca has remarked that "even rude and uncultivated minds are struck, as it were, with those short but weighty sentences which anticipate all reasoning by flashing truths upon them at once." Wise men in all ages seem to have been fully aware of the advantage of condensing into pithy sentences the results of their observations of the course of human life; and the following selection of sayings of the Jewish Fathers, taken from the *Pirke Aboth* (the 41st treatise of the Talmud, compiled by Nathan of Babylon, A.D. 200), and other sources, will be found to be quite as sagacious as the aphorisms of the most celebrated philosophers of India and Greece:

This world is like an ante-chamber in comparison with the world to come; prepare thyself in the ante-chamber, therefore, that thou mayest enter into the dining-room.

Be humble to a superior, and affable to an inferior, and receive all men with cheerfulness.

Be not scornful to any, nor be opposed to all things; for there is no man that hath not his hour, nor is there anything which hath not its place.

Attempt not to appease thy neighbour in the time of his anger, nor comfort him in the time when his dead is lying before him, nor ask of him in the time of his vowing, nor desire to see him in the time of his calamity.[96]

Hold no man responsible for his utterances in times of grief.

Who gains wisdom? He who is willing to receive instruction from all sources. Who is rich? He who is content with his lot. Who is deserving of honour? He who honoureth mankind. Who is the mighty man? He who subdueth his temper.[97]

When a liar speaks the truth, he finds his punishment in being generally disbelieved.

The physician who prescribes gratuitously gives a worthless prescription.

He who hardens his heart with pride softens his brains with the same.

The day is short, the labour vast; but the labourers are still slothful, though the reward is great, and the Master presseth for despatch.[98]

He who teacheth a child is like one who writeth on new paper; and he who teacheth old people is like one who writeth on blotted paper.[99]

First learn and then teach.

Teach thy tongue to say, "I do not know."

The birds of the air despise a miser.

If thy goods sell not in one city, take them to another.

Victuals prepared by many cooks will be neither cold nor hot.[100]

Two pieces of money in a large jar make more noise than a hundred.[101]

Into the well which supplies thee with water cast no stones.[102]

When love is intense, both find room enough upon one bench; afterwards, they may find themselves cramped in a space of sixty cubits.[103]

The place honours not the man; it is the man who gives honour to the place.

Few are they who see their own faults.[104]

Thy friend has a friend, and thy friend's friend has a friend: be discreet.[105]

Poverty sits as gracefully upon some people as a red saddle upon a white horse.

Rather be thou the tail among lions than the head among foxes.[106]

The thief who finds no opportunity to steal considers himself an honest man.

Use thy noble vase to-day, for to-morrow it may perchance be broken.

Descend a step in choosing thy wife; ascend a step in choosing thy friend.

A myrtle even in the dust remains a myrtle.[107]

Every one whose wisdom exceedeth his deeds, to what is he like? To a tree whose branches are many and its roots few; and the wind cometh and plucketh it up, and overturneth it on its face.[108]

If a word spoken in time be worth one piece of money, silence in its place is worth two.[109]

Silence is the fence round wisdom.[110]

A saying ascribed to Esop has been frequently cited with admiration. The sage Chilo asked Esop what God was doing, and he answered that he was "depressing the proud and exalting the humble." A parallel to this is presented in the answer of Rabbi Jose to a woman who asked him what God had been doing since the creation: "He makes ladders on which he causes the poor to ascend and the rich to descend," in other words, exalts the lowly and humbles the haughty.

The lucid explanation of the expression, "I, God, am a jealous God," given by a Rabbi, has been thus elegantly translated by Coleridge:[111]

"Your God," said a heathen philosopher to a Hebrew Rabbi, "in his Book calls himself a jealous God, who can endure no other god besides himself, and on all occasions makes manifest his abhorrence of idolatry. How comes it, then, that he threatens and seems to hate the worshippers of false gods more than the false gods themselves?"

"A certain king," said the Rabbi, "had a disobedient son. Among other worthless tricks of various kinds, he had the baseness to give his dogs his father's names and titles. Should the king show anger with the prince or his dogs?"

"Well-turned," replied the philosopher; but if God destroyed the objects of idolatry, he would take away the temptation to it."

"Yea," retorted the Rabbi; "if the fools worshipped such things only as were of no farther use than that to which their folly applied them—if the idol were always as worthless as the idolatry is contemptible. But they worship the sun, the moon, the host of heaven, the rivers, the sea, fire, air, and what not. Would you that the Creator, for the sake of those fools, should ruin his own works, and disturb the laws applied to nature by his own wisdom? If a man steal grain and sow it, should the seed not shoot up out of the earth because it was stolen? O no! The wise Creator lets nature run its own course, for its course is his own appointment. And what if the children of folly abuse it to evil? The day of reckoning is not far off, and men will then learn that human actions likewise reappear in their consequences by as certain a law as that which causes the green blade to rise up out of the buried cornfield."

Not less conclusive was the form of illustration employed by Rabbi Joshuah in answer to the emperor Trajan. "You teach," said Trajan, "that your God is everywhere. I should like to see him." "God's presence," replied the Rabbi, "is indeed everywhere, but he cannot be seen. No mortal can behold his glory." Trajan repeated his demand. "Well," said the Rabbi, "suppose we try, in the first place, to look at one of his ambassadors." The emperor consented, and Joshuah took him into the open air, and desired him to look at the sun in its meridian splendour. "I cannot," said Trajan; "the light dazzles me." "Thou canst not endure the light of one of his creatures," said the Rabbi, "yet dost thou expect to behold the effulgent glory of the Creator!"

Our selections from the sayings of the Hebrew Fathers might be largely extended, but we shall conclude them with the following: A Rabbi, being asked why God dealt out manna to the Israelites day by day, instead of giving them a supply sufficient for a year, or more, answered by a parable to this effect: There was once a king who gave a certain yearly allowance to his son, whom he saw, in consequence, but once a year, when he came to receive it; so the king changed his plan, and paid him his allowance daily, and thus had the pleasure of seeing his son each day. And so with the manna: had God given the people a supply for a year they would have forgotten their divine benefactor, but by sending them each day the requisite quantity, they had God constantly in their minds.

There can be no doubt that the Rabbis derived the materials of many of their legends and tales of Biblical characters from foreign sources; but their beautiful moral stories and parables, which "hide a rich truth in a tale's pretence," are probably for the most part of their own invention; and the fact that the Talmud was partially, if not wholly, translated into Arabic shortly after the settlement of the Moors in Spain sufficiently accounts for the early introduction of rabbinical legends into Muhammedan works, apart from those found in the Kurán.

ADDITIONAL NOTES

ADAM AND THE OIL OF MERCY

In the apocryphal Revelation of Moses, which appears to be of Rabbinical extraction, Adam, when near his end, informs his sons; that, because of his transgression, God had laid upon his body seventy strokes, or plagues. The trouble of the first stroke was injury to the eyes; the trouble of the second stroke, of the hearing; and so on, in succession, all the strokes should overtake him. And Adam, thus speaking to his sons, groaned out loud, and said, "What shall I do? I am in great grief." And Eve also wept, saying: "My lord Adam, arise; give me the half of thy disease, and let me bear it, because through me this has happened to thee; through me thou art in distresses and troubles." And Adam said to Eve: "Arise, and go with our son Seth near Paradise, and put earth upon your heads, and weep, beseeching the Lord that he may have compassion upon me, and send his angel to Paradise, and give me of the tree out of which flows the oil, that thou mayest bring it unto me; and I shall anoint myself and have rest, and show thee the manner in which we were deceived at first.".... And Seth went with his mother Eve near Paradise, and they wept there, beseeching God to send his angel to give them the Oil of Compassion. And God sent to them the archangel Michael, who said to them these words: "Seth, man of God, do not weary thyself praying in this supplication about the tree from which flows the oil to anoint thy father Adam; for it will not happen to thee now, but at the last times.... Do thou again go to thy father, since the measure of his life is fulfilled, saving three days."

The Revelation, or Apocalypse, of Moses, remarks Mr. Alex. Walker (from whose translation the foregoing is extracted: *Apocryphal Gospels, Acts, and Revelations*, 1870), "belongs rather to the Old Testament than to the New. We have been unable to find in it any reference to any Christian writing. In its form, too, it appears to be a portion of some larger work. Parts of it at least are of an ancient date, as it is very likely from this source that the celebrated legend of the Tree of Life and the Oil of Mercy was derived"—an account of which, from the German of Dr. Piper, is given in the *Journal of Sacred Literature*, October, 1864, vol. vi (N.S.), p. 30 ff.

MUSLIM LEGEND OF ADAM'S PUNISHMENT, PARDON, DEATH, AND BURIAL

When "our first parents" were expelled from Paradise, Adam fell upon the mountain in Ceylon which still retains his name ("Adam's Peak"), while Eve descended at Júddah, which is the port of Mecca, in Arabia. Seated on the pinnacle of the highest mountain in Ceylon, with the orisons of the angelic choirs still vibrating in his ears, the fallen progenitor of the human race had sufficient leisure to bewail his guilt, forbearing all food and sustenance for the space of forty days.[112] But Allah, whose mercy ever surpasses his indignation, and who sought not the death of the wretched penitent, then despatched to his relief the angel Gabriel, who presented him with a quantity of wheat, taken from that fatal tree[113] for which he had defied the wrath of his Creator, with the information that it was to be for food to him and to his children. At the same time he was directed to set it in the earth, and afterwards to grind it into flour. Adam obeyed, for it was part of his penalty that he should toil for sustenance; and the same day the corn sprang up and arrived at maturity, thus affording him an immediate resource against the evils of hunger and famine. For the benevolent archangel did not quit him until he had farther taught him how to construct a mill on the side of the mountain, to grind his corn, and also how to convert the flour into dough and bake it into bread.

With regard to the forlorn associate of his guilt, from whom a long and painful separation constituted another article in the punishment of his disobedience, it is briefly related that, experiencing also for the first time the craving of hunger, she instinctively dipped her hand into the sea and brought out a fish, and laying it on a rock in the sun, thus prepared her first meal in this her state of despair and destitution.

Adam continued to deplore his guilt on the mountain for a period of one hundred years, and it is said that from his tears, with which he moistened the earth during this interval of remorse, there grew up that useful variety of plants and herbs which in after times by their medicinal qualities served to alleviate the afflictions of the human race; and to this circumstance is to be ascribed the fact that the most useful drugs in the *materia medica* continue to this day to be supplied from the peninsula of India and the adjoining islands. The angel Gabriel had now tamed the wild ox of the field, and Allah himself had discovered to Adam in the caverns of the same mountain that most important of minerals, iron, which he soon learned to fashion into a variety of articles necessary to the successful prosecution of his increasing labours. At the termination of one hundred years, consumed in toil and sorrow, Adam having been instructed by the angel Gabriel in a penitential formula by which he might hope yet to conciliate Allah, the justice of Heaven was satisfied, and his repentance was finally accepted by the Most High. The joy of Adam was now as intense as his previous sorrow had been extreme, and another century passed, during which the tears with which Adam—from very different emotions—now bedewed the earth were not less effectual in producing every species of fragrant and aromatic flower and shrub, to delight the eye and gratify the sense of smell by their odours, than they were formerly in the generation of medicinal plants to assuage the sufferings of humanity.

Tradition has ascribed to Adam a stature so stupendous that when he stood or walked his forehead brushed the skies; and it is stated that he thus partook in the converse of the angels, even after his fall. But this, by perpetually holding to his view the happiness which he had lost, instead of alleviating, contributed in a great degree to aggravate his misery, and to deprive him of all repose upon earth. Allah, therefore, in pity of his sufferings, shortened his stature to one hundred cubits, so that the harmony of the celestial hosts should no longer reach his ear.

Then Allah caused to be raised up for Adam a magnificent pavilion, or temple, constructed entirely of rubies, on the spot which is now occupied by the sacred Kaába at Mecca, and which is in the centre of the earth and immediately beneath the throne of Allah. The forlorn Eve—whom Adam had almost forgotten amidst his own sorrows—in the course of her weary wanderings came to the palace of her spouse, and, once more united, they returned to Ceylon. But Adam revisited the sacred pavilion at Mecca every year until his death. And wherever he set his foot there arose, and exists to this day, some city, town, or village, or other place to indicate the presence of man and of human cultivation. The spaces between his footsteps—three days' journey—long remained barren wilderness.

On the twentieth day of that disorder which terminated the earthly existence of Adam, the divine will was revealed to him through the angel Gabriel, that he was to make an immediate bequest of his power as Allah's vicegerent on earth to Shayth, or Seth, the discreetest and most virtuous of all his sons, which having done, he resigned his soul to the Angel of Death on the following day. Seth buried his venerable parent on the summit of the mountain in Ceylon ("Adam's Peak"); but some writers assert that he was buried under Mount Abú Kebyss, about three miles from Mecca. Eve died a twelvemonth after her husband, and was buried in his grave. Noah conveyed their remains in the ark, and afterwards interred them in Jerusalem, at the spot afterwards known as Mount Calvary.

The foregoing is considerably abridged from *An Essay towards the History of Arabia, antecedent to the Birth of Mahommed, arranged from the 'Tarikh Tebry' and other authentic sources*, by Major David Price, London, 1824, pp. 4, 11.—We miss in this curious legend the brief but pathetic account of the expulsion of Adam and Eve from the Garden of Eden, as found in the last two verses of the 3rd chapter of Genesis, which suggested to Milton the fine conclusion of his *Paradise Lost*: how "some natural tears they dropped," as the unhappy pair went arm-in-arm out of Paradise—and "the world was all before them, where to choose." Adam's prolonged residence at the top of a high mountain in Ceylon seems to be of purely Muhammedan invention; and assuredly the Arabian Prophet did not obtain from the renegade Jew who is said to have assisted him in the composition of the Kurán the "information" that Allah taught Adam the mystery of working in iron, since in the Book of Genesis (iv, 22) it is stated that Tubal-cain was "an instructor of every artificer in brass and iron," as his brother Jubal was "the father of all such as handle the harp and the organ" (21).—The disinterment of the bones of Adam and Eve by Noah before the Flood began and their subsequent burial at the spot on which Jerusalem was afterwards built, as also the stature of Adam, are, of course, derived from Jewish tradition.

MOSES AND THE POOR WOODCUTTER

The following interesting legend is taken from Mrs. Meer Hassan Ali's *Observations on the Mussulmans of India* (1832), vol. i, pp. 170-175. It was translated by her husband (an Indian Muslim) from a commentary on the history of Músa, or Moses, the great Hebrew lawgiver, and in all probability is of rabbinical origin:

When the prophet Músa—to whose spirit be peace!—was on earth, there lived near him a poor but remarkably religious man, who had for many years supported himself and his wife by the daily occupation of cutting wood for his richer neighbours, four small copper coins being the reward of his toil, which at best afforded the poor couple but a scanty meal after his day's exertions. One morning the Prophet Músa, passing the woodcutter, was thus addressed: "O Músa! Prophet of the Most High! behold I labour each day for my coarse and scanty meal. May it please thee, O Prophet! to make petition for me to our gracious God, that he may, in his mercy, grant me at once the whole supply for my remaining years, so that I shall enjoy one day of earthly happiness, and then, with my wife, be transferred to the place of eternal rest." Músa promised, and made the required petition. His prayer was thus answered from Mount Tor: "This man's life is long, O Músa! Nevertheless, if he be willing to surrender life when his supply is exhausted, tell him thy prayer is heard, the petition accepted, and the whole amount shall be found beneath his prayer-carpet after his morning prayers."

The woodcutter was satisfied when Músa told him the result of his petition, and, the first duties of the morning being performed, he failed not in looking for the promised gift, and to his surprise found a heap of silver coins in the place indicated. Calling his wife, he told her what he had acquired of the Lord through his holy prophet Músa, and they both agreed that it was very good to enjoy a short life of happiness on earth and depart in peace; although they could not help again and again recurring to the number of years on earth they had thus sacrificed. "We will make as many hearts rejoice as this the Lord's gift will permit," they both agreed; "and thus we shall secure in our future state the blessed abode promised to those who fulfil the commands of God in this life, since to-morrow it must close for us."

The day was spent in procuring and preparing provisions for the feast. The whole sum was expended on the best sorts of food, and the poor were made acquainted with the rich treat the woodcutter and his wife were cooking for their benefit. The food being cooked, allotments were made to each hungry applicant, and the couple reserved to themselves one good substantial meal, which was to be eaten only after the poor were all served and satisfied. It happened at the very moment they were seated to enjoy this their last meal, as they believed, a voice was heard, saying: "O friend! I have heard of your feast; I am late, yet it may be that you have still a little to spare, for I am hungry to my very heart. The blessing of God be on him who relieves my present sufferings from hunger!" The woodcutter and his wife agreed that it would be much better for them to go to Paradise with half a meal than to leave one fellow creature famishing on earth. So they shared their own portion with him who had none, and he went away from them rejoicing. "Now," said the happy pair, "we shall eat of our half-share with unmixed delight, and with thankful hearts. By to-morrow evening we shall be transferred to Paradise."

They had scarcely raised the savoury food to their mouths when a bewailing voice arrested their attention, and stayed the hands already charged with food. A poor creature who had not tasted food for two days moaned his piteous tale, in accents which drew tears from the woodcutter and his wife; their eyes met and the sympathy was mutual: they were more willing to depart for Paradise without the promised benefit of one earthly enjoyment, than suffer the hungry man to die from want of that meal they had before them. The dish was promptly tendered to the unfortunate one, and the woodcutter and his wife consoled each other with reflecting that, as the time of their departure was now so near at hand, the temporary enjoyment of a meal was not worth one moment's consideration: "To-morrow we die; then of what consequence is it to us whether we depart with full or empty stomachs?"

And now their thoughts were set on the place of eternal rest. They slept, and arose to their morning orisons with hearts reposing humbly on their God, in the fullest expectation that this was their last day on earth. The prayer was concluded, and the woodcutter was in the act of rolling up his carpet, on which he had prostrated himself with gratitude, reverence, and love to his Creator, when he perceived a fresh heap of silver on the floor. He could scarcely believe but it was a dream. "How wonderful art thou, O God!" cried he. "This is thy bounteous gift, that I may indeed enjoy one day before I quit this earth." And Músa, when he came to him, was satisfied with the goodness and the power of God. But he retired again to the Mount, to inquire of God the cause of the woodcutter's respite. The reply which Músa received was as follows: "That man has faithfully applied the wealth given in answer to his petition. He is worthy to live out his numbered years on earth who, receiving my bounty, thought not of his own enjoyments whilst his fellow men had wants which he could supply." And to the end of the wood-cutter's long life God's bounty lessened not in substance; neither did the pious man relax in his charitable duties of sharing with the indigent all that he had, and with the same disregard of his own enjoyments.

PRECOCIOUS SAGACITY OF SOLOMON

Commentators on the Kurán state that while Solomon was still a mere youth he frequently upset the decisions of the judges in open court, and they became displeased with his interference, though they could not but confess to themselves that his judgment was always superior to theirs. Having prevailed upon King David to permit the sagacity of his son to be publicly tested, they plied him with what they deemed very difficult questions, which, however, were hardly uttered before he answered them correctly, and at length they became silent and shame-faced. Then Solomon rose and said (I take the paragraph which follows from the English translation of Dr. Weil's interesting work, *The Bible, the Korán, and the Talmud*, 1846, p. 165 f.):

"You have exhausted yourselves in subtleties, in the hope of manifesting your superiority over me before this great assembly. Permit me now also to put to you a very few simple questions, the solution of which needs no manner of study, but only a little intellect and understanding. Tell me: What is Everything, and what is Nothing? Who is Something, and who is less than Nothing?" Solomon waited long, and when the judge whom he had addressed was not able to answer, he said: "Allah, the Creator, is Everything, and the world, the creature, is Nothing. The believer is Something, but the hypocrite is less than Nothing." Turning to another, Solomon inquired: "Which are the most in number, and which are the fewest? What is the sweetest, and what is the most bitter?" But as the second judge also was unable to find proper answers to these questions, Solomon said: "The most numerous are the doubters, and they who possess a perfect assurance of faith are fewest in number. The sweetest is the possession of a virtuous wife, excellent children, and a respectable competency; but a wicked wife, undutiful children, and poverty are the most bitter." Finally Solomon put this question to a third judge: "Which is the vilest, and which is the most beautiful? What is the most certain, and what is the least so?" But these questions also remained unanswered until Solomon said: "The vilest thing is when a believer apostasises, and the most beautiful is when a sinner repents. The most certain thing is death and the last judgment, and the most uncertain, life and the fate of the soul after the resurrection. You perceive," he continued, "it is not the oldest and most learned that are always the wisest. True wisdom is neither of years nor of learned books, but only of Allah, the All-wise."

The judges were full of admiration, and unanimously lauded the unparalleled sagacity of the future ruler of Israel.—The Queen of Sheba's "hard questions" (already referred to, p. 218) were probably of a somewhat similar nature. Such "wit combats" seem to have been formerly common at the courts and palaces of Asiatic monarchs and nobles; and a curious, but rather tedious, example is furnished in the *Thousand and One Nights*, in the story of Abú al-Husn and his slave Tawaddad, which will be found in vol. iv of Mr. John Payne's and vol. v of Sir R. F. Burton's complete translations.

SOLOMON AND THE SERPENT'S PREY

A curious popular tradition of Solomon, in French verse, is given by M. Emile Blémont in *La Tradition* (an excellent journal of folklore, etc., published at Paris) for March 1889, p. 73: Solomon, we are informed, in very ancient times ruled over all beings [on the earth], and, if we may believe our ancestors, was the King of magicians. One day Man appeared before him, praying to be delivered from the Serpent, who ever lay in wait to devour him. "That I cannot do," said Solomon; "for he is my preceptor, and I have given him the privilege to eat whatsoever he likes best." Man responded: "Is that so? Well, let him gorge himself without stint; but he has no right to devour me." "So you say," quoth Solomon; "but are you sure of it?" Said Man: "I call the light to witness it; for I have the high honour of being in this world superior to all other creatures." At these words the whole of the assembly [of animals] protested. "And I!" said the Eagle, with a loud voice, as he alighted on a rock. "Corcorico!" chanted the Cock. The Monkey was scratching himself and admiring his grinning phiz in the water, which served him for a looking-glass. Then the Buzzard was beside himself [with rage]. And the Cuckoo was wailing. The Ass rolled over and over, crying: "Heehaw! how ugly Man is!" The Elephant stamped about with his heavy feet, his trumpet raised towards the heavens. The Bear assumed dignified airs, while the Peacock was showing off his wheel-like tail. And in the distance the Lion was majestically exhaling his disdain in a long sigh.

Then said Solomon: "Silence! Man is right: is he not the only beast who gets drunk at all seasons? But, to accede to his request, as an honest prince, I ought to be able to give the Serpent something preferable, or at least equal, to his favourite prey. Therefore hear my decision: Let the Gnat—the smallest of animals—find out in what creature circulates the most exquisite blood in the world; and that creature shall belong to you, O Serpent. And I summon you all to appear here, without fail, on this day twelvemonths hence, that the Gnat may tell us the result of his experiments."

The year past, the Gnat—subtle taster—was slowly winging his way back when he met the Swallow. "Good day, friend Swallow," says he. "Good day,

139

friend Gnat," replies the Swallow. "Have you accomplished your mission?" "Yes, my dear," responded the Gnat. "Well, what is then the most delicious blood under the heavens?" "My dear, it is that of Man." "What!—of him? I haven't heard. Speak louder." The Gnat was beginning to raise his voice, and opened his mouth to speak louder, when the Swallow quickly fell upon him and nipped off his tongue in the middle of a word. Spite of this, the Gnat continued his way, and arrived next day at the general assembly, where Solomon was already seated. But when the king questioned him, he had no means of proving his zeal. Said the king: "Give us thy report." "Bizz! bizz! bizz!" said the poor fellow. "Speak out, and let thy talk be clear," quoth the king. "Bizz! bizz! bizz!" cried the other again. "What's the matter with the little stupid?" exclaimed the king, in a rage. Here the Swallow intervened in a sweet and shrill tone: "Sire, it is not his fault. Yesterday we were flying side by side, when suddenly he became mute. But, by good luck, down there about the sacred springs, before he met with this misfortune, he told me the result of his investigations. May I depone in his name?" "Certainly," replied Solomon. "What is the best blood, according to thy companion?" "Sire, it is the blood of the Frog."

Everybody was astonished: the Gnat was mad with rage. "I hold," said Solomon, "to all that I promised. Friend Serpent, renounce Man henceforth—that food is bad. The Frog is the best meat; so eat as much Frog as you please." So the Serpent had to submit to his deplorable lot, and I leave you to think how the bile was stirred up within the rascally reptile. As the Swallow was passing him—mocking and sneering—the Serpent darted at her, but the bird swiftly passed beyond reach, and with little effort cleft the vast blue sky and ascended more than a league. The Serpent snapped only the end of the bird's tail, and that is how the Swallow's tail is cloven to this day; but, so far from finding it an inconvenience, she is thereby the more lively and beautiful. And Man, knowing what he owes to her, is full of gratitude. She has her abode under the eaves of our houses, and good luck comes wherever she nestles. Her gay cries, sweet and shrill, rouse the springtide. Is she not a bird-fairy—a good angel? On the other hand, the crafty Serpent hardly knows how to get out of the mud, and drags himself along, climbing and climbing; while the Swallow, free and light, flies in the gold of the day. For she is faithful Friendship—the little sister of Love.

M. Blémont does not say in what part of France this legend is current, but it is doubtless of Asiatic extraction—whether Jewish or Muhammedan.

THE CAPON-CARVER

A variant of the same incident occurs in No. IV of M. Emile Legrand's *Receuil de Contes Populaires Grecs* (Paris, 1881), where a prince sets out in quest of some maiden acquainted with "figurative language," whom he

140

would marry. He comes upon an old man and his daughter, and overhears the latter address her father in metaphorical terms, which she has to explain to the old man, at which the prince is highly pleased, and following them to their hut desires and obtains shelter for the night. "As there was not much to eat, the old man bade them kill a cock, and when it was roasted it was placed on the table. Then the young girl got up and carved the fowl. She gave the head to her father; the body to her mother; the wings to the prince; and the flesh to the children. The old man, seeing his daughter divide the fowl in this manner, turned and looked at his wife, for he was ashamed to speak of it before the stranger. But when they were going to bed he said to his daughter: 'Why, my child, did you cut up the fowl so badly? The stranger has gone starving to bed.' 'Ah, my father,' she replied, 'you have not understood it; wait till I explain: I gave the head to you, because you are the head of this house; to my mother I gave the body, because, like the body of a ship, she has borne us in her sides; I gave the wings to the stranger, because to-morrow he will take his flight and go away; and lastly, to us the children I gave the bits of flesh, because we are the true flesh of the house. Do you understand it now, my good father?'"— The remainder of the story is so droll that, though but remotely related to the Capon-carver, I think it worth while to give a translation of it:

"As the room wherein the girl spoke with her father was adjacent to that in which the stranger lay, the latter heard all that she said. Great was his joy, and he said to himself that he would well like for wife one who could thus speak figurative language. And when it was day he rose, took his leave, and went away. On his return to the palace he called a servant and gave him in a sack containing 31 loaves, a whole cheese, a cock stuffed and roasted, and a skin of wine; and indicating to him the position of the cabin where he had put up, told him to go there and deliver these presents to a young girl of 18 years.

"The servant took the sack and set out to execute the orders of his master.—But, pardon me, ladies [quoth the story-teller], if I have forgotten to tell you this: Before setting out, the servant was ordered by the prince to say these words to the young girl: 'Many, many compliments from my master. Here is what he sends you: the month has 31 days; the moon is full; the chorister of the dawn is stuffed and roasted; the he-goat's skin is stretched and full.'—The servant then went towards the cabin, but on the way he met some friends. 'Good day, Michael. Where are you going with this load, and what do you carry?' 'I'm going over the mountain to a cabin where my master sends me.' 'And what have you got in there? The smell of it makes our mouths water.' 'Look, here are loaves, cheese, wine, and a roasted cock. It's a present which my master has given me to take to a poor girl.' 'O indeed, simpleton! Sit down, that we may eat a little. How should thy master ever know of it?' Down they sat on the green mountain sward and fell-to. The more they ate the keener their appetites grew, so that our fine fellows cleared away 13 loaves, half the cheese, the whole cock, and nearly half the wine. When they had eaten and drank their fill, the servant took up the remainder and resumed his way to the cabin. Arrived, he found the young girl, gave her the presents, and repeated the words which his master had ordered him to say.

"The girl took what he brought and said to him: 'You shall say to your master: "Many, many compliments. I thank him for all that he has sent me; but the month has only 18 days, the moon is only half full, the chorister of dawn was not there, and the he-goat's skin is lank and loose. But, to please the partridge, let him not beat the sow."' (That is to say, there were only 18 loaves, half a cheese, no roasted cock, and the wine-skin was scarcely half full; but that, to please the young girl, he was not to beat the servant, who had not brought the gift entire.)

"The servant left and returned to the palace. He repeated to the prince what the young girl had said to him, except the last clause, which he forgot. Then the prince understood all, and caused another servant to give the rogue a good beating. When the culprit had received such a caning that his skin and bones were sore, he cried out: 'Enough, prince, my master! Wait until I tell you another thing that the young girl said to me, and I have forgotten to tell you.' 'Come, what have you to say?—be quick.' 'Master, the young girl added, "But, to please the partridge, let him not beat the sow."' 'Ah, blockhead!' said the prince to him. 'Why did you not tell me this before? Then you would not have tasted the cane. But so be it.' A few days later the prince married the young girl, and fêtes and great rejoicings were held."

THE FOX AND THE BEAR

In no other version of this fable does the Fox take a stone with him when he enters one of the buckets and then throw it away—nor indeed does he go into the bucket at all; he simply induces the other animal to descend into the well, in order to procure the "fine cheese." La Fontaine gives a variant of the fable, in which a fox goes down into a well with the same purpose, and gets out by asking a wolf to come down and feast on the "cheese": as the wolf descends in one bucket he draws up the fox in the other one, and so the wolf, like Lord Ullin, is "left lamenting."[114] M. Bérenger-Féraud thinks this version somewhat analogous to a fable in his French collection of popular Senegambian Tales,[115] of the Clever Monkey and the Silly Wolf, of which, as it is short, I may offer a free translation, as follows:

A proud lion was pacing about a few steps forward, then a side movement, then a grand stride backward. A monkey on a tree above imitates the movements, and his antics enrage the lion, who warns him to desist. The

142

monkey however goes on with the caricature, and at last falls off the tree, and is caught by the lion, who puts him into a hole in the ground, and having covered it with a large stone goes off to seek his mate, that they should eat the monkey together. While he is absent a wolf comes to the spot, and is pleased to hear the monkey cry, for he had a grudge against him. The wolf asks why the monkey cries. "I am singing," says the monkey, "to aid my digestion. This is a hare's retreat, and we two ate so heartily this morning that I cannot move, and the hare is gone out for some medicine. We have lots of more food." "Let me in," says the wolf; "I am a friend." The monkey, of course, readily consents, and just as the wolf enters he slips out, and, replacing the stone, imprisons the wolf. By-and-by the lion and his mate come up. "We shall have monkey to-day," says the lion, lifting the stone—"faith! we shall only have wolf after all!" So the poor wolf is instantly torn into pieces, while the clever monkey once more overhead re-enacts his lion-pantomime.[116]

Strange as it may appear, there is a variant of the fable of the Fox and the Bear current among the negroes in the United States, according to *Uncle Remus*, that most diverting collection. In No. XVI, "Brer Rabbit" goes down in a bucket into a well, and "Brer Fox" asks him what he is doing there. "O I'm des a fishing, Brer Fox," says he; and Brer Fox goes into the bucket while Brer Rabbit escapes and chaffs his comrade.

THE DESOLATE ISLAND

There is a tale in the *Gesta Romanorum* (ch. 74 of the text translated by Swan) which seems to have been suggested by the Hebrew parable of the Desolate Island, and which has passed into general currency throughout Europe: A dying king bequeaths to his son a golden apple, which he is to give to the greatest fool he can find. The young prince sets out on his travels, and after meeting with many fools, none of whom, however, he deemed worthy of the "prize," he comes to a country the king of which reigns only one year, and finds him indulging in all kinds of pleasure. He offers the king the apple, explaining the terms of his father's bequest, and saying that he considers him the greatest of all fools, in not having made a proper use of his year of sovereignty.—A common oral form of this story is to the effect that a court jester came to the bedside of his dying master, who told him that he was going on a very long journey, and the jester inquiring whether he had made due preparation was answered in the negative. "Then," said the fool, "prithee take my bauble, for thou art truly the greatest of all fools."

OTHER RABBINICAL LEGENDS AND TALES

As analogues, or variants, of incidents in several wide-spread European popular tales, other Hebrew legends are cited in some of my former books;

e.g.: The True Son, in *Popular Tales and Fictions*, vol. i, p. 14; Moses and the Angel (the ways of Providence: the original of Parnell's "Hermit"), vol. i, p. 25; a mystical hymn, "A kid, a kid, my Father bought," the possible original of our nursery cumulative rhyme of "The House that Jack built," vol. i, p. 291; the Reward of Sabbath observance, vol. i, p. 399; the Intended Divorce, vol. ii, p. 328, of which, besides the European variants there cited, other versions will be found in Prof. Crane's *Italian Popular Tales*: "The Clever Girl" and Notes; the Lost Camel, in *A Group of Eastern Romances and Stories*, p. 512. In *Originals and Analogues of some of Chaucer's 'Canterbury Tales'* (for the Chaucer Society) I have cited two curious Jewish versions of the Franklin's Tale, in the paper entitled "The Damsel's Rash Promise," pp. 315, 317. A selection of Hebrew Facetiæ is given at the end of the papers on Oriental Wit and Humour in the present volume (p. 117); and an amusing story, also from the Talmud, is reproduced in my *Book of Sindibád*, p. 103, *note*, of the Athenian and the witty Tailor; and in the same work, p. 340, *note*, reference is made to a Jewish version of the famous tale of the Matron of Ephesus. There may be more in these books which I cannot call to mind.

AN ARABIAN TALE OF LOVE

Lovers and madmen have such seething brains,
Such shaping fantasies, that apprehend
More than cool reason ever comprehends.
Midsummer Night's Dream.

Every land has its favourite tale of love: in France, that of Abelard and
Eloisa, in Italy, of Petrarch and Laura; all Europe has the touching tale of
Romeo and Juliet in common; and Muslims have the ever fresh tale of the
loves and sorrows of Majnún and Laylá. Of the ten or twelve Persian poems
extant on this old tale those by Nizámí, who died A.D. 1211, and Jámí, of
the 15th century, are considered as by far the best; though Hátifí's version
(*ob.* 1520) is highly praised by Sir William Jones. The Turkish poet Fazúlí
(*ob.* 1562) also made this tale the basis of a fine mystical poem, of which
Mr. Gibb has given some translated specimens—reproducing the original
rhythm and rhyme-movement very cleverly—in his *Ottoman Poems.* The
following is an epitome of the tale of Majnún and Laylá:

Kays (properly, Qays), the handsome son of Syd Omri, an Arab chief of
Yemen, becomes enamoured of a beauteous maiden of another tribe: a
damsel bright as the moon,[117] graceful as the cypress;[118] with locks dark as
night, and hence she was called Laylá;[119] who captivated all hearts, but
chiefly that of Kays. His passion is reciprocated, but soon the fond lovers
are separated. The family of Laylá remove to the distant mountains of
Nejd, and Kays, distracted, with matted locks and bosom bare to the
scorching sun, wanders forth into the desert in quest of her abode, causing
the rocks to echo his voice, constantly calling upon her name. His friends,
having found him in woeful plight, bring him home, and henceforth he is
called Majnún—that is, one who is mad, or frantic, from love. Syd Omri,
his father, finding that Majnún is deaf to good counsel—that nothing but
the possession of Laylá can restore him to his senses—assembles his
followers and departs for the abode of Laylá's family, and presenting
himself before the maiden's father, proposes in haughty terms the union of
his son with Laylá; but the offer is declined, on the ground that Syd Omri's
son is a maniac, and he will not give his daughter to a man bereft of his
senses; but should he be restored to his right mind he will consent to their
union. Indignant at this answer, Syd Omri returns home, and after his
friends had in vain tried the effect of love-philtres to make Laylá's father
relent, as a last resource they propose that Majnún should wed another
damsel, upon which the demented lover once more seeks the desert, where

they again find him almost at the point of death, and bring him back to his tribe.

Now the season of pilgrimage to Mecca draws nigh, and it is thought that a visit to the holy shrine and the waters of the Zemzem[120] might cure his frenzy. Accordingly Majnún, weak and helpless, is conveyed to Mecca in a litter. Most fervently his sorrowing father prays in the Kaába for his recovery, but all in vain, and they return home. Again Majnún escapes to the desert, whence his love-plaints, expressed in eloquent verse, find their way to Laylá, who contrives to reply to them, also in verse, assuring her lover of her own despair, and of her constancy.

One day a gallant young chief, Ibn Salám, chances to pass near the dwelling of Laylá, and, seeing the beauteous maiden among her companions, falls in love with her, and straightway asks her in marriage of her parents. Laylá's father does not reject the handsome and wealthy suitor, who scatters his gold about as if it were mere sand, but desires him to wait until his daughter is of proper age for wedlock, when the nuptials should be duly celebrated; and with this promise Ibn Salám departs.

Meanwhile, Noufal, the chief in whose land Majnún has taken up his abode, while hunting one day comes upon the wretched lover, and, struck with his appearance, inquires the cause of his distress. Noufal conceives a warm friendship for Majnún, and sends a messenger to Laylá's father to demand her in marriage with his friend. But the damsel's parent scornfully refused to comply, and Noufal then marches with his followers against him. A battle ensues, in which Noufal is victorious. The father of Laylá then comes to Noufal, and offers submission; but he declares that rather than consent to his daughter's union with Majnún he would put her to death before his face. Seeing the old man thus resolute, Noufal abandons his enterprise and returns to his own country.

And now Ibn Salám, having waited the appointed time, comes with his tribesmen to claim the hand of Laylá; and, spite of her tears and protestations, she is married to the wealthy young chief. Years pass on— weary years of wedded life to poor Laylá, whose heart is ever true to her wandering lover. At length a stranger seeks out Majnún, and tells him that his beloved Laylá wishes to have a brief interview with him, near her dwelling. At once the frantic lover speeds towards the rendezvous; but when Laylá is informed of his arrival, her sense of duty overcomes the passion of her life, and she resolves to forego the dangerous meeting, and poor Majnún departs without having seen his darling. Henceforth he is a constant dweller in the desert, having for his companions the beasts and birds of the wilderness—his clothes in tatters, his hair matted, his body wasted to a shadow, his bare feet lacerated with thorns. After the lapse of many more years the husband of Laylá dies, and the beautiful widow

146

passes the prescribed period of separation (*'idda*),[121] after which Majnún hastens to embrace his beloved. Overpowered by the violence of their emotions, both are for a space silent; at length Laylá addresses Majnún in tender accents; but when he finds voice to reply it is evident that the reaction has completely extinguished the last spark of reason: Majnún is now a hopeless maniac, and he rushes from the arms of Laylá and seeks the desert once more. Laylá never recovered from the shock occasioned by this discovery. She pined away, and with her last breath desired her mother to convey the tidings of her death to Majnún, and to assure him of her constant, unquenchable affection. When Majnún hears of her death he visits her tomb, and, exhausted with his journey and many privations, he lays himself down on the turf that covered her remains, and dies—the victim of pure, ever-during love.

Possibly, readers of a sentimental turn—oft inclined to the "melting" mood—may experience a kind of pleasing sadness in perusing a rhythmical prose translation of the passage in Nizámí's poem in which

Majnún bewails the Death of Laylá

When Zayd,[122] with heart afflicted, heard that in the silent tomb that moon[123] had set, he wept and mourned, and sadly flowed his tears. Who in this world is free from grief and tears? Then, clothed in sable garments, like one oppressed who seeks redress, he, agitated, and weeping like a vernal cloud, hastened to the grave of Laylá; but, as he o'er it hung, ask not how swelled his soul with grief; while from his eyes the tears of blood incessant flowed, and from his sight and groans the people fled. Sometimes he mourned with grief so deep and sad that from his woe the sky became obscure. Then from the tomb of that fair flower he to the desert took his way. There sought the wanderer from the paths of man him whose night was now in darkness veiled, as that bright lamp was gone; and, seated near him, weeping and sighing, he beat his breast and struck upon the earth his head. When Majnún saw him thus afflicted he said: "What has befallen thee, my brother, that thy soul is thus overpowered? and why so pale that cheek? and why these sable robes?" He thus replied: "Because that fortune now has changed: a sable stream has issued from the earth, and even death has burst its iron gates; a storm of hail has on the garden poured, and not a leaf of all our rose-bower now remains. The moon has fallen from the firmament, and prostrate on the mead that waving cypress lies! Laylá was, but from the world has now departed; and from the wound thy love had caused she died."

Scarce had these accents reached his listening ear e'er, senseless, Majnún fell as one by lightning struck. A short time, fainting, thus he lay; recovered, then he raised his head to heaven and thus exclaimed: "O merciless! what fate severe is this on one so helpless? Why such wrath?

147

Why blast a blade of grass with lightning, and on the ant [*i.e.* himself] thy power exert? One ant and a thousand pains of hell, when one single spark would be enough! Why thus with blood the goblet crown, and all my hopes deceive? I burned with flames that by that lamp were fed; and by that breath which quenched its light I too expire." Thus, like Asra, did he complain, and, like Wamik, traversed on every side the desert,[124] his heart broken, and his garments rent; while, as the beasts gazed on him, his tears so constant flowed, that in their eyes the tear-drop stood; and like a shadow Zayd his footsteps still pursued. When, weeping and mourning, Majnún thus o'er many a hill and many a vale had passed, as grief his path directed, he wished to view the tomb of all he loved; and then inquired of Zayd where was the spot that held her grave, and where the turf that o'er it grew.

But soon as to the tomb he came, struck with its view, his senses fled. Recovering, then he thus exclaimed: "O Heaven! what shall I do, or what resource attempt, as like a lamp I waste away? Alas! that heart-enslaver was all that in this world I prized: and now, alas! in wrath, dire Fate with ruthless blow has snatched her from me. In my hand I held a lovely flower; the wind came and scattered all its leaves. I chose a cypress that in the garden graceful grew; but soon the wind of fate destroyed it. Spring bade a blossom bloom; but Fortune would not guard the flower. A group of lilies I preserved, pure as the thoughts that in my bosom rose; but one unjust purloined them. I sowed, but he the harvest reaped."

Then, resting within the tomb his head, he mourning wept, and said: "O lovely floweret, struck by autumn's blast, and from this world departed ere thou knewest it! A garden once in bloom, but now laid waste! O fruit matured, but not enjoyed! To earth's mortality can such as thou be subject, and such as thou within the darkness of the tomb repose? And where is now that mole which seemed a grain of musk?[125] And where those eyes soft as the gazelle's? Where those ruby lips? And where those curling ringlets? In what bright hues is now thy form adorned? And through the love of whom does now thy lamp consume? To whose fond eyes are now thy charms displayed? And whom to captivate do now thy tresses wave? Beside the margin of what stream is now that cypress seen? And in what bower is now the banquet spread? Ah, can such as thou have felt the pangs of death, and be reclined within this narrow cave?[126] But o'er thy cell I mourn, as thou wast all I loved; and ere my grief shall cease, the grave shall be my friend. Thou wast agitated like the sand of the desert; but now thou reposest as the water of the lake. Thou, like the moon, hast disappeared; but, though unseen, the moon is still the same; and now, although thy form from me is hid, still in my breast remains the loved remembrance. Though far removed beyond my aching sight, still is thy image in my heart beheld. Thy form is now departed, but grief eternal fills its place. On thee my soul was fixed, and never will thy memory be forgot. Thou art gone, and from this wilderness escaped, and now reposest in the bowers of Paradise. I, too, after some little time will shake off these bonds, and there rejoin thee. Till then, faithful to the love I vowed, around thy tomb my footsteps will I bend. Until I come to thee within this narrow cell, pure be thy shroud! May Paradise everlasting be thy mansion blest! And be thy soul received into the mercy of thy God! And may thy spirit by his grace be vivified to all eternity!"

"This," methinks I hear some misogynist exclaim, after reading it—"this is rank nonsense—it is stark lunacy!" And so it is, perhaps. At all events, these impassioned words are supposed to be uttered by a poor youth who had gone mad from love. Our misogynist—and may I venture to include the experienced married man?—will probably retort, that all love between young folks is not only folly but sheer madness; and he will be the more confirmed in this opinion when he learns that, according to certain grave Persian writers, Laylá was really of a swarthy visage, and far from being the beauty her infatuated lover conceived her to be: thus verifying the dictum of our great dramatist, in the ever-fresh passage where he makes "the lunatic, the lover, and the poet" to be "of imagination all compact," the lover seeing "Helen's beauty in the brow of Egypt!"—Notwithstanding all this, the ancient legend of Laylá and Majnún has proved an inspiring theme to more than one great poet of Persia, during the most flourishing period of the literature of that country—for which let us all be duly thankful.

ADDITIONAL NOTES

'WAMIK AND ASRA,'

This is the title of an ancient Persian poem, composed in the reign of Núshírván, A.D. 531-579, of which some fragments only now remain, incorporated with an Arabian poem. In 1833, Von Hammer published a German translation, at Vienna: *Wamik und Asra; das ist, Glühende und die Blühende. Das älteste Persische romantische Gedicht. Jun fünftelsaft abgezogen*, von Joseph von Hammer (Wamik and Asra; that is, the Glowing and the Blowing. The most ancient Persian Romantic Poem. Transfer the Fifth, etc.) The hero and heroine, namely, Wamik and Asra, are personifications of the two great principles of heat and vegetation, the vivifying energy of heaven and the correspondent productiveness of earth.—This noble poem is the subject of a very interesting article in the *Foreign Quarterly Review*, vol. xviii, 1836-7, giving some of the more striking passages in English verse, of which the following may serve as a specimen:

'The Blowing One' Asra was justly named,
For she, in mind and form, a blossom stood;

149

Of beauty, youth, and grace divinely framed,
Of holiest spirit, filled with heavenly good.
The Spring, when warm, in fullest splendour showing,
Breathing gay wishes to the inmost core
Of youthful hearts, and fondest influence throwing,
Yet veiled its bloom, her beauty's bloom before;
For her the devotee his very creed forswore.
Her hair was bright as hyacinthine dyes;
Her cheek was blushing, sheen as Eden's rose;
The soft narcissus tinged her sleeping eyes,
And white her forehead, as the lotus shows
'Gainst Summer's earliest sunbeams shimmering fair.

A curious story is related by Dawlat Sháh regarding this poem, which bears a close resemblance to the story of the destruction of the Alexandrian Library, by order of the fanatical khalíf 'Umar: One day when Amír Abdullah Tahir, governor of Khurasán under the Abbasside khalífs, was giving audience, a person laid before him a book, as a rare and valuable present. He asked: "What book is this?" The man replied: "It is the story of Wamik and Asra." The Amír observed: "We are the readers of the Kurán, and we read nothing except that sacred volume, and the traditions of the Prophet, and such accounts as relate to him, and we have therefore no use for books of this kind. They are besides compositions of infidels, and the productions of worshippers of fire, and are therefore to be rejected and contemned by us." He then ordered the book to be thrown into the water, and issued his command that whatever books could be found in the kingdom which were the composition of the Persian infidels should be immediately burnt.

ANOTHER FAMOUS ARABIAN LOVER

Scarcely less celebrated than the story of Majnún and Laylá—among the Arabs, at least—is that of the poet Jamíl and the beauteous damsel Buthayna. It is said that Jamíl fell in love with her while he was yet a boy, and on attaining manhood asked her in marriage, but her father refused. He then composed verses in her honour and visited her secretly at Wádi-'l Kura, a delightful valley near Medína, much celebrated by the poets. Jamíl afterwards went to Egypt, with the intention of reciting to Abdu-'l Azíz Ibn Marwán a poem he had composed in his honour. This governor admitted Jamíl into his presence, and, after hearing his eulogistic verses and rewarding him generously, he asked him concerning his love for Buthayna, and was told of his ardent and painful passion. On this Abdu-'l Azíz promised to unite Jamíl to her, and bade him stay at Misr (Cairo), where he assigned him a habitation and furnished him with all he required. But Jamíl died there shortly after, A.H. 82 (A.D. 701).

The following narrative is given in the *Kitabal-Aghání*, on the authority of the famous poet and philologist Al-Asma'í, who flourished in the 8th century:

A person who was present at the death of Jamíl in Egypt relates that the poet called him and said: "If I give you all I leave after me, will you perform one thing which I shall enjoin you?" "By Allah, yes," said the other. "When I am dead," said Jamíl, "take this cloak of mine and put it aside, but keep everything else for yourself. Then go to Buthayna's tribe, and when you are near them, saddle this camel of mine and mount her; then put on my cloak and rend it, and mounting on a hill, shout out these verses: 'A messenger hath openly proclaimed the death of Jamíl. He hath now a dwelling in Egypt from which he will never return. There was a time when, intoxicated with love, he trained his mantle proudly in the fields and palm-groves of Wádi-'l Kura! Arise, Buthayna! and lament aloud: weep for the best of all thy lovers!'" The man did what Jamíl ordered, and had scarcely finished the verses when Buthayna came forth, beautiful as the moon when it appears from behind a cloud. She was muffled in a cloak, and on coming up to him said: "Man, if what thou sayest be true, thou hast killed me; if false, thou hast dishonoured me!" [*i.e.* by associating her name with that of a strange man, still alive.] He replied: "By Allah! I only tell the truth," and he showed her Jamíl's mantle, on seeing which she uttered a loud cry and smote her face, and the women of the tribe gathered around, weeping with her and lamenting her lover's death. Her strength at length failed her, and she swooned away. After some time she revived, and said [in verse]: "Never for an instant shall I feel consolation for the loss of Jamíl! That time shall never come. Since thou art dead, O Jamíl, son of Mamar! the pains of life and its pleasures are alike to me." And quoth the lover's messenger: "I never saw man or woman weep more than I saw that day."— Abridged from Ibn Khallikan's great Biographical Dictionary as translated by Baron De Slane, vol. i, pp. 331-326.

APOCRYPHAL LIFE OF ESOP,
THE FABULIST

The origin of the Beast-Fable is still a vexed question among scholars, some of whom ascribe it to the doctrine of metempsychosis, or the transmigration of human souls into different animal forms; others, again, are of the opinion that beasts and birds were first adopted as characters of fictitious narratives, in order to safely convey reproof or impart wholesome counsel to the minds of absolute princes, who would signally resent "plain speaking."[127] Several nations of antiquity—notably the Greeks, the Hindús, the Egyptians—have been credited with the invention of the beast-fable, and there is no reason to believe that it may not have been independently devised in different countries. It is very certain, however, that Esop was not the inventor of this kind of narrative in Greece, while those fables ascribed to him, which have been familiar to us from our nursery days, are mostly spurious, and have been traced to ancient Oriental sources. The so-called Esopic apologue of the Lion and the House is found in an Egyptian papyrus preserved at Leyden.[128] Many of them are quite modern *rechauffés* of Hindú apologues, such as the Milkmaid and her Pot of Milk, which gave rise to our popular saying, "Don't count your chickens until they be hatched." Nevertheless, genuine fables of Esop were current in Athens at the best period of its literary history, though it does not appear that they existed in writing during his lifetime. Aristophanes represents a character in one of his plays as learning Esop's fables from oral recitation. When first reduced to writing they were in prose, and Socrates is said to have turned some of them into verse, his example being followed by Babrius, amongst others, of whose version but few fables remain entire. The most celebrated of his Latin translators is Phædrus, who takes care to inform us that

> If any thoughts in these Iambics shine,
> The invention's Esop's, and the verse is mine.[129]

Little is authentically known regarding the career of the renowned fabulist, who is supposed to have been born about B.C. 620, and, as in the case of Homer, various places are assigned as that of his nativity--Samos, Sardis, Mesembria in Thrace, and Cotiæium in Phrygia. He is said to have been brought as a slave to Athens when very young, and after serving several masters was enfranchised by Iadmon, the Samian. His death is thus related by Plutarch: Having gone to Delphos, by the order of Crœsus, with a large

152

quantity of gold and silver, to offer a costly sacrifice to Apollo and to distribute a considerable sum among the inhabitants, a quarrel arose between him and the Delphians, which induced him to return the money, and inform the king that the people were unworthy of the liberal benefaction he had intended for them. The Delphians, incensed, charged him with sacrilege, and, having procured his condemnation, precipitated him from a rock and caused his death.--The popular notion that Esop was a monster of ugliness and deformity is derived from a "Life" of the fabulist, prefixed to a Greek collection of fables purporting to be his, said to have been written by Maximus Planudes, a monk of the 14th century, which, however apocryphal, is both curious and entertaining, from whatever sources the anecdotes may have been drawn.

According to Planudes,[130] Esop was born at Amorium, in the Greater Phrygia, a slave, ugly exceedingly: he was sharp-chinned, snub-nosed, bull-necked, blubber-lipped, and extremely swarthy (whence his name, *Ais-ôpos*, or *Aith-ôpos*: burnt-face, blackamoor); pot-bellied, crook-legged, and crook-backed; perhaps uglier even than the Thersites of Homer; worst of all, tongue-tied, obscure and inarticulate in his speech; in short, everything but his mind seemed to mark him out for a slave. His first master sent him out to dig one day. A husbandman having presented the master with some fine fresh figs, they were given to a slave to be set before him after his bath. Esop had occasion to go into the house; meanwhile the other slaves ate the figs, and when the master missed them they accused Esop, who begged a moment's respite: he then drank some warm water and caused himself to vomit, and as he had not broken his fast his innocence was thus manifest. The same test discovered the thieves, who by their punishment illustrated the proverb:

> Whoso against another worketh guile
> Thereby himself doth injure unaware.[131]

Next day the master goes to town. Esop works in the field, and entertains with his own food some travellers who had lost their way, and sets them on the right road again. They are really priests of Artemis, and having received their blessing he falls asleep, and dreams that Tychê (*i.e.* Fortune) looses his tongue, and gives him eloquence. Waking, he finds he can say *bous, onos, dikella*, (ox, ass, mattock). This is the reward of piety, for "well-doing is full of good hopes." Zenas, the overseer, is rebuked by Esop for beating a slave. This is the first time he has been heard to speak distinctly. Zenas goes to his master and accuses Esop of having blasphemed him and the gods, and is given Esop to sell or give away as he pleases. He sells him to a trader for three obols (4½d.), Esop pleading that, if useless for aught else, he will do for a bugbear to keep his children quiet. When they arrive home the little ones begin to cry. "Was I not right?" quoth Esop, and the other slaves think he has been bought to avert the Evil Eye.

The merchant sets out for Asia with all his house-hold. Esop is offered the lightest load, as being a raw recruit. From among the bags, beds, and baskets he chooses a basket full of bread—"a load for two men." They laugh at his folly, but let him have his will, and he staggers under the burden to the wonder of his master. But at the first halt for *ariston*, or breakfast, the basket is half-emptied, and by the evening wholly so, and then Esop marches triumphantly ahead, all commending his wit. At Ephesus the merchant sells all his slaves, excepting a musician, a scribe, and Esop. Thence he goes to Samos, where he puts new garments on the two former (he had none left for Esop), and sets them out for sale, Esop between them. Xanthus, the philospher, lived at Samos. He goes to the slave market, and, seeing the three, praises the dealer's cunning in making the two look handsomer than they were by contrast with the ugly one. Asking the scribe and the musician what they know, their answer is, "Everything," upon which Esop laughs. The price of the musician (1000 obols, or six guineas) and of the scribe (three times that sum) prevents the philosopher from buying them, and he turns to Esop to see what he is made of. He gives him the customary salutation, "Khaire!" (Rejoice). "I wasn't grieving," retorts Esop. "I greet thee," says Xanthus. "And I thee," replies Esop. "What are thou?" "Black." "I don't mean that, but in what sort of place wast thou born?" "My mother didn't tell me whether in the second floor or the cellar." "What can you do?" "Nothing." "How?" "Why, these fellows here say they know how to do everything, and they haven't left me a single thing." "By Jove," cries Xanthus, "he has answered right well; for there is no man who knows everything. That was why he laughed, it is clear." In the end, Xanthus buys Esop for sixty obols (about 7s. 6d.) and takes him home, where his wife (who is "very cleanly") receives him only on sufferance.

One day Xanthus, meeting friends at the bath, sends Esop home to boil pease (idiomatically using the word in the singular), for his friends are coming to eat with him. Esop boils *one* pea and sets it before Xanthus, who tastes it and bids him serve up. The water is then placed on the table, and Esop justifies himself to his distracted master, who then sends him for four pig's feet. While they boil, Xanthus slyly abstracts one, and when Esop discovers this he takes it for a plot against him of the other slaves. He runs into the yard, cuts a foot from the pig feeding there, and tosses it into the pot. Presently the other foot is put back, and Esop is confounded to see *five* trotters on the boil. He serves them up, however, and when Xanthus asks him what the five mean he replies: "How many feet have two pigs?" Xanthus saying, "Eight," quoth Esop: "Then here are five, and the porker feeding below goes on three." On being reproached he urges: "But, master, there is no harm in doing a sum in addition and subtraction, is there?" For very shame Xanthus forbears whipping him.

One morning Xanthus gives a breakfast, for which Esop is sent to buy "the best and most useful." He buys tongues, and the guests (philosophers all)

154

have nothing else. "What could be better for man than tongue?" quoth Esop. Another time he is ordered to get "the worst and most worthless"; again he brings tongues, and again is ready with a similar defence.[132] A guest reviles him, and Esop retorts that he is "malicious and a busybody." On hearing this Xanthus commands him to find some one who is not a busybody. In the road Esop finds a simple soul and brings him home to his master, who persuades his wife to bear with him in anything he should pretend to do to her; if the guest is a busybody (or one who meddles) Esop will get a beating. The plan fails; for the good man continues eating and takes no notice of the wife-cuffing going on, and when his host seems about to burn her, he only asks leave to bring his own wife to be also placed on the pile.

At a symposium Xanthus takes too much wine, and in bravado wagers his house and all that it contains that he will drink up the waters of the sea. Out of this scrape Esop rescues him by suggesting that he should demand that all the rivers be stopped from flowing into the sea, for he did not undertake to drink them too, and the other party is satisfied.[133]

A party of scientific guests are coming to dinner one day, and Esop is set just within the door to keep out "all but the wise." When there is a knock at the door Esop shouts: "What does the dog shake?" and all save one go away in high dudgeon, thinking he means them; but this last answers: "His tail," and is admitted.

At a public festival an eagle carries off the municipal ring, and Esop obtains his freedom by order of the state for his interpretation of this omen—that some king purposes to annex Samos. This, it turns out, is Crœsus, who sends to claim tribute. Hereupon Esop relates his first fable, that of the Wolf, the Dog, and the Sheep, and, going on an embassy to Crœsus, that of the Grasshopper who was caught by the Locust-gatherer. He brings home "peace with honour." After this Esop travels over the world, showing his wisdom and wit. At Babylon he is made much of by the king. He then visits Egypt and confounds the sages in his monarch's behalf. Once more he returns to Greece, and at Delphi is accused of stealing a sacred golden bowl and condemned to be hurled from a rock. He pleads the fables of the Matron of Ephesus,[134] the Frog and the Mouse, the Beetle and the Eagle, the Old Farmer and his Ass-waggon, and others, but all is of no avail, and the villains break his neck.

Such are some of the apocryphal sayings and doings of Esop the fabulist— the manner of his death being the only circumstance for which there is any authority. The idea of his bodily deformity is utterly without foundation, and may have been adopted as a foil to his extraordinary shrewdness and wit, as exhibited in the anecdotes related of him by Planudes. That there was nothing uncouth in the person of Esop is evident from the fact that the

Athenians erected a fine statue of him, by the famed sculptor Lysippus.—
The Latin collection of the fables ascribed to Esop was first printed at
Rome in 1473 and soon afterwards translated into most of the languages of
Europe. About the year 1480 the Greek text was printed at Milan. From a
French version Caxton printed them in English at Westminster in 1484,
with woodcuts: "Here begynneth the Book of the subtyl History and Fables
of Esope. Translated out of Frenssche into Englissche, by William Caxton,"
etc. In this version Planudes' description of Esop's personal appearance is
reproduced[135] He was "deformed and evil shapen, for he had a great head,
large visage, long jaws, sharp eyes, a short neck, curb backed, great belly,
great legs, and large feet; and yet that which was worse, he was dumb and
could not speak; but, notwithstanding all this, he had a great wit and was
greatly ingenious, subtle in cavillection and joyous in words"—an
inconsistency which is done away in a later edition by the statement that
afterwards he found his tongue.—It is curious to find the Scottish poet
Robert Henryson (15th century), in one of the prologues to his metrical
versions of some of the Fables, draw a very different portrait of Esop.[136] He
tells us that one day in the midst of June, "that joly sweit seasoun," he went
alone to a wood, where he was charmed with the "noyis of birdis richt
delitious," and "sweit was the smell of flowris quhyte and reid," and,
sheltering himself under a green hawthorn from the heat of the sun, he fell
asleep:

> And, in my dreme, methocht come throw the schaw[137]
> The fairest man that ever befoir I saw.
>
> His gowne wes of ane claith als quhyte as milk,
> His chymeris[138] wes of chambelote purpour broun;
> His hude[139] of scarlet, bordourit[140] weill with silk,
> On hekellit-wyis,[141] untill his girdill doun;
> His bonat round, and of the auld fassoun,[142]
> His beird was quhyte, his ene was greit and gray,
> With lokker[143] hair, quilk ouer his schulderis lay.
>
> Ane roll of paper in his hand he bair,
> Ane swannis pen stikkand[144] under his eir,
> Ane inkhorne, with ane prettie gilt pennair,[145]
> Ane bag of silk, all at his belt can beir:
> Thus was he gudelie graithit[146] in his geir.
> Of stature large, and with ane feirfull[147] face;
> Evin quhair I lay, he came ane sturdie pace.

The Arabian sage Lokinan is represented by tradition to have been a black
slave, and of hideous appearance, from which, and from the identity of the
apologues in the Arabian collection that bears his name as the author with
the so-called Esopic fables, some writers have supposed that Esop and
Lokman are simply different names of one and the same individual. But

the fables ascribed to Lokman have been for the most part (if not indeed entirely) derived from the Greek; and there is no authority whatever that Lokman composed any apologues. Various traditions exist regarding Lokman's origin and history. It is said that he was an Ethiopian, and was sold as a slave to the Israelites during the reign of David. According to one version, he was a carpenter; another describes him as having been originally a tailor; while a third account states that he was a shepherd. If the Arabs may be credited, he was nearly related to the patriarch Job. Among the anecdotes which are recounted of his amiable disposition is the following: His master once gave him a bitter lemon to eat. Lokman ate it all, upon which his master, greatly astonished, asked him: "How was it possible for you to eat so unpalatable a fruit?" Lokman replied: "I have received so many favours from you, that it is no wonder I should once in my life eat a bitter melon from your hand." Struck with this generous answer, the master, it is said, immediately gave him his freedom.—A man of eminence among the Jews, observing a great crowd around Lokman, eagerly listening to his discourse, asked him whether he was not the black slave who lately tended the sheep of such a person, to which Lokman replying in the affirmative, "How was it possible," continued his questioner, "for thee to attain so exalted a degree of wisdom and piety?" Lokman answered: "By always speaking the truth; keeping my word; and never intermeddling in affairs that did not concern me."—Being asked from whom he had learned urbanity, he replied: "From men of rude manners, for whatever I saw in them that was disagreeable I avoided doing myself." And when asked from whom he had acquired his philosophy, he said: "From the blind, who never advance a step until they have tried the ground." Lokman is also credited with this apothegm: "Be a learned man, a disciple of the learned, or an auditor of the learned; at least, be a lover of knowledge and desirous of improvement."—In Persian and Turkish tales Lokman sometimes figures as a highly skilled physician, and "wise as Lokman" is proverbial throughout the Muhammedan world.

ADDITIONAL NOTE

DRINKING THE SEA DRY

The same jest is also found in *Aino Folk-Tales*, translated by Prof. Basil Hall Chamberlain, and published in the *Folk-Lore Journal*, 1888, as follows:

There was the Chief of the Mouth of the River and the Chief of the Upper Current of the River. The former was very vain-glorious, and therefore wished to put the latter to shame or to kill him by engaging him in an attempt to perform something impossible. So he sent for him and said: "The sea is a useful thing, in so far as it is the original home of the fish which come up the river. But it is very destructive in stormy weather, when it beats wildly upon the beach. Do you now drink it dry, so that there may be rivers and dry land only. If you cannot do so, then forfeit all your possessions." The other said, greatly to the vain-glorious man's surprise: "I accept the challenge." So, on their going down to the beach, the Chief of the Upper Current of the River took a cup and scooped up a little of the sea-water with it, drank a few drops, and said: "In the sea-water itself there is no harm. It is some of the rivers flowing into it that are poisonous. Do you, therefore, first close the mouths of all the rivers both in Aino-land and in Japan, and prevent them from flowing into the sea, and then I will undertake to drink the sea dry." Hereupon the Chief of the Mouth of the River felt ashamed, acknowledged his error, and gave all his treasures to his rival.

Such an idea as this of first "stopping the rivers" might well have been conceived independently by different peoples, but surely not by such a race so low in the scale of humanity as the Ainos, who must have got the story from the Japanese, who in their turn probably derived it from some Indian-Buddhist source—perhaps a version of the Book of Sindibád. Of course, the several European versions and variants have been copied out of one book into another, and independent invention is out of the question.

IGNORANCE OF THE CLERGY IN THE MIDDLE AGES

Orl. Whom ambles Time withal?

Ros. With a priest that lacks Latin; for he sleeps easily, because he cannot study, lacking the burden of lean and wasteful learning.—*As You Like It.*

During the 7th and 8th centuries the state of letters throughout Christian Europe was so low that very few of the bishops could compose their own discourses, and some of those Church dignitaries thought it no shame to publicly acknowledge their inability to write their own names. Numerous instances occur in the Acts of the Councils of Ephesus and Chalcedon of an inscription in these words: "I, ——, have subscribed by the hand of ——, because I cannot write"; and such a bishop having thus confessed that he could not write, there followed: "I, ——, whose name is underwritten, have therefore subscribed for him."

Alfred the Great—who was twelve years of age before a tutor could be found competent to teach him the alphabet—complained, towards the close of the 9th century, that "from the Humber to the Thames there was not a priest who understood the liturgy in his mother-tongue, or could translate the easiest piece of Latin"; and a correspondent of Abelard, about the middle of the 12th century, complimenting him upon a resort to him of pupils from all countries, says that "even Britain, distant as she is, sends her savages to be instructed by you."

Henri Etienne, in the Introduction to his Apology for Herodotus,[148] says that "the most brutish and blockish ignorance was to be found in friars' cowls, especially mass-mongering priests, which we are the less to wonder at, considering that which Menot twits them in the teeth withal, that instead of books there was nothing to be found in their chambers but a sword, or a long-bow, or a cross-bow, or some such weapon. But how could they send *ad ordos* such ignorant asses? You must note, sir, that they which examined them were as wise as woodcocks themselves, and therefore judged of them as penmen of pikemen and blind men of colours. Or were it that they had so much learning in their budgets as that they could make a shift to know their inefficiency, yet to pleasure those that recommended them they suffered them to pass. One is famous among the rest, who being asked by the bishop sitting at the table: 'Es tu dignus?' answered, 'No, my Lord, but I shall dine anon with your men.' For he thought that *dignus* (that is, worthy) signified to dine."

Etienne gives another example, which, however, belongs rather to the class of simpleton stories: A young man going to the bishop for admission into holy orders, to test his *learning*, was asked by the prelate, "Who was the father of the Four Sons of Aymon?"[149] and not knowing what answer to make, this promising candidate was refused as inefficient. Returning home, and explaining why he had not been ordained, his father told him that he must be an ass if he could not tell who was the father of the four sons of Aymon. "See, I pray thee," quoth he, "yonder is Great John, the smith, who has four sons; if a man should ask thee who was their father, wouldst thou not say it was Great John, the smith?" "Yes," said the brilliant youth; "now I understand it." Thereupon he went again before the bishop, and being asked a second time, "Who was the father of the Four Sons of Aymon?" he promptly replied: "Great John, the smith."[150]

The same author asks who but the churchmen of those days of ignorance corrupted and perverted the text of the New Testament? Thus, in the parable of the lost piece of money, *evertit domum*, "she overturned the house," was substituted for *everrit domum*, "she *swept* the house." And in the Acts of the Apostles, where Saul (or Paul) is described as being let down from the house on the wall of Damascus in a basket, for *demissus per sportam* was substituted *demissus per portam*, a correction which called forth a rather witty Latin epigram to this effect:

> This way the other day did pass
> As jolly a carpenter as ever was;
> So strangely skilful in his trade,
> That of a *basket* a *door* he made.

Among the many curious anecdotes told in illustration of the gross ignorance of the higher orders of the clergy in medieval times the two following are not the least amusing:

About the year 1330 Louis Beaumont was bishop of Durham. He was an extremely illiterate French nobleman, so incapable of reading that he could not, although he had studied them, read the bulls announced to the people at his consecration. During that ceremony the word "metropoliticæ" occurred. The bishop paused, and tried in vain to repeat it, and at last remarked: "Suppose that said." Then he came to "enigmate," which also puzzled him. "By St. Louis!" he exclaimed in indignation, "it could be no gentleman who wrote that stuff!"

Our second anecdote is probably more generally known: Andrew Forman, who was bishop of Moray and papal legate for Scotland, at an entertainment given by him at Rome to the Pope and cardinals, blundered so in his Latinity when he said grace that his Holiness and the cardinals lost their gravity. The disconcerted bishop concluded his blessing by giving "a' the fause carles to the de'il," to which the company, not understanding his Scotch Latinity, said "Amen!"

When such was the condition of the bishops, it is not surprising to find that few of the ordinary priests were acquainted with even the rudiments of the Latin tongue, and they consequently mumbled over masses which they did not understand. A rector of a parish, we are told, going to law with his parishioners about paving the church, cited these words, *Paveant illi, non paveam ego*, which, ascribing them to St. Peter, he thus construed: "They are to pave the church, not I"—and this was allowed to be good law by a judge who was himself an ecclesiastic.

We have an amusing example of the ignorance of the lower orders of churchmen during the "dark [ages" in No. xii of *A Hundred Mery Talys*, as follows: "The archdekyn of Essex, that had ben longe in auctorite, in a tyme of vysytacyon, whan all the prestys apperyd before hym, called aside iii. of the yonge prestys which were acusyd that they could not wel say theyr dyvyne service, and askyd of them, when they sayd mas, whether they sayd corpus meus or corpum meum. The fyrst prest sayde that he sayd corpus meus. The second sayd that he sayd corpum meum. And than he asked of the thyrd how he sayde; whyche answered and sayd thus: Sir, because it is so great a dout, and dyvers men be in dyvers opynyons, therfore, because I wolde be sure I wolde not offende, whan I come to the place I leve it clene out and say nothynge therfore. Wherfore the bysshoppe than openly rebuked them all thre. But dyvers that were present thought more defaut in hym, because he hym selfe beforetyme had admytted them to be prestys." And assuredly they were right in so thinking, and the worthy archdeacon (or bishop, as he is also styled), who had probably passed the three young men "for value received" from their fathers, should have refrained from publicly examining them afterwards.

The covetousness and irreverence of the churchmen in former times are well exemplified in another tale given in the same old jest-book, No. lxxi, which, with spelling modernised, goes thus: "Sometime there dwelled a priest in Stratford-on-Avon, of small learning, which undevoutly sang mass and oftentimes twice on one day. So it happened on a time, after his second mass was done in short space, not a mile from Stratford there met him divers merchantmen, which would have heard mass, and desired him to sing mass and he should have a groat, which answered them and said: 'Sirs, I will say mass no more this day; but I will say you two gospels for one groat, and that is dog-cheap for a mass in any place in England.'" The story-teller does not inform us whether the pious merchants accepted of the business-like compromise offered by "Mass John."

Hagiolatry was quite as much in vogue among the priesthood in medieval times as mariolatry has since been the special characteristic of the Romish Church, to the subordination (one might almost say, the suppression) of the only true object of worship; in proof of which, here is a droll anecdote from another early English collection, *Mery Tales, Wittie Questions, and Quicke Answeres, very pleasant to be readde* (No. cxix): "A friar, preaching to the people, extolled Saint Francis above confessors, doctors, virgins, martyrs, prophets—yea, and above one more than prophets, John the Baptist, and finally above the seraphical order of angels; and still he said, 'Yet let us go higher.' So when he could go no farther, except he should put Christ out of his place, which the good man was half afraid to do, he said aloud, 'And yet we have found no fit place for him.' And, staying a little while, he cried out at last, saying, 'Where shall we place the holy father?' A froward fellow standing among the audience,[151] said, 'If thou canst find none other, then set him here in my place, for I am weary,' and so he went his way."—This "froward fellow's" unexpected reply will doubtless remind the reader of the old man's remark in the mosque, about the "calling of Noah," *ante*.[152]

Probably not less than one third of the jests current in Europe in the 16th century turned on the ignorance of the Romish clergy—such, for instance, as that of the illiterate priest who, finding *salta per tria* (skip over three leaves) written at the foot of a page in his mass-book, deliberately jumped down three of the steps before the altar, to the great astonishment of the congregation; or that of another who, finding the title of the day's service indicated only by the abbreviation *Re.*, read the mass of the Requiem instead of the service of the Resurrection; or that of yet another, who being so illiterate as to be unable to pronounce readily the long words in his ritual always omitted them, and pronounced the word Jesus, which he said was much more devotional.

There is a diverting tale of a foolish curé of Brou, which is well worthy of reproduction, in *Les Contes; ou, les Nouvelles Récréations et Joyeux Devis*, by Bonaventure des Periers—one of the best story-books of the 16th century (Bonaventure succeeded the celebrated poet Clement Marot as *valet-de-chambre* to Margaret, queen of Navarre):

It happened that a lady of rank and importance, on her way to Châteaudun to keep there the festival of Easter, passed through Brou on Good Friday, about ten o'clock in the morning, and, wishing to hear service, she went into the church. When the curé came to the Passion he said it in his own peculiar manner, and made the whole church ring when he said, "*Quem, quæritis?*" But when it came to the reply, "*Jesum, Nazarenum,*"[153] he

162

spoke as low as he possibly could, and in this manner he continued the Passion. The lady, who was very devout and, for a woman, well-informed, in the Holy Scriptures [the reader will understand this was early in the 16th century], and attentive to ecclesiastical ceremonies, felt scandalised at this mode of chanting, and wished that she had never entered the church. She had a mind to speak to the curé, and tell him what she thought of it, and for this purpose sent for him to come to her after service. When he was come, "Monsieur le Curé," she said to him, "I don't know where you have learned to officiate on a day like this, when the people ought to be all humility. But to hear you perform the service is enough to drive away anybody's devotion." "How so, madame?" said the curé. "How so?" responded the lady. "You have said a Passion contrary to all rules of decency. When our Lord speaks you cry as if you were in the town-hall, and when it is Caiaphas, or Pilate, or the Jews, you speak softly like a young bride. Is this becoming in one like you? Are you fit to be a curé? If you had what you deserve, you would be turned out of your benefice, and then you would be made to know your fault." When the curé had very attentively listened to the good lady, "Is this what you have to say to me, madame?" said he. "By my soul! it is very true what you say, and the truth is, there are many people who talk of things which they do not understand. Madame, I believe I know my office as well as another, and beg all the world to know that God is as well served in this parish according to its condition as in any place within a hundred leagues of it. I know very well that the other curés chant the Passion quite differently. I could easily chant it like them if I would; but they don't understand their business at all. I should like to know if it becomes those rogues of Jews to speak as loud as our Lord? No, no, madame; rest assured that in my parish it is my will that God be master, and he shall be as long as I live, and let others do in their parishes according to their understanding."

This is another of Des Periers' comical tales at the expense of the clerical orders: There was a priest of a village who was as proud as might be because he had seen a little more than his Cato. And this made him set up his feathers and talk very grand, using words that filled his mouth in order to make people think him a great doctor. Even at confession he made use of terms which astonished the poor people. One day he was confessing a poor working man, of whom he asked: "Here, now, my friend, tell me, art thou not ambitious?" The poor man said, "No," thinking this was a word which belonged to great lords, and almost repented of having come to confess to this priest; for he had already heard that he was such a great clerk and that he spoke so grandly that nobody understood him, which he knew by the word *ambitious*; for although he might have heard it somewhere, yet he knew not at all what it meant. The priest went on to ask: "Art thou not a gourmand?" Said the labourer, who understood as little as before: "No." "Art thou not superbe" [proud]? "No." "Art thou not iracund" [passionate]? "No." The priest, seeing the man always answer, "No," was somewhat surprised. "Art thou not concupiscent?" "No." "And what are thou, then?" said the priest. "I am," said he, "a mason—here's my trowel."

Readers acquainted with the *fabliaux* of the minstrels (the Trouvères) of Northern France know that those light-hearted gentry very often launched their satirical shafts at the churchmen of their day. One of the *fabliaux* in Barbazan's collection relates how a doltish, thick-headed priest was officiating in his church on Good Friday, and when about to read the service for that day he discovered that he had lost his book-mark ("*mais il ot perdu ses festuz.*")[154] Then he began to go back and turn over the leaves, but until Ascension Day he found not the Passion service. And the assembled peasants fretted and complained that he made them fast too long, since it was time for the festival. "Had he but said them the service," interjects the *fableur*, "should I make you a longer story?" So much did they grumble on all sides, that the priest began on them and fell to saying very rapidly, first in a loud and then in a low tone of voice, "*Dixit Dominus Domino meo*" (the Lord said unto my Lord); "but," says the *fableur*, "I cannot find here any sequel." The priest having read the text as chance might lead him, read the vespers for Sunday;—and you must know he travailed hard, that the offerings should be worth something to him. Then he fell to crying, "Barabbas!"—no crier could have cried a ban so loud as he cried to them; and everyone began to confess his sins aloud (*i.e.*, struck up "*mea culpa*") and cried, "Mercy!" The priest, who read on the sequence of his Psalter, once more began to cry out, saying, "Crucify him!" So that both men and women prayed God that he would defend them from torment. But it sorely vexed the clerk, who said to the priest, "Make an end"; but he answered, "Make no end, friend, till 'unto the marvellous works'"— referring to a passage in the Psalter. The clerk then said that a long Passion service boots nothing, and that it is never a gain to keep the people too long. And as soon as the offerings of the people were collected he finished the Passion.—"By this tale," adds the *raconteur*, "I would show you how— by the faith of Saint Paul!—it as well befits a fool to talk folly and sottishness as it becomes a wise man to speak wisely. And he is a fool who believes me not."[155]—A commentary, this, which recalls the old English saying, that "it is as great marvel to see a woman weep as to see a goose go barefoot."

They were bold fellows, those Trouvères. Not content with making the ignorance and the gross vices of the clerical orders the subjects of their *fabliaux*, they did not scruple to ridicule their superstitious teachings, as witness the satire on saint-worship, entitled "Du vilain [*i.e.*, peasant] qui conquist Paradis par plait," the substance of which is as follows: A poor peasant dies suddenly, and his soul escapes at a moment when neither angel nor demon was on the watch, so that, unclaimed and left to his own discretion, the peasant follows St. Peter, who happened to be on his way to Paradise, and enters the gate with him unperceived. When the saint finds that the soul of such a low person has found its way into Paradise he is angry, and rudely orders the peasant out. But the latter accuses St. Peter of denying his Saviour, and, conscience-stricken, the gate-keeper of heaven applies to St. Thomas, who undertakes to drive away the intruder. The peasant, however, disconcerts St. Thomas by reminding him of his disbelief, and St. Paul, who comes next, fares no better—he had persecuted the saints. At length Christ hears of what had occurred, and comes himself. The Saviour listens benignantly to the poor soul's pleading, and ends by forgiving the peasant his sins, and allowing him to remain in Paradise.[156]

There exists a very singular English burlesque of the unprofitable sermons of the preaching friars in the Middle Ages, which is worthy of Rabelais himself, and of which this is a modernised extract:

Mollificant olera durissima crusta.—"Friends, this is to say to your ignorant understanding, that hot plants and hard crusts make soft hard plants. The help and the grace of the gray goose that goes on the green, and the wisdom of the water wind-mill, with the good grace of a gallon pitcher, and all the salt sausages that be sodden in Norfolk upon Saturday, be with us now at our beginning, and help us in our ending, and quit you of bliss and both your eyes, that never shall have ending. Amen. My dear curst creatures, there was once a wife whose name was Catherine Fyste, and she was crafty in court, and well could carve. Hence she sent after the four Synods of Rome to know why, wherefore, and for what cause that Alleluja was closed before the cup came once round. Why, believest thou not, forsooth, that there stood once a cock on St. Paul's steeple-top, and drew up the strapples of his breech? How provest thou that tale? By all the four doctors of Wynberryhills—that is to say, Vertas, Gadatryne, Trumpas, and Dadyltrymsert—the which four doctors say there was once an old wife had a cock to her son, and he looked out of an old dove-cot, and warned and charged that no man should be so hardy either to ride or go on St. Paul's steeple-top unless he rode on a three-footed stool, or else that he brought with him a warrant of his neck"—and so on, in this fantastical style.

The meaning of the phrase "benefit of clergy" is not perhaps very generally understood. The phrase had its origin in those days of intellectual darkness, when the state of letters was so low that anyone found guilty in a court of justice of a crime which was punishable with death, if he could prove himself able to read a verse in a Latin Bible he was pardoned, as being a man of learning, and therefore likely to be useful to the state; but if he could not read he was sure to be hanged. This privilege, it is said, was granted to all offences, excepting high treason and sacrilege, till after the year 1350. At first it was extended not only to the clergy but to any person that could read, who, however, had to vow that he would enter into holy orders; but with the increase of learning this "benefit to clergy" was restricted by several Acts of Parliament, and it was finally abolished only so late as the reign of George IV.

In *Pasquils Jests and Mother Bunches Merriments*, a book of *facetiæ* very popular in the 16th century, a story is told of a criminal at the Oxford Assizes who "prayed his clergy," and a Bible was accordingly handed to him that he might read a verse. He could not read a word, however, which a scholar who chanced to be present observing, he stood behind him and prompted him with the verse he was to read; but coming towards the end, the man's thumb happened to cover the remaining words, and so the scholar, in a low voice, said: "Take away thy thumb," which words the man, supposing them to form part of the verse he was reading, repeated aloud, "Take away thy thumb"—whereupon the judge ordered him to be taken away and hanged. And in Taylor's *Wit and Mirth* (1630): "A fellow having his book [that is, having read a verse in the Bible] at the sessions, was burnt in the hand, and was commanded to say: 'May God save the King.' 'The King!' said he, 'God save my grandam, that taught me to read; I am sure I had been hanged else.'"

The verse in the Bible which a criminal was required to read, in order to entitle him to the "benefit of clergy" (the beginning of the 51st Psalm, "Miserere mei"), was called the "neck-verse," because his doing so saved his neck from the gallows. It is sometimes jestingly alluded to in old plays. For example, in Massinger's *Great Duke of Florence*, Act iii, sc. 1:

> *Cataminta.*—How the fool stares!
> *Fiorinda.*—And looks as if he were conning his neck-verse;

and in the same dramatist's play of *The Picture*:

> Twang it perfectly,
> As if it were your neck-verse.

In the anonymous *Pleasant Comedy of Patient Grissell* (1603), Act ii, sc. 1, we find this custom again referred to:

> *Farnese.*—Ha, hah! Emulo not write and read?
> *Rice.*—Not a letter, an you would hang him.
> *Urcenze.*—Then he'll never be saved by his book.

In Scott's *Lay of the Last Minstrel*, the moss-trooper, William of Deloraine, assures the lady, who had warned him not to look into what he should receive from the Monk of St. Mary's Aisle, "be it scroll or be it book," that

166

"Letter nor line know I never a one,
Were't my neck-verse at Haribee"—

the place where such Border rascals were usually executed.

It was formerly the custom to sing a psalm at the gallows before a criminal was "turned off." And there is a good story, in Zachary Gray's notes to *Hudibras*, told of one of the chaplains of the famous Montrose; how, being condemned in Scotland to die for attending his master in some of his expeditions, and being upon the ladder and ordered to select a psalm to be sung, expecting a reprieve, he named the 119th Psalm, with which the officer attending the execution complied (the Scottish Presbyterians were great psalm-singers in those days), and it was well for him he did so, for they had sung it half through before the reprieve came. Any other psalm would certainly have hanged him! Cotton, in his *Virgil Travestie*, thus alludes to the custom of psalm-singing at the foot of the gallows:

> Ready, when Dido gave the word,
> To be advanced into the halter,
> Without the benefit on's Psalter.
> Then 'cause she would, to part the sweeter,
> A portion have of Hopkins' metre,
> As people use at execution,
> For the decorum of conclusion,
> Being too sad to sing, she says.[157]

If the clergy in medieval times had, as they are said to have had, all the learning among themselves, what a blessed state of ignorance must the laity have been in! And so, indeed, it appears, for there is extant an old Act of Parliament which provides that a nobleman shall be entitled to the "benefit of clergy," even though he could not read. And another law sets forth that "the command of the sheriff to his officer by word of mouth, and without writing is good; for it may be that neither the sheriff nor his officer can write or read!" Many charters are preserved to which persons of great dignity, even kings, have affixed the sign of the cross, because they were not able to write their names, and hence the term of *signing*, instead of subscribing. In this respect a ten-year-old Board School boy in these "double-distilled" days is vastly superior to the most renowned of the "barons bold."

THE BEARDS OF OUR FATHERS

'Tis merry in the hall when beards wag all.—*Old Song*.

Among the harmless foibles of adolescence which contribute to the quiet amusement of folks of mature years is the eager desire of youths to have their smooth faces adorned with that "noble" distinction of manhood—a beard. And no wonder. For, should a clever lad, getting out of his "teens," venture to express opinions contrary to those of his elders present, is he not at once snubbed by being called "a beardless boy"? A boy! Bitter taunt! He very naturally feels that he is grossly insulted, and all because his "dimpled chin never has known the barber's shear." Full well does our ingenuous youth know that a man is not wise in consequence of his beard—that, as the Orientals say of women's long hair, it often happens that men with long beards have short wits; nevertheless, had he but a beard himself, he should then be free from such a wretched "argument"— such an implied accusation of his lack of wit, as that he is beardless. The young Roman watched the first appearance of the downy precursor of his beard with no little solicitude, and applied the household oil to his face— there were no patent specifics in those days for "infallibly producing luxuriant whiskers and moustaches in a few weeks"—to promote its tardy growth, and entitle him, from the incipient fringe, to be styled "barbatulus." When his beard was full-grown he was called "barbatus."

It would seem that the beard was held in the highest esteem, especially in Asiatic countries, from the earliest period of which any records have been preserved. The Hebrew priests are commanded in the Book of Leviticus, ch. xix, not to shave off the corners of their beards; and the first High Priest, Aaron, probably wore a magnificent beard, since the amicable relations between brethren are compared, in the 133rd Psalm, to "the precious ointment upon the head, that ran down upon the beard, even Aaron's beard; that went down to the skirts of his garments." The Assyrian kings intertwined gold thread with their fine beards—and, judging from mural sculptures, curling tongs must have been in considerable demand with them. In ancient Greece the beard was universally worn, and it is related of Zoilus, the founder of the anti-Homeric school, that he shaved the crown of his head, in order that all the virtue should go to the nourishment of his beard. Persius could not think of a more complimentary epithet to apply to Socrates than that of "Magistrum Barbatum," or Bearded Master—the notion being that the beard was the

168

symbol of profound sagacity.[158] Alexander the Great, however, caused his soldiers to shave off their beards, because they furnished their enemies with handles whereby to seize hold of them in battle. The beard was often consecrated to the deities, as the most precious offering. Chaucer, in his *Knight's Tale*, represents Arcite as offering his beard to Mars:

> And evermore, unto that day I dye,
> Eternè fyr I wol bifore the fynde,
> And eek to this avow I wol me bynde,
> My berd, myn heer, that hangeth long a doun,
> That neuer yit ne felt offensioun
> Of rasour ne of schere, I wol ye giue,
> And be thy trewè seruaunt whiles I lyue.[159]

Selim I was the first Turkish sultan who shaved his beard after his accession to the throne; and when his muftis remonstrated with him for this *dangerous* innovation, he facetiously replied that he had removed his beard in order that his vazírs should not have wherewith to *lead* him. The beards of modern Persian soldiers were abolished in consequence of a singular accident, which Morier thus relates in his *Second Journey*: When European discipline was introduced into the Persian army, Lieutenant Lindsay raised a corps of artillery. His zeal was only equalled by the encouragement of the king, who liberally adopted every method proposed. It was only upon the article of shaving off the beards of the Persian soldiers that the king was inexorable; nor would the sacrifice have ever taken place had it not happened that, in discharging the guns before the prince, a powder-horn exploded in the hand of a gunner who had been gifted with a very long beard, which in an instant was blown away from his chin. Lieutenant Lindsay, availing himself of this lucky opportunity to prove his argument on the inconvenience of beards to soldiers, immediately produced the scorched gunner before the prince, who was so much struck with his woeful appearance that the abolition of military beards was at once decided upon.

It was customary for the early French monarchs to place three hairs of their beard under the seal attached to important documents; and there is still extant a charter of the year 1121, which concludes with these words: "Quod ut ratum et stabile perseveret in posterum, præsentis scripto sigilli mei robur apposui cum tribus pilis barbæ meæ."—In obedience to his spiritual advisers, Louis VII of France had his hair cut close and his beard shaved off. But his consort Eleanor was so disgusted with his smooth face and cropped head that she took her own measures to be revenged, and the poor king was compelled to obtain a divorce from her. She subsequently gave her hand to the Count of Anjou, afterwards Henry II of England, and the rich provinces of Poitou and Guienne were her dowry. From this sprang those terrible wars which continued for three centuries, and cost

France untold treasure and three millions of men—and all because Louis did not consult his consort before shaving off his beard!

Charles the Fifth of Spain ascending the throne while yet a mere boy, his courtiers shaved their beards in compliment to the king's smooth face. But some of the shaven Dons were wont to say bitterly, "Since we have lost our beards, we have lost our souls!" Sully, the eminent statesman and soldier, scorned, however, to follow the fashion, and, being one day summoned to Court on urgent business of State, his beard was made the subject of ridicule by the foppish courtiers. The veteran thus gravely addressed the king: "Sire, when your father, of glorious memory, did me the honour to consult me in grave State matters, he first dismissed the buffoons and stage-dancers from the presence-chamber." It may be readily supposed that after this well-merited rebuke the grinning courtiers at once disappeared.

Julius II, one of the most warlike of all the Roman Pontiffs, was the first Pope who permitted his beard to grow, to inspire the faithful with still greater respect for his august person. Kings and their courtiers were not slow to follow the example of the Head of the Church and the ruler of kings, and the fashion soon spread among people of all ranks.

So highly prized was the beard in former times that Baldwin, Prince of Edessa, as Nicephorus relates in his Chronicle, pawned his beard for a large sum of money, which was redeemed by his father Gabriel, Prince of Melitene, to prevent the ignominy which his son must have suffered by its loss. And when Juan de Castro, the Portuguese admiral, borrowed a thousand pistoles from the citizens of Goa he pledged one of his whiskers, saying, "All the gold in the world cannot equal this natural ornament of my valour." And it is said the people of Goa were so much affected by the noble message that they remitted the money and returned the whisker—though of what earthly use it could prove to the gallant admiral, unless, perhaps, to stuff a tennis ball, it is not easy to say.

To deprive a man of his beard was a token of ignominious subjection, and is still a common mode of punishment in some Asiatic countries. And such was the treatment that the conjuror Pinch received at the hands of Antipholus of Ephesus and his man, in the *Comedy of Errors*, according to the servant's account of the outrage, who states that not only had they "beaten the maids a-row," but they

> bound the doctor,
> Whose beard they have singed off with brands of fire;
> And ever as it blazed they threw on him
> Great pails of puddled mire to quench the hair (v, 1).

In Persia and India when a wife is found to have been unfaithful, her hair—the distinguishing ornament of woman, as the beard is considered to be that of man—is shaved off, among other indignities.

Don Sebastian Cobbarruvius gravely relates the following marvellous legend to show that nothing so much disgraced a Spaniard as pulling his beard: "A noble of that nation dying (his name Cid Lai Dios), a Jew, who hated him much in his lifetime, stole privately into the room where his body was laid out, and, thinking to do what he never durst while living, stooped down and plucked his beard; at which the body started up, and drawing out half way his sword, which lay beside him, put the Jew in such a fright that he ran out of the room as if a thousand devils had been behind him. This done, the body lay down as before to rest; and," adds the veracious chronicler, "the Jew after that turned Christian."—In the third of Don Quevedo's Visions of the Last Judgment, we read that a Spaniard, after receiving sentence, was taken into custody by a pair of demons who happened to disorder the set of his moustache, and they had to re-compose them with a pair of curling-tongs before they could get him to proceed with them!

By the rules of the Church of Rome, lay monks were compelled to wear their beards, and only the priests were permitted to shave.[160] The clergy at length became so corrupt and immoral, and lived such scandalous lives, that they could not be distinguished from the laity except by their close-shaven faces. The first Reformers, therefore, to mark their separation from the Romish Church, allowed their beards to grow. Calvin, Fox, Cranmer, and other leaders of the Reformation are all represented in their portraits with long flowing beards. John Knox, the great Scottish Reformer, wore, as is well known, a beard of prodigious length.

The ancient Britons shaved the chin and cheeks, but wore their moustaches down to the breast. Our Saxon ancestors wore forked beards. The Normans at the Conquest shaved not only the chin, but also the back of the head. But they soon began to grow very long beards. During the Wars of the Roses beards grew "small by degrees and beautifully less."

Queen Mary of England, in the year 1555, sent to Moscow four accredited agents, who were all bearded; but one of them, George Killingworth, was particularly distinguished by a beard five feet two inches long, at the sight of which, it is said, a smile crossed the grim features of Ivan the Terrible himself; and no wonder. But the longest beard known out of fairy tales was that of Johann Mayo, the German painter, commonly called "John the Bearded." His beard actually trailed on the ground when he stood upright, and for convenience he usually kept it tucked in his girdle. The emperor Charles V, it is said, was often pleased to cause Mayo to unfasten his beard and allow it to blow in the faces of his courtiers.—A worthy clergyman in the time of Queen Elizabeth gave as the best reason he had for wearing a beard of enormous length, "that no act of his life might be unworthy of the gravity of his appearance."

Queen Elizabeth, in the first year of her reign, made an abortive attempt to abolish her subjects' beards by an impost of 3s. 4d. a year (equivalent to four times that sum in these "dear" days) on every beard of more than a fortnight's growth. And Peter the Great also laid a tax upon beards in Russia: nobles' beards were assessed at a rouble, and those of commoners at a copeck each. "But such veneration," says Giles Fletcher, "had this people for these ensigns of gravity that many of them carefully preserved their beards in their cabinets to be buried with them, imagining perhaps that they should make but an odd figure in their grave with their naked chins."

The beard of the renowned Hudibras was portentous, as we learn from Butler, who thus describes the Knight's hirsute honours:

> His tawny beard was th' equal grace
> Both of his wisdom and his face;
> In cut and dye so like a tile,
> A sadden view it would beguile:
> The upper part whereof was whey,
> The nether orange mixt with grey.
> This hairy meteor did denounce
> The fall of sceptres and of crowns;
> With grisly type did represent
> Declining age of government,
> And tell, with hieroglyphic spade,
> Its own grave and the state's were made.

Philip Nye, an Independent minister in the time of the Commonwealth, and one of the famous Assembly of Divines, was remarkable for the singularity of his beard. Hudibras, in his Heroical Epistle to the lady of his "love," speaks of

> Amorous intrigues
> In towers, and curls, and periwigs,
> With greater art and cunning reared
> Than Philip Nye's *thanksgiving beard.*

Nye opposed Lilly the astrologer with no little virulence, for which he was rewarded with the privilege of holding forth upon Thanksgiving Day, and so, as Butler says, in some MS. verses,

He thought upon it and resolved to put
His beard into as wonderful a cut.

Butler even honoured Nye's beard with a whole poem, entitled "On Philip Nye's Thanksgiving Beard," which is printed in his *Genuine Remains*, edited by Thyer, vol. i, p. 177 ff., and opens thus:

A beard is but the vizard of the face,
That nature orders for no other place;
The fringe and tassel of a countenance
That hides his person from another man's,
And, like the Roman habits of their youth,
Is never worn until his perfect growth.

And in another set of verses he has again a fling at the obnoxious beard of the same preacher:

This reverend brother, like a goat,
Did wear a tail upon his throat;
The fringe and tassel of a face
That gives it a becoming grace,
But set in such a curious frame,
As if 'twere wrought in filograin;
And cut so even as if 't had been
Drawn with a pen upon the chin.

As it was customary among the peoples of antiquity who wore their beards to cut them off, and for those who shaved to allow their beards to grow, in times of mourning, so many of the Presbyterians and Independents vowed not to cut their beards till monarchy and episcopacy were utterly destroyed. Thus in a humorous poem, entitled "The Cobler and the Vicar of Bray," we read:

This worthy knight was one that swore,
    He would not cut his beard
Till this ungodly nation was
    From kings and bishops cleared.

Which holy vow he firmly kept,
    And most devoutly wore
A grisly meteor on his face,
    Till they were both no more.

In *Pericles, Prince of Tyre*, when the royal hero leaves his infant daughter Marina in charge of his friend Cleon, governor of Tharsus, to be brought up in his house, he declares to Cleon's wife (Act iii, sc. 3):

Till she be married, madam,
By bright Diana, whom we honour all,
Unscissored shall this hair of mine remain,
Though I show well in't;

and that he meant his beard is evident from what he says at the close of the play, when his daughter is about to be married to Lysimachus, governor of Mitylene (Act v, sc. 3):

And now
This ornament, that makes me look so dismal,
Will I, my loved Marina, clip to form;
And what these fourteen years no razor touched,
To grace thy marriage day, I'll beautify.

Scott, in his *Woodstock*, represents Sir Henry Lee, of Ditchley, whilom Ranger of Woodstock Park (or Chase), as wearing his full beard, to indicate his profound grief for the death of the "Royal Martyr," which indeed was not unusual with elderly and warmly devoted Royalists until the "Happy Restoration"—save the mark!

Another extraordinary beard was that of Van Butchell, the quack doctor, who died at London in 1814, in his 80th year. This singular individual had his first wife's body carefully embalmed and preserved in a glass case in his "study," in order that he might enjoy a handsome annuity to which he was entitled "so long as his wife remained above ground." His person was for many years familiar to loungers in Hyde Park, where he appeared regularly every afternoon, riding on a little pony, and wearing a magnificent beard of twenty years' growth, which an Oriental might well have envied, the more remarkable in an age when shaving was so generally practised.—A jocular epitaph was composed on "Mary Van Butchell," of which these lines may serve as a specimen:

O fortunate and envied man!
To keep a wife beyond life's span;
Whom you can ne'er have cause to blame,
Is ever constant and the same;
Who, qualities most rare, inherits
A wife that's dumb, yet *full of spirits*.

The celebrated Dr. John Hunter is said to have embalmed the body of Van Butchell's first wife—for the bearded empiric married again—and the "mummy," in its original glass case, is still to be seen in the Museum of the Royal College of Surgeon's, Lincoln's-Inn-Fields, London.

It was once the fashion for gallants to dye their beards various colours, such as yellow, red, gray, and even green. Thus in the play of *Midsummer Night's Dream*, Bottom the weaver asks in what kind of beard he is to play the part of Pyramis—whether "in your straw-coloured beard, your orange-tawny beard, your purple-in-grain beard, or your French crown-coloured beard, your perfect yellow?" (Act i, sc. 2.) In ancient church pictures, and in the miracle plays performed in medieval times, both Cain and Judas Iscariot were always represented with yellow beards. In the *Merry Wives of Windsor*, Mistress Quickly asks Simple whether his master (Slender) does not wear "a great round beard, like a glover's paring-knife," to which he replies: "No, forsooth; he hath but a little wee face, with a little yellow beard—a Cain-coloured beard" (Act i, sc. 4).—Allusions to beards are of very frequent occurrence in Shakspeare's plays, as may be seen by reference to any good Concordance, such as that of the Cowden Clarkes.

Harrison, in his *Description of England*, ed. 1586, p. 172, thus refers to the vagaries of fashion of beards in his time: "I will saie nothing of our heads, which sometimes are polled, sometimes curled, or suffered to grow at length like womans lockes, manie times cut off, above or under the eares, round as by a woodden dish. Neither will I meddle with our varietie of beards, of which some are shaven from the chin like those of Turks, not a few cut short like to the beard of marques Otto, some made round like a rubbing brush, others with a *pique de vant* (O fine fashion!), or now and then suffered to grow long, the barbers being growen to be so cunning in this behalfe as the tailors. And therfore if a man have a leane and streight face, a marquesse Ottons cut will make it broad and large; if it be platter like, a long slender beard will make it seeme the narrower; if he be wesell becked, then much heare left on the cheekes will make the owner looke big like a bowdled hen, and so grim as a goose."[161]

Barnaby Rich, in the conclusion of his *Farewell to the Military Profession* (1581), says that the young gallants sometimes had their beards "cutte rounde, like a Philippes doler; sometymes square, like the kinges hedde in Fishstreate; sometymes so neare the skinne, that a manne might judge by his face the gentlemen had had verie pilde lucke."[162]

In Taylor's *Superbiae Flagellum* we find the following amusing description of the different "cuts" of beards:

> Now a few lines to paper I will put,
> Of mens Beards strange and variable cut:
> In which there's some doe take as vaine a Pride,
> As almost in all other things beside.
> Some are reap'd most substantiall, like a brush,
> Which makes a Nat'rall wit knowne by the bush:
> (And in my time of some men I have heard,

175

Whose wisedome have bin onely wealth and beard)
Many of these the proverbe well doth fit,
Which sayes Bush naturall, More haire then wit.
Some seeme as they were starched stiffe and fine,
Like to the bristles of some angry swine:
And some (to set their Loves desire on edge)
Are cut and prun'de like to a quickset hedge.
Some like a spade, some like a forke, some square,
Some round, some mow'd like stubble, some starke bare,
Some sharpe Steletto fashion, dagger like,
That may with whispering a mans eyes out pike:
Some with the hammer cut, or Romane T,[163]
Their beards extravagant reform'd must be,
Some with the quadrate, some triangle fashion,
Some circular, some ovall in translation,
Some perpendicular in longitude,
Some like a thicket for their crassitude,
That heights, depths, bredths, triforme, square, ovall, round,
And rules Ge'metricall in beards are found.
Besides the upper lip's strange variation,
Corrected from mutation to mutation;
As 'twere from tithing unto tithing sent,
Pride gives to Pride continuall punishment.
Some (spite their teeth) like thatch'd eves downeward grows,
And some growes upwards in despite their nose.
Some their mustatioes of such length doe keepe,
That very well they may a maunger sweepe:
Which in Beere, Ale, or Wine, they drinking plunge,
And sucke the liquor up, as 'twere a Spunge;
But 'tis a Slovens beastly Pride, I thinke,
To wash his beard where other men must drinke.
And some (because they will not rob the cup),
Their upper chaps like pot hookes are turn'd up;
The Barbers thus (like Taylers) still must be,
Acquainted with each cuts variety—
Yet though with beards thus merrily I play,
'Tis onely against Pride which I inveigh:
For let them weare their haire or their attire,
According as their states or mindes desire,
So as no puff'd up Pride their hearts possesse,
And they use Gods good gifts with thankfulnesse.[164]

The staunch Puritan Phillip Stubbes, in the second part of his *Anatomie of Abuses* (1583), thus rails at the beards and the barbers of his day:

"There are no finer fellowes under the sunne, nor experter in their noble science of barbing than they be. And therefore in the fulnes of their overflowing knowledge (oh ingenious heads, and worthie to be dignified with the diademe of follie and vaine curiositie), they have invented such strange fashions and monstrous maners of cuttings, trimings, shavings and washings, that you would wonder to see. They have one maner of cut called the French cut, another the Spanish cut, one called the Dutch cut, another the Italian, one the newe cut, another the old, one of the bravado fashion, another of the meane fashion. One a gentlemans cut, another the common cut, one cut of the court, another of the country, with infinite the like vanities, which I overpasse. They have also other kinds of cuts innumerable; and therefore when you come to be trimed, they will aske you whether you will be cut to looke terrible to your enimie, or amiable to your freend, grime and sterne in countenance, or pleasant and demure (for they have divers kinds of cuts for all these purposes, or else they lie). Then when they have done all their feats, it is a world to consider, how their mowchatowes [*i.e.*, moustaches] must be preserved and laid out, and from one cheke to another, yea, almost from one eare to another, and turned up like two hornes towards the forehead. Besides that, when they come to the cutting of the haire, what snipping and snapping of the cycers is there, what tricking and toying, and all to tawe out mony, you may be sure. And when they come to washing, oh how gingerly they behave themselves therein. For then shall your mouth be bossed with the lather or fome that riseth of the balle (for they have their sweet balles wherewith-all they use to washe), your eyes closed must be anointed therewith also. Then snap go the fingers ful bravely, God wot. Thus this tragedy ended, comes me warme clothes, to wipe and dry him withall; next the eares must be picked and closed againe togither artificially forsooth. The haire of the nostrils cut away, and every thing done in order comely to behold. The last action in this tragedie is the paiment of monie. And least these cunning barbers might seeme unconscionable in asking much for their paines, they are of such a shamefast modestie, as they will aske nothing at all, but standing to the curtisie and liberalitie of the giver, they will receive all that comes, how much soever it be, not giving anie againe, I warrant you: for take a barber with that fault, and strike off his head. No, no, such fellowes are *Rarae aves in terris, nigrisque similimi cygnis*, Rare birds upon the earth, and as geason as blacke swans. You shall have also your orient perfumes for your nose, your fragrant waters for your face, wherewith you shall bee all to besprinkled, your musicke againe, and pleasant harmonic, shall sound in your eares, and all to tickle the same with vaine delight. And in the end your cloke shall be brushed, and 'God be with you Gentleman!'"[165]

A very curious Ballad of the Beard, of the time of Charles I, if not earlier, is reproduced in *Satirical Songs and Poems on Costume*, edited by F. W. Fairholt, for the Percy Society, in which "the varied forms of beards which characterised the profession of each man are amusingly descanted on":

The beard, thick or thin, on the lip or the chin,
  Doth dwell so near the tongue,
That her silence in the beards defence
  May do her neighbour wrong.
Now a beard is a thing that commands in a king,
  Be his sceptre ne'er so fair:
Where the beard bears the sway the people obey,
  And are subject to a hair.

'Tis a princely sight, and a grave delight,
  That adorns both young and old;
A well-thatcht face is a comely grace,
  And a shelter from the cold.

When the piercing north comes thundering forth,
  Let a barren face beware;
For a trick it will find, with a razor of wind,
  To shave a face that's bare.

But there's many a nice and strange device
  That doth the beard disgrace;
But he that is in such a foolish sin
  Is a traitor to his face.

Now of beards there be such company,
  And fashions such a throng,
That it is very hard to handle a beard,
  Tho' it be never so long.

The Roman T, in its bravery,
  Both first itself disclose,
But so high it turns, that oft it burns
  With the flames of a torrid nose.

The stiletto-beard, oh, it makes me afear'd,
  It is so sharp beneath,
For he that doth place a dagger in 's face,
  What wears he in his sheath?

But, methinks, I do itch to go thro' the stitch
  The needle-beard to amend,
Which, without any wrong, I may call too long,
  For a man can see no end.

The soldier's beard doth march in shear'd,
  In figure like a spade,
With which he'll make his enemies quake,

And think their graves are made.

What doth invest a bishop's breast,
    But a milk-white spreading hair?
Which an emblem may be of integrity
    Which doth inhabit there.

But oh, let us tarry for the beard of King Harry,
    That grows about the chin,
With his bushy pride, and a grove on each side,
    And a champion ground between.

"Barnes in the defence of the Berde" is another curious piece of verse, or rather of arrant doggrel, printed in the 16th century. It is addressed to Andrew Borde, the learned and facetious physician, in the time of Henry VIII, who seems to have written a tract against the wearing of beards, of which nothing is now known. In the second part Barnes (whoever he was) says:

But, syr, I praye you, yf you tell can,
Declare to me, when God made man,
(I meane by our forefather Adam)
Whyther he had a berde than;
And yf he had, who dyd hym shave,
Syth that a barber he coulde not have.
Well, then, ye prove hym there a knave,
Bicause his berde he dyd so save:
        I fere it not.

Sampson, with many thousandes more
Of auncient phylosophers (!), full great store,
Wolde not be shaven, to dye therefore;
Why shulde you, then, repyne so sore?
Admit that men doth imytate
Thynges of antyquité, and noble state,
Such counterfeat thinges oftymes do mytygate
Moche ernest yre and debate:
        I fere it not.

Therefore, to cease, I thinke be best;
For berdyd men wolde lyve in rest.
You prove yourselfe a homly gest,
So folysshely to rayle and jest;
For if I wolde go make in ryme,
How new shavyd men loke lyke scraped swyne,
And so rayle forth, from tyme to tyme,
A knavysshe laude then shulde be myne:
        I fere it not.

179

What should this avail him? he asks; and so let us all be good friends, bearded and unbearded.[166]

But Andrew Borde, if he did ever write a tract against beards, must have formerly held a different opinion on the subject, for in his *Breviary of Health*, first printed in 1546, he says: "The face may have many impediments. The first impediment is to see a man having no beard, and a woman to have a beard." It was long a popular notion that the few hairs which are sometimes seen on the chins of very old women signified that they were in league with the arch-enemy of mankind—in plain English, that they were witches. The celebrated Three Witches who figure in *Macbeth*, "and palter with him in a double sense," had evidently this distinguishing mark, for says Banquo to the "weird sisters" (Act i, sc. 2):

> You should be women,
> And yet your beards forbid me to interpret
> That you are so.

And in the ever-memorable scene in the *Merry Wives of Windsor*, when Jack Falstaff, disguised as the fat woman of Brentford, is escaping from Ford's house, he is cuffed and mauled by Ford, who exclaims, "Hang her, witch!" on which the honest Cambrian Sir Hugh Evans sapiently remarks: "Py yea and no, I think the 'oman is a witch indeed. I like not when a 'oman has a great peard. I spy a great peard under her muffler!" (Act iv, sc. 2.)

There have been several notable bearded women in different parts of Europe. The Duke of Saxony had the portrait painted of a poor Swiss woman who had a remarkably fine, large beard. Bartel Græfjë, of Stuttgart, who was born in 1562, was another bearded woman. In 1726 there appeared at Vienna a female dancer with a large bushy beard. Charles XII of Sweden had in his army a woman who wore a beard a yard and a half in length. In 1852 Mddle. Bois de Chêne, who was born at Genoa in 1834, was exhibited in London: she had "a profuse head of hair, a strong black beard, and large bushy whiskers." It is not unusual to see dark beauties in our own country with a moustache which must be the envy of "young shavers." And, *apropos*, the poet Rogers is said to have had a great dislike of ladies' beards, such as this last described; and he happened to be in a circulating library turning over the books on the counter, when a lady, who seemed to cherish her beard with as much affection as the young gentlemen aforesaid, alighted from her carriage, and, entering the shop, asked the librarian for a certain book. The polite man of books replied that he was sorry he had not a copy at present. "But," said Roger, slily, "you have the *Barber of Seville*, have you not?" "O yes," said the bookseller, not seeing the poet's drift, "I have the *Barber of Seville*, very much at your ladyship's service." The lady drove away, evidently much offended, but the beard afterwards disappeared. Talking of barbers—but they deserve a whole paper to themselves, and they shall have it, from me, some day, if I live a little longer.

In No. 331 of the *Spectator*, Addison tells us how his friend Sir Roger de Coverley, in Westminster Abbey, pointing to the bust of a venerable old man, asked him whether he did not think "our ancestors looked much wiser in their beards than we without them. For my part," said he, "when I am walking in my gallery in the country, and see my ancestors, who many of them died before they were my age, I cannot forbear regarding them as so many patriarchs, and at the same time looking upon myself as an idle, smock-faced young fellow. I love to see your Abrahams, your Isaacs, and your Jacobs, as we have them in old pieces of tapestry, with beards below their girdles, that cover half the hangings."

During most part of last century close shaving was general throughout Europe. In France the beard began to appear on the faces of Bonaparte's "braves," and the fashion soon extended to civilians, then to Italy, Germany, Spain, Russia, and lastly to England, where, after the gradual enlargement of the side-whiskers, the full beard is now commonly worn—to the comfort and health of the wearers.

Footnotes

1. One reason, doubtless, for Persian and Turkish poets adopting a *takhallus* is the custom of the poet introducing his name into every ghazal he composes, generally towards the end; and as his proper name would seldom or never accommodate itself to purposes of verse he selects a more suitable one.
2. A dínar is a gold coin, worth about ten shillings of our money.
3. Referring to the custom of throwing small coins among crowds in the street on the occasion of a wedding. A dirham is a coin nearly equal in value to sixpence of our money.
4. The nightingale.
5. In the original Turkish:

> *Dinleh bulbul kissa sen kim gildi eiyami behár!*
> *Kurdi her bir baghda hengamei hengami behár;*
> *Oldi sim afshan ana ezhari badami behár:*
> *Ysh u nush it kim gicher kalmaz bu eiyami behár.*

Here we have an example of the *redíf*, which is common in Turkish and Persian poetry, and "consists of one or more words, always the same, added to the end of every rhyming line in a poem, which word or words, though counting in the scansion, are not regarded as the true rhyme, which must in every case be sought for immediately before them. The lines—

> There shone such truth about thee,
> I did not dare to doubt thee—

furnish an example of this in English poetry." In the opening verse of Mesíhí's ode, as above transliterated in European characters, the *redíf* is "behár," or spring, and the word which precedes it is the true rhyme-ending. Sir William Jones has made an elegant paraphrase of this charming ode, in which, however, he diverges considerably from the original, as will be seen from his rendering of the first stanza:

> Hear how the nightingale, on every spray,
> Hails in wild notes the sweet of May!
> The gale, that o'er yon waving almond blows,

182

The verdant bank with silver blossoms strows;
The smiling season decks each flowery glade—
Be gay; too soon the flowers of spring will fade.

6. Hátim was chief of the Arabian tribe of Taï, shortly before Muhammed began to promulgate Islám, renowned for his extraordinary liberality.

7. Auvaiyár, the celebrated poetess of the Tamils (in Southern India), who is said to have flourished in the ninth century, says, in her poem entitled *Nalvali*:

> Mark this: who lives beyond his means
> Forfeits respect, loses his sense;
> Where'er he goes through the seven births,
> All count him knave; him women scorn.

8. "All perishes except learning."—*Auvaiyár*.

9. "Learning is really the most valuable treasure.—A wise man will never cease to learn.—He who has attained learning by free self-application excels other philosophers.—Let thy learning be thy best friend.—What we have learned in youth is like writing cut in stone.—If all else should be lost, what we have learned will never be lost.—Learn one thing after another, but not hastily.—Though one is of low birth, learning will make him respected."—*Auvaiyár*.

10. There is a similar story to this in one of our old English jest-books, *Tales and Quicke Answeres*, 1535, as follows (I have modernised the spelling): As an astronomer [*i.e.* an astrologer] sat upon a time in the market place, and took upon him to divine and to show what their fortunes and chances should be that came to him, there came a fellow and told him (as it was indeed) that thieves had broken into his house, and had borne away all that he had. These tidings grieved him so sore that, all heavy and sorrowfully, he rose up and went his way. When the fellow saw him do so, he said: "O thou foolish and mad man! goest thou about to divine other men's matters, and art ignorant of thine own?"

11. The sayings of Buzurjmihr, the sagacious prime minister of King Núshírván, are often cited by Persian writers, and a curious story of his precocity when a mere youth is told in the *Latá'yif at-Taw'áyif*, a Persian collection, made by Al-Káshifí, of which a translation will be found in my "Analogues and Variants" of the Tales in vol. iii of Sir R. F. Burton's *Supplemental Arabian Nights*, pp. 567-9—too long for reproduction here.

12. Simonides used to say that he never regretted having held his tongue, but very often had he felt sorry for having spoken.—*Stobæus*: Flor. xxxiii, 12.

13. The name of a musical instrument.

14. The fancied love of the nightingale for the rose is a favourite theme of Persian poets.
15. Cf. the fable of Anianus: After laughing all summer at her toil, the Grasshopper came in winter to borrow part of the Ant's store of food. "Tell me," said the Ant, "what you did in the summer?" "I sang," replied the Grasshopper. "Indeed," rejoined the Ant. "Then you may dance and keep yourself warm during the winter."
16. Auvaiyár, the celebrated Indian poetess, in her *Nalvali*, says:

> Hark! ye who vainly toil and wealth
> Amass—O sinful men, the soul
> Will leave its nest; where then will be
> The buried treasure that you lose?

17. "Comprehensive talkers are apt to be tiresome when we are not athirst for information; but, to be quite fair, we must admit that superior reticence is a good deal due to the lack of matter. Speech is often barren, but silence does not necessarily brood over a full nest. Your still fowl, blinking at you without remark, may all the while be sitting on one addled nest-egg; and when it takes to cackling will have nothing to announce but that addled delusion."—George Eliot's *Felix Holt*.
18. The cow is sacred among the Hindús.
19. Thus also Jámí, in his *Baháristán* (Second "Garden"): "With regard to a secret divulged and one kept concealed, there is in use an excellent proverb, that the one is an arrow still in our possession, and the other is an arrow sent from the bow." And another Persian poet, whose name I have not ascertained, eloquently exclaims: "O my heart! if thou desirest ease in this life, keep thy secrets undisclosed, like the modest rose-bud. Take warning from that lovely flower, which, by expanding its hitherto hidden beauties when in full bloom, gives its leaves and its happiness to the winds."
20. Is such a thing as an emerald made worse than it was if it is not praised?—*Marcus Aurelius*.

> If glass be used to decorate a crown,
> While gems are taken to bedeck a foot,
> 'Tis not that any fault lies in the gem,
> But in the want of knowledge of the setter.
> —*Panchatantra*, a famous Indian book of Fables.

21. The Súfís are the mystics of Islám, and their poetry, while often externally anacreontic—bacchanalian and erotic—possesses an esoteric, spiritual signification: the sensual world is employed to symbolise that which is to be apprehended only by the *inward*

sense. Most of the great poets of Persia, Afghanistán, and Turkey are generally understood to have been Súfís.

22. Sir Gore Ouseley's *Biographical Notices of Persian Poets*.

23. Cf. these lines, from Herrick's "Hesperides":

> But you are *lovely leaves*, where we
> May read, how soon things have
> Their end, tho' ne'er so brave;
> And after they have shown their pride,
> Like you, a while, they glide
> Into the grave.

24. "In the name of God" is part of the formula employed by pious Muslims in their acts of worship, and on entering upon any enterprise of danger or uncertainty—*bi'smi'llahi ar-rahman ar-rahimi*, "In the name of God, the Merciful, the Compassionate!" These words are usually placed at the beginning of Muhammedan books, secular as well as religions; and they form part of the Muslim Confession of Faith, used in the last extremity: "In the name of God, the Merciful, the Compassionate! There is no strength nor any power save in God, the High, the Mighty. To God we belong, and verily to him we !"

25. "Bear in mind," says Thorkel to Bork, in the Icelandic saga of Gisli the Outlaw, "bear in mind that a woman's counsel is always unlucky."—On the other hand, quoth Panurge, "Truly I have found a great deal of good in the counsel of women, chiefly in that of the old wives among them."

26. The Khoja was contemporary with the renowned conqueror of nations, Tímúr, or Tímúrleng, or, as the name is usually written in this country, Tamarlane, though there does not appear to be any authority that he was the official jester at the court of that monarch, as some writers have asserted. The pleasantries ascribed to the Khoja—the title now generally signifies Teacher, or School-master, but formerly it was somewhat equivalent to our "Mr," or, more familiarly, "Goodman"—have been completely translated into French. Of course, a large proportion of the jests have been taken from Arabian and Persian collections, though some are doubtless genuine; and they represent the Khoja as a curious compound of shrewdness and simplicity. A number of the foolish sayings and doings fathered on him are given in my *Book of Noodles*, 1888.

27. This is how the same story is told in our oldest English jest-book, entitled *A Hundred Mery Talys* (1525): A certain merchant and a courtier being upon a time at dinner, having a hot custard, the courtier, being somewhat homely of manner, took part of it and put it in his mouth, which was so hot that it made him shed tears.

The merchant, looking on him, thought that he had been weeping, and asked him why he wept. This courtier, not willing it to be known that he had brent his mouth with the hot custard, answered and said, "Sir," quod he, "I had a brother which did a certain offence, wherefore he was hanged." The merchant thought the courtier had said true, and anon, after the merchant was disposed to eat of the custard, and put a spoonful of it into his mouth, and brent his mouth also, that his eyes watered. This courtier, that perceiving, spake to the merchant; and said, "Sir," quod he, "why do ye weep now?" The merchant perceived how he had been deceived, and said, "Marry," quod he, "I weep because thou wast not hanged when that thy brother was hanged."

28. What may be an older form of this jest is found in the *Kathá Manjarí*, a Canarese collection, where a wretched singer dwelling next door to a poor woman causes her to weep and wail bitterly whenever he begins to sing, and on his asking her why she wept, she explains that his "golden voice" recalled to her mind her donkey that died a month ago.—The story had found its way to our own country more than three centuries since. In *Mery Tales and Quicke Answeres* (1535), under the title "Of the Friar that brayde in his Sermon," the preacher reminds a "poure wydowe" of her ass—all that her husband had left her—which had been devoured by wolves, for so the ass was wont to bray day and night.

29. Messrs. W. H. Allen & Co., London, have in the press a new edition of this work, to be entitled *"Tales of the Sun; or, Popular Tales of Southern India."* I am confident that the collection will be highly appreciated by many English readers, while its value to story-comparers can hardly be over-rated.

30. A similar incident is found in the 8th chapter of the Spanish work, *El Conde Lucanor*, written, in the 14th century, by Prince Don Juan Manuel, where a pretended alchemist obtains from a king a large sum of money in order that he should procure in his own distant country a certain thing necessary for the transmutation of the baser metals into gold. The impostor, of course, did not , and so on, much the same as in the above.—Many others of Don Manuel's tales are traceable to Eastern sources; he was evidently familiar with the Arabic language, and from his long intercourse with the Moors doubtless became acquainted with Asiatic story-books. His manner of telling the stories is, however, wholly his own, and some of them appear to be of his own invention.—There is a variant of the same story in *Pasquils Jests and Mother Bunches Merriments*, in which a servant enters his master's name in a list of all the fools of his acquaintance, because he had lately lent his cousin twenty pounds.

31. A variant of this occurs in the *Heptameron*, an uncompleted work in imitation of the *Decameron*, ascribed to Marguerite, queen of Navarre (16th century), but her *valet de chambre* Bonaventure des

Periers is supposed to have had a hand in its composition. In Novel 55 it is related that a merchant in Saragossa on his death-bed desired his wife to sell a fine Spanish horse for as much as it would fetch and give the money to the mendicant friars. After his death his widow did not approve of such a legacy, but, in order to obey her late husband's will, she instructed a servant to go to the market and offer the horse for a ducat and her cat for ninety-nine ducats, both, however, to be sold together. A gentleman purchased the horse and the cat, well knowing that the former was fully worth a hundred ducats, and the widow handed over one ducat—for which the horse was nominally sold—to the mendicant friars.

32. Cardonne took this story from a Turkish work entitled "*Ajá'ib el-ma'ásir wa ghará'ib en-nawádir* (the Wonders of Remarkable Incidents and Rarities of Anecdotes)," by Ahmed ibn Hemdem Khetkhody, which was composed for Sultan Murád IV, who reigned from A.D. 1623 to 1640.

33. This story has been taken from Arab Sháh into the Breslau printed Arabic text of the *Thousand and One Nights*, where it is related at great length. The original was rendered into French under the title of "Ruses des Femmes" (in the Arabic *Ked-an-Nisa*, Stratagems of Women) by Lescallier, and appended to his version of the Voyages of Sindbád, published at Paris in 1814, long before the Breslau text of *The Nights* was known to exist. It also forms part of one of the Persian Tales (*Hazár ú Yek Rúz*, 1001 Days) translated by Petis de la Croix, where, however, the trick is played on the kází, not on a young merchant.

34. A variant of this story is found in Le Grand's *Fabliaux et Contes*, ed. 1781, tome iv, p. 119, and it was probably brought from the East during the Crusades: Maimon was a valet to a count. His master, ing home from a tourney, met him on the way, and asked him where he was going. He replied, with great coolness, that he was going to seek a lodging somewhere. "A lodging!" said the count. "What then has happened at home?" "Nothing, my lord. Only your dog, whom you love so much, is dead." "How so?" "Your fine palfrey, while being exercised in the court, became frightened, and in running fell into the well." "Ah, who startled the horse?" "It was your son, Damaiseau, who fell at its feet from the window." "My son!—O Heaven! Where, then, were his servant and his mother? Is he injured?" "Yes, sire, he has been killed by falling. And when they went to tell it to madame, she was so affected that she fell dead also without speaking." "Rascal! in place of flying away, why hast thou not gone to seek assistance, or why didst thou not remain at the chateau?" "There is no more need, sire; for Marotte, in watching madame, fell asleep. A light caused the fire, and there remains nothing now."—Truly a delicate way of "breaking ill news"!

35. *The Dabistán, or School of Manners*. Translated from the original Persian, by David Shea and Anthony Troyer. 3 vols. Published by the Oriental Translation Fund, 1843. Vol. i, 198-200. The author of this work is said to be Moshan Fáni, who flourished at Hyderábád about the end of the 18th century.

36. Pedro Alfonso (the Spanish form of his adopted name) was originally a Jewish Rabbi, and was born in 1062, at Huesca, in the kingdom of Arragon. He was reputed a man of very great learning, and on his being baptised (at the age of 44) was appointed by Alfonso XV, king of Castile and Leon, physician to the royal household. His work, above referred to, is written in Latin, and has been translated into French, but not as yet into English. An outline of the tales, by Douce, will be found prefixed to Ellis' *Early English Metrical Romances*.

37. This is also the subject of one of the *Fabliaux*.—In a form similar to the story in Alfonsus it is current among the Milanese, and a Sicilian version is as follows: Once upon a time there was a prince who studied and racked his brains so much that he learned magic and the art of finding hidden treasures. One day he discovered a treasure in Daisisa. "O," he says, "now I am going to get it out." But to get it out it was necessary that ten million million of ants should cross the river one by one in a bark made of the half-shell of a nut. The prince puts the bark in the river, and makes the ants pass over—one, two, three; and they are still doing it. Here the story-teller pauses and says: "We will finish the story when the ants have finished crossing the river."—Crane's *Italian Popular Tales*, p. 156.

38. This last jest reappears in the apocryphal Life of Esop, by Planudes, the only difference being that Esop's master is invited to a feast, instead of receiving a present of game, upon which Esop exclaims: "Alas! I see two crows, and I am beaten; you see one, and are asked to a feast. What a delusion is augury!"

39. This tale is found in the early Italian novelists, slightly varied, and it was doubtless introduced by Venetian merchants from the Levant: A parrot belonging to Count Fiesco was discovered one day stealing some roast meat from the kitchen. The enraged cook, overtaking him, threw a kettle of boiling water at him, which completely scalded all the feathers from his head, and left the poor bird with a bare poll. Some time afterwards, as Count Fiesco was engaged in conversation with an abbot, the parrot, observing the shaven crown of his reverence, hopped up to him and said: "What! do *you* like roast meat too?"

In another form the story is orally current in the North of England. Dr. Fryer tells it to this effect, in his charming *English Fairy Tales from the North Country*: A grocer kept a parrot that used to cry out to the customers that the sugar was sanded and the butter mixed with lard. For this the bird had her neck wrung and was thrown upon an ash-heap; but reviving and seeing a dead cat beside her she cried: "Poor Puss! have you, too, suffered for telling the truth?"

There is yet another variant of this droll tale, which has been popular for generations throughout England, and was quite recently reproduced in an American journal as a genuine "nigger" story: In olden times there was a roguish baker who made many of his loaves less than the regulation weight, and one day, on observing the government inspector coming along the street, he concealed the light loaves in a closet. The inspector having found the bread on the counter of the proper weight, was about to leave, when a parrot, which the baker kept in his shop, cried out: "Light bread in the closet!" This caused a search to be made, and the baker was heavily fined. Full of fury, the baker seized the parrot, wrung its neck, and threw it in his back yard, near the carcase of a pig that had died of the measles. The parrot, coming to itself again, observed the dead porker and inquired in a tone of sympathy: "O poor piggy, didst thou, too, tell about light bread in the closet?"

40. In the Rev. J. Hinton Knowles' *Folk-Tales of Kashmír* a merchant gives his stupid son a small coin with which he is to purchase something to eat, something to drink, something to gnaw, something to sow in the garden, and some food for the cow. A clever young girl advises him to buy a water-melon, which would answer all the purposes required.—P. 145.
41. Ziyáu-'d-Dín Nakhshabí, so called from Nakhshab, or Nasaf, the modern Kashí, a town situated between Samarkand and the Oxus, led a secluded life in Badá'um, and died, as stated by 'Abdal-Hakk, A.H. 751 (A.D. 1350-1).—Dr. Rieu's *Catalogue of Persian MSS. in the British Museum.*—In 1792 the Rev. B. Gerrans published an English translation of twelve of the fifty-two tales comprised in the *Túti Náma*, but the work is now best known in Persia and India from an abridgment made by Kádirí in the last century, which was printed, with a translation, at London in 1801.
42. "He that has money in the scales," says Saádí, "has strength in his arms, and he who has not the command of money is destitute of friends in the world."—Hundreds of similar sarcastic observations on the power of wealth might be cited from the Hindú writers, such as: "He who has riches has friends; he who has riches has relations; he who has riches *is even a sage!*" The following verses in praise of money are, I think, worth reproducing, if only for their whimsical arrangement:

Honey,
Our Money
We find in the end
Both relation and friend;
'Tis a helpmate for better, for worse.
Neither father nor mother,
Nor sister nor brother,
Nor uncles nor aunts,
Nor dozens
Of cousins,
Are like a friend in the purse.
Still regard the main chance;
'Tis the clink
Of the chink
Is the music to make the heart dance.

43. In a Telúgú MS., entitled *Patti Vrútti Mahima* (the Value of Chaste Wives), the minister of Chandra Pratápa assumes the form of a bird owing to a curse pronounced against him by Siva, and is sold to a merchant named Dhanadatta, whose son, Kuvéradatta, is vicious. The bird by moral lessons reformed him for a time. They went to a town called Pushpamayuri, where the king's son saw the wife of Kuveradatta when he was absent from home. An illicit amour was about to begin, when the bird interposed by relating tales of chaste wives, and detained the wanton lady at home till her husband ed.

44. Many Asiatic stories relate to the concealing of treasure—generally at the foot of a tree, to mark the spot—by two or more companions, and its being secretly stolen by one of them. The device of the carpenter in the foregoing tale of abducting the rascally goldsmith's two sons, and so on, finds an analogue in the *Panchatantra*, the celebrated Sanskrit collection of fables (Book I, Fab. 21, of Benfey's German translation), where we read that a young man, who had spent the wealth left to him by his father, had only a heavy iron balance remaining of all his possessions, and depositing it with a merchant went to another country. When he ed, after some time, he went to the merchant and demanded back his balance. The merchant told him it had been eaten by rats; adding: "The iron of which it was composed was particularly sweet, and so the rats ate it." The young man, knowing that the merchant spoke falsely, formed a plan for the recovery of his balance. One day he took the merchant's young son, unknown to his father, to bathe, and left him in the care of a friend. When the merchant missed his son he accused the young man of having stolen him, and summoned him to appear in the king's judgment-hall. In answer to the merchant's accusation, the young man asserted that a kite had carried away the boy; and when the

officers of the court declared this to be impossible, he said: "In a country where an iron balance was eaten by rats, a kite might well carry off an elephant, much more a boy." The merchant, having lost his cause, ed the balance to the young man and received back his boy.

45. So, too, Bœthius, in his *De Consolatione Philosophiæ*, says, according to Chaucer's translation: "All thynges seken ayen to hir [*i.e.* their] propre course, and all thynges rejoysen on hir retournynge agayne to hir nature."—A tale current in Oude, and given in *Indian Notes and Queries* for Sept. 1887, is an illustration of the maxim that "everything s to its first principles": A certain prince chose his friends out of the lowest class, and naturally imbibed their principles and habits. When the death of his father placed him on the throne, he soon made his former associates his courtiers, and exacted the most servile homage from the nobles. The old vazír, however, despised the young king and would render none. This so exasperated him that he called his counsellors together to advise the most excruciating of tortures for the old man. Said one: "Let him be flayed alive and let shoes be made of his skin." The vazír ejaculated on this but one word, "Origin." Said the next: "Let him be hacked into pieces and his limbs cast to the dogs." The vazír said, "Origin." Another advised: "Let him be forthwith executed, and his house be levelled to the ground." Once more the vazír simply said, "Origin." Then the king turned to the rest, who declared each according to his opinion, the vazír noticing each with the same word. At last a young man, who had not spoken hitherto, was asked. "May it please your Majesty," said he, "if you ask my opinion, it is this: Here is an aged man, and honourable from his years, family, and position; moreover, he served in the king your father's court, and nursed you as a boy. It were well, considering all these matters, to pay him respect, and render his old age comfortable." Again the vazír uttered the word "Origin." The king now demanded what he meant by it. "Simply this, your Majesty," responded the vazír: "You have here the sons of shoemakers, butchers, executioners, and so forth, and each has expressed himself according to his father's trade. There is but one noble-born among them, and he has made himself conspicuous by speaking according to the manner of his race." The king was ashamed, and released the vazír.—A parallel to this is found in the Turkish *Qirq Vezír Taríkhí*, or History of the Forty Vezírs (Lady's 4th Story): according to Mr. Gibb's translation, "All things to their origin."

46. Originally, Rúmelia (Rúm Eyli) was only implied by the word *Rúm*, but in course of time it was employed to designate the whole Turkish empire.

47. If the members severed from the golden image were to be instantly replaced by others, what need was there for the daily appearance of the "fakír," as promised?—But *n'importe!*

48. Ralston's *Russian Folk-Tales*, p. 224, *note*.

49. The same story is given by the Comte de Caylus—but, like Noble, without stating where the original is to be found—in his *Contes Orientaux*, first published in 1745, under the title of "Histoire de Dervich Abounadar." These entertaining tales are reproduced in *Le Cabinet des Fées*, ed. 1786, tome xxv.—It will be observed that the first part of the story bears a close resemblance to that of our childhood's favourite, the Arabian tale of "Aladdin and the Wonderful Lamp," of which many analogues and variants, both European and Asiatic, are cited in the first volume of my *Popular Tales and Fictions*, 1887;—see also a supplementary note by me on Aladdin's Lamp in *Notes and Queries*, Jan. 5, 1889, p. 1.

50. That is, hell. Properly, it is Je-Hinnon, near Jerusalem, which seems to have been in ancient times the cremation ground for human corpses.

51. The italicised passages which occur in this tale are verses in the original Persian text.

52. There is a very similar story in the Tamil *Alakésa Kathá*, a tale of a King and his Four Ministers, but the conclusion is different: the rájá permits all his subjects to partake of the youth-bestowing fruit;—I wonder whether they are yet alive! A translation of the romance of the King and his Four Ministers—the first that has been made into English—will be found in my *Group of Eastern Romances and Stories*, 1889.

53. In one Telúgú version, entitled *Totí Náma Cat'halú*, the lady kills the bird after hearing all its tales; and in another the husband, on ing home and learning of his wife's intended intrigue, cuts off her head and becomes a devotee.

54. Captain R. C. Temple's *Legends of the Panjáb*, vol. i, p. 52 ff.; and "Four Legends of Rájá Rasálú," by the Rev. C. Swynnerton, in the *Folk-Lore Journal*, 1883, p. 141 ff.

55. In midsummer, 1244, twenty waggon loads of copies of the Talmud were burnt in France. This was in consequence of, and four years after, a public dispute between a certain Donin (afterwards called Nicolaus), a converted Jew, with Rabbi Yehiel, of Paris, on the contents of the Talmud.—See *Journal of Philology*, vol. xvi, p. 133.—In the year 1569, the famous Jewish library in Cremona was plundered, and 12,000 copies of the Talmud and other Jewish works were committed to the flames.—*The Talmud*, by Joseph Barclay, LL. D., London, 1875, p. 14.

56. Introductory Essay to *Hebrew Tales*, by Hyman Hurwitz; published at London in 1826.

57. Commentators on the Kurán say that Adam's beard did not grow till after his fall, and it was the result of his excessive sorrow and

penitence. Strange to say, he was ashamed of his beard, till he heard a voice from heaven calling to him and saying: "The beard is man's ornament on earth; it distinguishes him from the feeble woman." Thus we ought to—should we not?—regard our beards as the offshoots of what divines term "original sin"; and cherish them as mementoes of the Fall of Man. Think of this, ye effeminate ones who use the razor!

58. The notion of man being at first androgynous, or man-woman, was prevalent in most of the countries of antiquity. Mr. Baring-Gould says that "the idea, that man without woman and woman without man are imperfect beings, was the cause of the great repugnance with which the Jews and other nations of the East regarded celibacy." (*Legends of the Old Testament*, vol. i, p. 22.) But this, I think, is not very probable. The aversion of Asiatics from celibacy is rather to be ascribed to their surroundings in primitive times, when neighbouring clans were almost constantly at war with each other, and those chiefs and notables who had the greatest number of sturdy and valiant sons and grandsons would naturally be best able to hold their own against an enemy. The system of concubinage, which seems to have existed in the East from very remote times, is not matrimony, and undoubtedly had its origin in the passionate desire which, even at the present day, every Asiatic has for male offspring. By far the most common opening of an Eastern tale is the statement that there was a certain king, wise, wealthy, and powerful, but though he had many beautiful wives and handmaidens, Heaven had not yet blest him with a son, and in consequence of this all his life was embittered, and he knew no peace day or night.

59. Professor Charles Marelle, of Berlin, in an interesting little collection, *Affenschwanz, &c.; Variants orales de Contes Populaires, Français et Etrangers* (Braunschweig, 1888), gives an amusing story, based evidently on this rabbinical legend: The woman formed from Adam's tail proved to be as mischievous as a monkey, and gave her spouse no peace; whereupon another was formed from a part of his breast, and she was a decided improvement on her sister. All the giddy girls in the world are descended from the woman who was made from Adam's tail.

60. You and I, good reader, must therefore have been seen by the Father of Mankind.

61. *Legends of Old Testament Characters*, by S. Baring-Gould, vol. i, pp. 78, 79.

62. The Muhammedan legend informs us that Cain was afterwards slain by the blood-avenging angel. But the Jewish traditionists say that God was at length moved by Cain's contrition and placed on his brow a seal, which indicated that the fratricide was fully pardoned. Adam happened to meet him, and observing the seal on his forehead, asked him how he had turned aside the wrath of God.

He replied: "By confession of my sin and sincere repentance." On hearing this Adam exclaimed, beating his breast: "Woe is me! Is the virtue of repentance so great and I knew it not?"

63. A garbled version of this legend is found in the Latin *Gesta Romanorum* (it does not occur in the Anglican versions edited by Sir F. Madden for the Roxburghe Club, and by Mr. S. J. Herrtage for the Early English Text Society), Tale 179, as follows: "Josephus, in his work on 'The Causes of Things,' says that Noah discovered the vine in a wood, and because it was bitter he took the blood of four animals, viz., of a lion, a lamb, a pig, and a monkey. This mixture he united with earth and made a kind of manure, which he deposited at the roots of the trees. Thus the blood sweetened the fruit, with the juice of which he afterwards intoxicated himself, and lying naked was derided by his youngest son."

64. Luminous jewels figure frequently in Eastern tales, and within recent years, from experiments and observations, the phosphorescence of the diamond, sapphire, ruby, and topaz has been fully established.

65. Did the Talmudist borrow this story from the Greek legend of the famous robber of Attica, Procrustes, who is said to have treated unlucky travellers after the same barbarous fashion?

66. There are two Italian stories which bear some resemblance to this queer legend: In the fourth novel of Arienti an advocate is fined for striking his opponent in court, and "takes his change" by repeating the offence; and in the second novel of Sozzini, Scacazzone, after dining sumptuously at an inn, and learning from the waiter that the law of that town imposed a fine of ten livres for a blow on the face, provokes the landlord so that he gets a slap from him on the cheek, upon which he tells Boniface to pay himself out of the fine he should have had to pay for the blow if charged before the magistrate, and give the rest of the money to the waiter.—A similar story is told in an Arabian collection, of a half-witted fellow and the kází.

67. The commentators on the Kurán have adopted this legend. But according to the Kurán it was not Isaac, but Ishmael, the great progenitor of the Arabs, who was to be sacrificed by Abraham.

68. Commentators on the Kurán inform us that when Joseph was released from prison, after so satisfactorily interpreting Pharaoh's two dreams, Potiphar was degraded from his high office. One day, while Joseph was riding out to inspect a granary beyond the city, he observed a beggar-woman in the street, whose whole appearance, though most distressing, bore distinct traces of former greatness. Joseph approached her compassionately, and held out to her a handful of gold. But she refused it, and said aloud: "Great prophet of Allah, I am unworthy of this gift, although my transgression has been the stepping-stone to thy present fortune." At these words Joseph regarded her more closely, and,

behold, it was Zulaykhá, the wife of his lord. He inquired after her husband, and was told that he had died of sorrow and poverty soon after his deposition. On hearing this, Joseph led Zulaykhá to a relative of the king, by whom she was treated like a sister, and she soon appeared to him as blooming as at the time of his entrance into her house. He asked her hand of the king, and married her, with his permission.

Zulaykhá was the name of Potiphar's wife, if we may believe Muhammedan legends, and the daughter of the king of Maghrab (or Marocco), who gave her in marriage to the grand vazír of the king of Egypt, and the beauteous princess was disgusted to find him, not only very old, but, as a modest English writer puts it, very mildly, "belonged to that unhappy class which a practice of immemorial antiquity in the East excluded from the pleasures of love and the hope of posterity." This device of representing Potiphar as being what Byron styles "a neutral personage" was, of course, adopted by Muslim traditionists and poets in order to "white-wash" the frail Zulaykhá.—There are extant many Persian and Turkish poems on the "loves" of *Yúsuf wa Zulaykhá*, most of them having a mystical signification, and that by the celebrated Persian poet Jámí is universally considered as by far the best.

69. Gen. xlii, 24.—It does not appear from the sacred narrative why Joseph selected his brother Simeon as hostage. Possibly Simeon was most eager for his death, before he was cast into the dry well and then sold to the Ishmaelites; and indeed both he and his brother Levi seem to have been "a bad lot," judging from the dying Jacob's description of them, Gen. xlix, 5-7.

70. "Jacob's grief" is proverbial in Muslim countries. In the Kurán, *sura* xii, it is stated that the patriarch became totally blind through constant weeping for the loss of Joseph, and that his sight was restored by means of Joseph's garment, which the governor of Egypt sent by his brethren.—In the *Makamat* of Al-Harírí, the celebrated Arabian poet (A.D. 1054-1122), Harith bin Hamman is represented as saying that he passed a night of "Jacobean sorrow," and another imaginary character is said to have "wept more than Jacob when he lost his son."

71. Muslims say that Pharaoh's seven daughters were all lepers, and that Bathia's sisters, as well as herself, were cured through her saving the infant Moses.

According to the Hebrew traditionists, nine human beings entered Paradise without having tasted of death, viz.: Enoch; Messiah; Elias; Eliezer, the servant of Abraham; the servant of the king of Kush; Hiram, king of Tyre; Jaabez, the son of the Prince, and the

Rabbi, Juda; Serach, the daughter of Asher; and Bathia, the daughter of Pharaoh.

The last of the race of genuine Dublin ballad-singers, who rejoiced in the *nom de guerre* of "Zozimus" (*ob.* 1846), used to edify his street patrons with a slightly different reading of the romantic story of the finding of Moses in the bulrushes, which has the merit of striking originality, to say the least:

> In Egypt's land, upon the banks of Nile,
> King Pharaoh's daughter went to bathe in style;
> She tuk her dip, then went unto the land,
> And, to dry her royal pelt, she ran along the strand.
> A bulrush tripped her, whereupon she saw
> A smiling babby in a wad of straw;
> She tuk it up, and said, in accents mild,
> *"Tare an' agers, gyurls, which av yez owns this child?"*

The story of the finding of Moses has its parallels in almost every country—in the Greek and Roman legends of Perseus, Cyrus, and Romulus—in Indian, Persian, and Arabian tales—and a Babylonian analogue is given, as follows, by the Rev. A. H. Sayce, in the *Folk-Lore Journal* for 1883: "Sargon, the mighty monarch, the king of Agané, am I. My mother was a princess; my father I knew not. My father's brother loved the mountain land. In the city of Azipiranu, which on the bank of the Euphrates lies, my mother, the princess, conceived me; in an inacessible spot she brought me forth. She placed me in a basket of rushes; with bitumen the door of my ark she closed. She launched me on the river, which drowned me not. The river bore me along; to Akki, the irrigator, it brought me. Akki, the irrigator, in the tenderness of his heart, lifted me up. Then Akki, the irrigator, as his gardener appointed me, and in my gardenership the goddess Istar loved me. For forty-five years the kingdom I have ruled, and the black-headed (Akkadian) race have governed."

72. That the arch-fiend could, and often did, assume various forms to lure men to their destruction was universally believed throughout Europe during mediæval times and even much later; generally he appeared in the form of a most beautiful young woman; and there are still current in obscure parts of Scotland wild legends of his having thus tempted even godly men to sin.—In Asiatic tales rákshasas, ghúls (ghouls), and such-like demons frequently assume the appearance of heart-ravishing damsels in order to delude and devour the unwary traveller. In many of our old European romances fairies are represented as transforming

themselves into the semblance of deer, to decoy into sequestered places noble hunters of whom they had become enamoured.

73. The "Great Name" (in Arabic, *El-Ism el-Aazam*, "the Most Great Name"), by means of which King David was saved from a cruel death, as above, is often employed in Eastern romances for the rescue of the hero from deadly peril, as well as to enable him to perform supernatural exploits. It was generally engraved on a signet-ring, but sometimes it was communicated orally to the fortunate hero by a holy man, or by a king of the genii—who was, of course, a good Muslim.

74. At the "mill" the man who was plagued with a bad wife doubtless saw some labourers threshing corn, since *grinding* corn would hardly suggest the idea of *beating* his provoking spouse.—By the way, this man had evidently never heard the barbarous sentiment, expressed in the equally barbarous English popular rhyme— composed, probably, by some beer-sodden bacon-chewer, and therefore, in those ancient times, *non inventus*—

> A woman, a dog, and a walnut tree,
> The more you beat 'em, the better they be—

else, what need for him to consult King Solomon about his paltry domestic troubles?

75. A variant of this occurs in the *Decameron* of Boccaccio, Day ix, Nov. 9, of which Dunlop gives the following outline: Two young men repair to Jerusalem to consult Solomon. One asks how he may be well liked, the other how he may best manage a froward wife. Solomon advised the first to "love others," and the second to "repair to the mill." From this last counsel neither can extract any meaning; but it is explained on their road home, for when they came to the bridge of that name they meet a number of mules, and one of these animals being restive its master forced it on with a stick. The advice of Solomon, being now understood, is followed, with complete success.

Among the innumerable tales current in Muhammedan countries regarding the extraordinary sagacity of Solomon is the following, which occurs in M. René Basset's *Contes Populaires Berbèrs* (Paris, 1887): Complaint was made to Solomon that some one had stolen a quantity of eggs. "I shall discover him," said Solomon. And when the people were assembled in the mosque (*sic*), he said: "An egg-thief has come in with you, and he has got feathers on his head." The thief in great fright raised his hand to his head, which Solomon perceiving, he cried out: "There is the culprit—seize him!" There are many variants of this story in Persian and Indian collections, where a kází, or judge, takes the place of Solomon, and it had found its way into our own jest-books early in the 16th century. Thus in *Tales and Quicke Answeres*, a man has a goose stolen from him and complains to the priest, who promises to find out the thief. On Sunday the priest tells the congregation to sit down, which they do accordingly. Then says he, "Why are ye not all seated?" Say they, "We *are* all seated." "Nay," quoth Mass John, "but he that stole the goose sitteth not down." "But I *am* seated," says the witless goose-thief.

76. Among the Muhammedan legends concerning Solomon and the Queen of Sheba, it is related that, after he had satisfactorily answered all her questions and solved her riddles, "before he would enter into more intimate relations with her, he desired to clear up a certain point respecting her, and to see whether she actually had cloven feet, as several of his demons would have him to believe; or whether they had only invented the defect from fear lest he should marry her, and beget children, who, as descendants of the genii [the mother of Bilkís is said to have been of that race of beings], would be even more mighty than himself. He therefore caused her to be conducted through a hall, whose floor was of crystal, and under which water tenanted by every variety of fish was flowing. Bilkís, who had never seen a crystal floor, supposed that there was water to be passed through, and therefore raised her robe slightly, when the king discovered to his great joy a beautifully shaped female foot. When his eye was satisfied, he called to her: 'Come hither; there is no water here, but only a crystal floor; and confess thyself to the faith in the one only God.' Bilkís approached the throne, which stood at the end of the hall, and in Solomon's presence abjured the worship of the sun. Solomon then married Bilkís, but reinstated her as Queen of Sába, and spent three days in every month with her."

77. According to the Muslim legend, eight angels appeared before Solomon in a vision, saying that Allah had sent them to surrender to him power over them and the eight winds which were at their command. The chief of the angels then presented him with a jewel bearing the inscription: "To Allah belong greatness and might." Solomon had merely to raise this stone towards the heavens and these angels would appear, to serve him. Four other angels next appeared, lords of all creatures living on the earth and in the waters. The angel representing the kingdom of birds gave him a jewel on which were inscribed the words: "All created things praise the Lord." Then came an angel who gave him a jewel conferring on the possessor power over earth and sea, having inscribed on it: "Heaven and earth are servants of Allah." Lastly, another angel appeared and presented him with a jewel bearing these words (the

formula of the Muslim Confession of Faith): "There is no God but *the* God, and Muhammed is his messenger." This jewel gave Solomon power over the spirit-world. Solomon caused these four jewels to be set in a ring, and the first use to which he applied its magical power was to subdue the demons and genii.—It is perhaps hardly necessary to remark here, with reference to the fundamental doctrine of Islám, said to have been engraved on the fourth jewel of Solomon's ring, that according to the Kurán, David, Solomon, and all the Biblical patriarchs and prophets were good Muslims, for Muhammed did not profess to introduce a new religion, but simply to restore the original and only true faith, which had become corrupt.

78. We are not told here how the demon came to part with this safeguard of his power. The Muslim form of the legend, as will be seen presently, is much more consistent, and corresponds generally with another rabbinical version, which follows the present one.

79. According to the Muslim version, Solomon's temporary degradation was in punishment for his taking as a concubine the daughter of an idolatrous king whom he had vanquished in battle, and, through her influence, bowing himself to "strange gods." Before going to the bath, one day, he gave this heathen beauty his signet to take care of, and in his absence the rebellious genie Sakhr, assuming the form of Solomon, obtained the ring. The king was driven forth and Sakhr ruled (or rather, misruled) in his stead; till the wise men of the palace, suspecting him to be a demon, began to read the Book of the Law in his presence, whereupon he flew away and cast the signet into the sea. In the meantime Solomon hired himself to some fishermen in a distant country, his wages being two fishes each day. He finds his signet in the maw of one of the fish, and so forth.

80. Is it possible that this "story" of the unicorn was borrowed and garbled from the ancient Hindú legend of the Deluge? "When the flood rose Manu embarked in the ship, and the fish swam towards him, and he fastened the ship's cable to its horn." But in the Hindú legend the fish (that is, Brahma in the form of a great fish) tows the vessel, while in the Talmudic legend the ark of Noah takes the unicorn in tow.

81. In a manuscript preserved in the Lambeth Palace Library, of the time of Edward IV, the height of Moses is said to have been "xiij. fote and viij. ynches and half"; and the reader may possibly find some amusement in the "longitude of men folowyng," from the same veracious work: "Cryste, vj. fote and iij. ynches. Our Lady, vj. fote and viij. ynches. Crystoferus, xvij. fote and viij. ynches. King Alysaunder, iiij. fote and v. ynches. Colbronde, xvij. fote and ij. ynches and half. Syr Ey., x. fote iij. ynches and half. Seynt Thomas of Caunterbery, vij. fote, save a ynche. Long Mores, a man of

Yrelonde borne, and servaunt to Kyng Edward the iiijth., vj. fote and x. ynches and half."—*Reliquæ Antiquæ*, vol i, p. 200.

82. *The Friend*, ed. 1850, vol. ii, p. 247.
83. Book of Job, i, 21.
84. Prov. xxxi, 10, 26.
85. The droll incident of dividing the capon, besides being found in Sacchetti, forms part of a popular story current in Sicily, and is thus related in Professor Crane's *Italian Popular Tales*, p. 311 ff., taken from Prof. Comparetti's *Fiabe, Novelle, e Racconti* (Palermo, 1875), No. 43, "La Ragazza astuta": Once upon a time there was a huntsman who had a wife and two children, a son and a daughter; and all lived together in a wood where no one ever came, and so they knew nothing about the world. The father alone sometimes went to the city, and brought back the news. The king's son once went hunting, and lost himself in that wood, and while he was seeking his way it became night. He was weary and hungry. Imagine how he felt. But all at once he saw a light shining in the distance. He followed it and reached the huntsman's house, and asked for lodging and something to eat. The huntsman recognised him at once and said: "Highness, we have already supped on our best; but if we can find anything for you, you must be satisfied with it. What can we do? We are so far from the towns that we cannot procure what we need every day." Meanwhile he had a capon cooked for him. The prince did not wish to eat it alone, so he called all the huntsman's family, and gave the head of the capon to the father, the back to the mother, the legs to the son, and the wings to the daughter, and ate the rest himself. In the house there were only two beds, in the same room. In one the husband and wife slept, in the other the brother and sister. The old people went and slept in the stable, giving up their bed to the prince. When the girl saw that the prince was asleep, she said to her brother: "I will wager that you do not know why the prince divided the capon among us in the manner he did." "Do you know? Tell me why." "He gave the head to our father, because he is the head of the family; the back to our mother, because she has on her shoulders all the affairs of the house; the legs to you, because you must be quick in performing the errands which are given you; and the wings to me, to fly away and catch a husband." The prince pretended to be asleep, but he was awake and heard these words, and perceived that the girl had much judgment, and as she was also pretty, he fell in love with her [and ultimately married this clever girl].
86. This story seems to be the original of a French popular tale, in which a gentleman secures his estate for his son by a similar device. The gentleman, dying at Paris while his son was on his travels, bequeathed all his wealth to a convent, on condition that they should give his son "whatever they chose." On the son's he received from the holy fathers a very trifling portion of the

paternal estate. He complained to his friends of this injustice, but they all agreed that there was no help for it, according to the terms of his father's will. In his distress he laid his case before an eminent lawyer, who told him that his father had adopted this plan of leaving his estate in the hands of the churchmen in order to prevent its misappropriation during his absence. "For," said the man of law, "your father, by will, has left you the share of his estate which the convent should choose (*le partie qui leur plairoit*), and it is plain that what they chose was that which they kept for themselves. All you have to do, therefore, is to enter an action at law against the convent for recovery of that portion of your father's property which they have retained, and, take my word for it, you will be successful." The young man accordingly sued the churchmen and gained his cause.

87. But the Book of Judges was probably edited after the time of Hesiod, whose fable of the Hawk and the Nightingale (*Works and Days*, B. i, v. 260) must be considered as the oldest extant fable.

88. This theory, though perhaps somewhat ingenious, is generally considered as utterly untenable.

89. Ezekiel, xviii, 2.

90. This wide-spread fable is found in the *Disciplina Clericalis* (No. 21) and in the collection of Marie de France, of the 13th century; and it is one of the many spurious Esopic fables.

91. This is similar to the 10th parable in the spiritual romance of Barlaam and Joasaph, written in Greek, probably in the first half of the 7th century, and ascribed to a monk called John of Damascus. Most of the matter comprised in this interesting work (which has not been translated into English) was taken from well-known Buddhist sources, and M. Zotenberg and other eminent scholars are of the opinion that it was first composed, probably in Egypt, before the promulgation of Islám. The 10th parable is to this effect: The citizens of a certain great city had an ancient custom, to take a stranger and obscure man, who knew nothing of the city's laws and traditions, and to make him king with absolute power for a year's space; then to rise against him all unawares, while he, all thoughtless, was revelling and squandering and deeming the kingdom his for ever; and stripping off his royal robes, lead him naked in procession through the city, and banish him to a long-uninhabited and great island, where, worn down for want of food and raiment, he bewailed this unexpected change. Now, according to this custom, a man was chosen whose mind was furnished with much understanding, who was not led away by sudden prosperity, and was thoughtful and earnest in soul as to how he should best order his affairs. By close questioning, he learned from a wise counsellor the citizens' custom, and the place of exile, and was instructed how he might secure himself. When he knew this, and that he must soon go to the island and leave his

acquired and alien kingdom to others, he opened the treasures of which he had for the time free and unrestricted use, and took an abundant quantity of gold and silver and precious stones, and giving them to some trusty servants sent them before him to the island. At the appointed year's end the citizens rose and sent him naked into exile, like those before him. But the other foolish and flitting kings had perished miserably of hunger, while he who had laid up that treasure beforehand lived in lusty abundance and delight, fearless of the turbulent citizens, and felicitating himself on his wise forethought. Think, then, the city this vain and deceitful world, the citizens the principalities and powers of the demons, who lure us with the bait of pleasure, and make us believe enjoyment will last for ever, till the sudden peril of death is upon us.—This parable (which seems to be of purely Hebrew origin) is also found in the old Spanish story-book *El Conde Lucanor*.

92. This is the 9th parable in the romance of Barlaam and Joasaph, where it is told without any variation.

93. Psalm cxix, 92.—By the way, it is probably known to most readers that the twenty-two sections into which this grand poem is divided are named after the letters of the Hebrew alphabet; but from the translation given in our English Bible no one could infer that in the original every one of the eight verses in each section begins with the letter after which it is named, thus forming a very long acrostic.

94. After Abraham had walked to and fro unscathed amidst the fierce flames for three days, the faggots were suddenly transformed into a blooming garden of roses and fruit-trees and odoriferous plants.—This legend is introduced into the Kurán, and Muslim writers, when they expatiate on the almighty power of Allah, seldom omit to make reference to Nimrod's flaming furnace being turned into a bed of roses.

95. Eccles., i, 2. The word Vanity (remarks Hurwitz, the translator) occurs twice in the plural, which the Rabbi considered as equivalent to four, and three times in the singular, making altogether *seven*.

96. "Do not," says Nakhshabí, "try to move by persuasion the soul that is afflicted with grief. The heart that is overwhelmed with the billows of sorrow will, by slow degrees, to itself."

97. "He who subdueth his temper is a mighty man," says the Talmudist; and Solomon had said so before him: "He that is slow to anger is better than the mighty, and he that ruleth his spirit than he that taketh a city" (Prov. xvi, 32). A curious parallel to these words is found in an ancient Buddhistic work, entitled *Buddha's Dhammapada*, or Path of Virtue, as follows: "If one man conquer in battle a thousand times a thousand men, and if another conquer himself, he is the greatest of conquerors." (Professor Max

Müller's translation, prefixed to *Buddhagosha's Parables*, translated by Captain Rogers.)

98. Cf. Saádí, *ante*, page 41, "Life is snow," etc.
99. Locke was anticipated not only by the Talmudist, as above, but long before him by Aristotle, who termed the infant soul *tabula rasa*, which was in all likelihood borrowed by the author of the Persian work on the practical philosophy of the Muhammedans, entitled *Akhlák-i-Jalaly*, who says: "The minds of children are like a clear tablet, equally open to all inscriptions."
100. Too many cooks spoil the broth.—*English Proverb*.
101.   Two farthings and a thimble
        In a tailor's pocket make a jingle.—*English Saying*.

102. "Don't speak ill of the bridge that bore you safe over the stream" seems to be the European equivalent.
103. Python, of Byzantium, was a very corpulent man. He once said to the citizens, in addressing them to make friends after a political dispute: "Gentlemen, you see how stout I am. Well, I have a wife at home who is still stouter. Now, when we are good friends, we can sit together on a very small couch; but when we quarrel, I do assure you, the whole house cannot contain us."—*Athenæus*, xii.
104. Compare Burns:

> O wad some power the giftie gie us
> To see oursels as ithers see us!

105. See the Persian aphorisms on revealing secrets, *ante*, Burns, in his "Epistle to a Young Friend," says:

> Aye free aff hand your story tell
> When wi' a bosom crony,
> But still keep something to yoursel'
> Ye scarcely tell to ony.

106. The very reverse of our English proverb, "Better to be the head of the commonalty than the tail of the gentry."
107. Saádí has the same sentiment in his *Gulistán*—see *ante*, p. 49.
108. See also Saádí's aphorisms on precept and practice, *ante*, p. 47.
109. Here we have a variant of Thomas Carlyle's favourite maxim, "Speech is silvern; silence is golden."
110. "Nothing is so good for an ignorant man as silence; and if he were sensible of this he would not be ignorant."—*Saádí*.
111. *The Friend*, ed. 1850, vol. ii, p. 249.
112. The number Forty occurs very frequently in the Bible (especially the Old Testament) in connection with important events, and also in Asiatic tales. It is, in fact, regarded with peculiar veneration

alike by Jews and Muhammedans. See notes to my *Group of Eastern Romances and Stories* (1889), pp. 140 and 456.

113. The "fruit of the forbidden tree" was not an apple, as we Westerns fondly believe, but *wheat*, say the Muslim doctors.

114. *Fables de La Fontaine*, Livre xie, fable v^e: "Le Loup et le Renard."

115. *Recueil de Contes Populaires de la Sénégambie*, recueillis par L.-J.-B.-Bérenger-Féraud. Paris, 1885. Page 51.

116. I have to thank my friend Dr. David Ross, Principal, E. C. Training College, Glasgow, for kindly drawing my attention to this diverting tale.

117. Nothing is more hackneyed in Asiatic poetry than the comparison of a pretty girl's face to the moon, and not seldom to the disparagement of that luminary. Solomon, in his love-songs, exclaims: "Who is she that looketh forth in the morning, fair as the moon, clear as the sun?" The greatest of Persian poets, Firdausí, says of a damsel:

> "Love ye the moon? Behold her face,
> And there the lucid planet trace."

And Kalidása, the Shakspeare of India (6th century B.C.), says:
> "Her countenance is brighter than the moon."

Amongst ourselves the epithet "moon-faced" is not usually regarded as complimentary, yet Spenser speaks of a beautiful damsel's "moon-like forehead."—Be sure, the poets are right!

118. The lithe figure of a pretty girl is often likened by Eastern poets to the waving cypress, a tree which we associate with the grave-yard.—"Who is walking there?" asks a Persian poet. "Thou, or a tall cypress?"

119. "Nocturnal."

120. The sacred well in the Kaába at Mecca, which, according to Muslim legends, miraculously sprang up when Hagar and her son Ishmael were perishing in the desert from thirst.

121. According to Muslim law, four months and ten days must elapse before a widow can marry again.

122. An attendant, who had always befriended Majnún.

123. "The moon," to wit, the unhappy Laylá.

124. See Note on 'Wamik and Asra' at the end of this paper.

125. A mole on the fair face of Beauty is not regarded as a blemish, but the very contrary, by Asiatics—or by Europeans either, else why did the ladies of the last century patch their faces, if not (originally) to set off the clearness of their complexion by contrast with the little black wafer?—though (afterwards) often to hide a

pimple! Eastern poets are for ever raving over the mole on a pretty face. Háfíz goes the length of declaring:

> "For the mole on the cheek of that girl of Shíráz
> I would give away Samarkand and Bukhárá"—

albeit they were none of his to give to anybody.

126. Cf. Shelley, in the fine opening of that wonderful poetical offspring of his adolescence, *Queen Mab*:

> "Hath, then, the gloomy Power
> Whose reign is in the tainted sepulchres
> Seized on her sinless soul?"

127. The reader may with advantage consult the article 'Beast-Fable,' by Mr. Thos. Davidson, in *Chambers's Encylopædia*, new edition.

128. But this papyrus might be of as late a period as the second century of our era.

129. For the most complete history of the Esopic Fable, see vol. i of Mr. Joseph Jacobs' edition of *The Fables of Aesop, as first printed by Caxton in 1484, with those of Avian, Alfonso, and Poggio*, recently published by Mr. David Nutt; where a vast amount of erudite information will be found on the subject in all its ramifications. Mr. Jacobs, indeed, seems to have left little for future gleaners: he has done his work in a thorough, Benfey-like manner, and students of comparative folk-lore are under great obligations to him for the indefatigable industry he has devoted to the valuable outcome of his wide-reaching learning.

130. *Fabulae Romanenses Graece conscriptae ex recensione et cum adnotationibus*, Alfredi Eberhard (Leipzig, 1872), vol. i, p. 226 ff.

131. It would have been well had the sultan Bayazíd compelled his soldier to adopt this plan when accused by an old woman of having drunk up all her supply of goat's milk. The soldier declared his innocence, upon which Bayazíd ordered his stomach to be cut open, and finding the milk not yet digested, quoth he to the woman: "Thou didst not complain without reason." And, having caused her to be recompensed for her loss, "Now go thy way," he added, "for thou hast had justice for the wrong done thee."

132. This story is also found in the *Liber de Donis* of Etienne de Bourbon (No. 246), a Dominican monk of the 14th century; in the *Summa Praedicantium* of John Bromyard, and several other medieval monkish collections of *exempla*, or stories designed for

the use of preachers: in these the explanation is that nothing can be better and nothing worse than *tongue*.

133. This occurs in the several Asiatic versions of the Book of Sindibád (Story of the Sandalwood Merchant); in the *Gesta Romanorum*; in the old English metrical *Tale of Beryn*; in one of the Italian *Novelle* of Sacchetti; and in the exploits of Tyl Eulenspiegel, the German Rogue.

134. Taken from Petronius Arbiter. The story is widely spread. It is found in the *Seven Wise Masters*, and—*mutatis mutandis*—is well known to the Chinese. Planudes takes some liberties with his original, substituting for the soldier guarding the suspended corpse of a criminal, who "comforts" the sorrowing widow, a herdsman with his beasts, which he loses in prosecuting his amour.

135. Mr. Jacobs was obliged to omit the Life of Esop in his reprint of Caxton's text of the Fables, as it would have unduly increased the bulk of his second volume. But those interested in the genealogy of popular tales and fables will be glad to have Mr. Jacobs' all but exhaustive account of the so-called Esopic fables, together with his excellent synopsis of parallels, in preference to the monkish collection of spurious anecdotes of the fabulist, of which the most noteworthy are given in the present paper.

136. Robert Henryson was a schoolmaster in Dunfermline in the latter part of the 15th century. His *Moral Fables*, edited by Dr. David Irving, were printed for the Maitland Club in 1832, and his complete works (Poems and Fables) were edited by Dr. David Laing, and published in 1865. His *Testament of Cresseid*, usually considered as his best performance, is a continuation of Chaucer's *Troilus and Cresseide*, which was derived from the Latin of an unknown author named Lollius. Henryson was the author of the first pastoral poem composed in the English (or Scottish) language—that of *Robin and Makyn*. "To his power of poetical conception," Dr. Laing justly remarks, "he unites no inconsiderable skill in versification: his lines, if divested of their uncouth orthography, might be mistaken for those of a more modern poet."

137. *Schaw*, a wood, a covert.

138. *Chymeris*, a short, light gown.

139. *Hude*, hood.

140. *Bordourit*, embroidered.

141. *Hekellit-wise*, like the feathers in the neck of a cock.

142. *Fassoun*, fashion.

143. *Lokker*, (?) gray.

144. *Stikkand*, sticking.

145. *Pennair*, pen-case.

146. *Graithit*, apparelled, arrayed.

147. *Feirfull*, awe-inspiring, dignified.

148. This is a work distinct from Henri Etienne's *Apologia pour Herodote*. An English translation of it was published at London in 1807, and at Edinburgh in 1808, under the title of "*A World of Wonders*; or, an Introduction to a Treatise touching the Conformitie of Ancient and Modern Wonders; or, a Preparative Treatise to the Apology for Herodotus," etc. For this book (the "Introduction") Etienne had to quit France, fearing the wrath of the clerics. His *Apologie pour Herodote* has not been rendered into English—and why not, it would be hard to say.

149. One of the Charlemagne Romances, translated by Caxton from the French, and printed by him about the year 1489, under the title of *The Right Pleasaunt and Goodly Historie of the Four Sonnes of Aymon*. It has been reprinted for the Early English Text Society, ably edited by Miss Octavia Richardson.

150. A slightly different version is found in *A Hundred Mery Talys*, No. lxix, "Of the franklyns sonne that cam to take orders." The bishop says that Noah had three sons, Shem, Ham, and Japheth;—who was the father of Japheth? When the "scholar" s home and tells his father how he had been puzzled by the bishop, he endeavours to enlighten his son thus: "Here is Colle, my dog, that hath three whelps; must not these three whelps have Colle for their sire?" Going back to the bishop, he informs his lordship that the father of Japheth was "Colle, my father's dogge."

151. There were no pews in the churches in those "good old times."

152. *Apropos* of saint-worship, quaint old Thomas Fuller relates a droll story in his *Church History*, ed. 1655, p. 278: A countryman who had lived many years in the Hercinian woods, in Germany, at last came into a populous city, demanding of the people therein, what God they did worship. They answered him, that they worshipped Jesus Christ. Whereupon the wild wood-man asked the names of the several churches in the city, which were all called by sundry saints, to whom they were consecrated. "It is strange," said he, "that you should worship Jesus Christ, and he not have a temple in all the city dedicated to him."

153. "Jesus, therefore, knowing all things that should come upon him, went forth, and said unto them, 'Whom seek ye?' They answered him, 'Jesus of Nazareth.'"—*Gospel of S. John*, xviii, 4, 5.

154. *Festueum*, the split straw so used in the Middle Ages.

155. See Méon's edition of Barbazan's *Fabliaux et Contes*, ed. 1808, tome ii, p. 442, and a prose *extrait* in Le Grand d'Aussy's collection, ed. 1781, tome iv, p. 101, "Du Prêtre qui dit la Passion."

156. See Méon's Barbazan, 1808, tome iv, p. 114; also Le Grand, 1781, tome ii, p. 190: "Du Vilain qui gagna Paradis en plaidant."

157. *Scarronides; or, Virgil Travestie*, etc., by Charles Cotton, Book iv. *Poetical Works*, 5th edition, London, 1765, pp. 122, 140.

158. The notion that a beard indicated wisdom on the part of the wearer is often referred to in early European literature. For

example, in Lib. v of Caxton's Esop, the Fox, to induce the sick King Lion to kill the Wolf, says he has travelled far and wide, seeking a good medicine for his Majesty, and "certaynly I have found no better counceylle than the counceylle of an auncyent Greke, with a grete and long berd, a man of grete wysdom, sage, and worthy to be praysed." And when the Fox, in another fable, leaves the too-credulous Goat in the well, Reynard adds insult to injury by saying to him, "O maystre goote, yf thow haddest be [*i.e.* been] wel wyse, with thy fayre berde," and so forth. (Pp. 153 and 196 of Mr. Jacobs' new edition.)—A story is told of a close-shaven French ambassador to the court of some Eastern potentate, that on presenting his credentials his Majesty made sneering remarks on his smooth face (doubtless he was himself "bearded to the eyes"), to which the envoy boldly replied: "Sire, had my master supposed that you esteem a beard so highly, instead of me, he would have sent your Majesty a goat as his ambassador."

159. Harleian MS. No. 7334, lines 2412-2418. Printed for the Early English Text Society.

160. In a scarce old poem, entitled, *The Pilgrymage and the Wayes of Jerusalem*, we read:

> The thyrd Seyte beyn prestis of oure lawe,
> That synge masse at the Sepulcore;
> At the same grave there oure lorde laye,
> They synge the leteny every daye.
> In oure manner is her [*i.e.* their] songe,
> Saffe, here [*i.e.* their] *berdys be ryght longe*,
> That is the geyse of that contre,
> *The lenger the berde the bettyr is he*;
> The order of hem [*i.e.* them] be barfote freeres.

161. Reprint for the Shakspere Society, 1877, B. ii, ch. vii, p. 169.

162. Reprint for the (old) Shakspeare Society, 1846, p. 217.

163. Formed by the moustache and a chin-tuft, as worn by Louis Napoleon and his imperialist supporters.

164. *Works of John Taylor, the Water Poet, comprised in the Folio edition of 1630.* Printed for the Spenser Society, 1869. "*Superbiae Flagellum*, or the Whip of Pride," p. 34.

165. Reprint for the Shakspere Society, Part ii (1882), pp. 50, 51.

166. *The Treatise answerynge the boke of Berdes, Compyled by Collyn Clowte, dedicated to Barnarde, Barber, dwellyng in Banbury*: "Here foloweth a treatyse made, Answerynge the treatyse of doctor Borde upon Berdes."—Appended to reprint of Andrew Borde's *Introduction of Knowledge*, edited by Dr. F. J. Furnivall, for the Early English Text Society, 1870—see pp. 314, 315.